EMPOWERING
TOM(

Empowering Leadership of Tomorrow examines leadership that enables and empowers others to coparticipate, cocreate, and experience the joy of creativity. It proposes a kind of leadership that fosters bottom-up dynamics, empowering people, groups, teams, and societies. Praszkier shows how this approach, called Empowering Leadership (EL), can drive success in business and, in the case of social entrepreneurship, have an immense social impact. Furthermore, he shows that EL style is also beneficial in other fields such as parenting and counseling.

The book presents diverse case studies from business and social arenas, as well as from family life. It establishes practical guidelines for leadership development, including methods to enhance creativity, and also casts an eye toward the future, demonstrating approaches to navigating future scenarios in a complex and unpredictable environment.

RYSZARD PRASZKIER is a researcher at the University of Warsaw, studying the dynamics of social change, namely, what makes change durable and irreversible. He is author and coauthor of many publications, including *Social Entrepreneurship: Theory and Practice* (Cambridge University Press, 2012). Delving into the mechanisms of synchronized relationships, he also authored the article "Empathy, Mirror Neurons and SYNC," which appears in *Mind and Society* and contributed the chapter "Social Entrepreneurs Open Closed Worlds: The Transformative Influence of Weak Ties" in *Complex Human Dynamics, From Mind to Societies* (2012). As a practitioner, he has worked for more than two decades for Ashoka: Innovators for the Public, an international association promoting social innovators. He has been a second-opinion reviewer for more than one hundred candidates for the Ashoka Fellowship on nearly all continents.

EMPOWERING LEADERSHIP OF TOMORROW

RYSZARD PRASZKIER

University of Warsaw

CAMBRIDGE
UNIVERSITY PRESS

CAMBRIDGE
UNIVERSITY PRESS

University Printing House, Cambridge CB2 8BS, United Kingdom

One Liberty Plaza, 20th Floor, New York, NY 10006, USA

477 Williamstown Road, Port Melbourne, VIC 3207, Australia

314–321, 3rd Floor, Plot 3, Splendor Forum, Jasola District Centre, New Delhi – 110025, India

79 Anson Road, #06–04/06, Singapore 079906

Cambridge University Press is part of the University of Cambridge.

It furthers the University's mission by disseminating knowledge in the pursuit of education, learning, and research at the highest international levels of excellence.

www.cambridge.org
Information on this title: www.cambridge.org/9781108433808
DOI: 10.1017/9781108380867

© Ryszard Praszkier 2018

First published 2018

Printed in the United States of America by Sheridan Books, Inc.

A catalogue record for this publication is available from the British Library.

ISBN 978-1-108-42214-7 Hardback
ISBN 978-1-108-43380-8 Paperback

Cambridge University Press has no responsibility for the persistence or accuracy of URLS for external or third-party internet websites referred to in this publication and does not guarantee that any content on such websites is, or will remain, accurate or appropriate.

Contents

Figures

Preface

Some leaders empower people and their bottom-up initiatives. From a Complexity Theory perspective, these leaders harness seemingly chaotic interactions and create an enabling environment to channel them into a higher-level order. They make a big impact through small investments, giving the appearance that they're creating "something out of nothing."

This book examines leadership that enables and empowers others to coparticipate, cocreate, and experience the joy of creativity. It reviews concepts of leadership in general and, specifically, the notion of Empowering Leadership. And it analyzes the ways in which complexity, social influence, and creativity facilitate leadership.

The book delineates theories of leadership and presents diverse case studies from the business and social arenas, as well as from family life. It also establishes practical guidelines for leadership development, including methods to enhance creativity. Firmly grounded in the present, this book also casts an eye toward the future, concluding with a discussion of ways to analyze future scenarios in a complex, and thus unpredictable, environment.

Merging theory with practice, *Empowering Leadership of Tomorrow* offers a structured blend of literature analysis, academic studies, and practical experience. It draws on conclusions from the book *Social Entrepreneurship: Theory and Practice* and other books and articles authored and coauthored by Ryszard Praszkier. In addition, much of the material comes from the author's experience with Ashoka: Innovators for the Public ((www.ashoka.org), an international association that promotes social innovators in more than eighty countries). As a second-opinion reviewer for the organization, he had in-depth conversations with more than one hundred innovators from around the world who were candidates for the Ashoka Fellowship. Moreover, he interviewed several business executives to better understand the bottom-up leadership model in use at their companies.

This book is suited for both academic and practical use. It examines the conceptual backbone and underlying mechanisms of Empowering Leadership for academicians and students and addresses basic "how-to" questions for practitioners. Intended to be accessible to a general audience, it may also appeal to those simply seeking to stay up to date on the latest trends in business and leadership.

Acknowledgments

First and foremost, I want to thank the Empowering Leaders who are the core source of knowledge for this book. Visiting with them, listening to their reflections, and exchanging ideas provided the cornerstone for this work.

Much of the inspiration for this book originated with the Ashoka founder and CEO William Drayton and with Professor Andrzej Nowak, whose insightful observations seeded many of my ideas. It's also a pleasure to thank friends who have been critically important advisers throughout this endeavor. In particular, I am grateful for the mentorship of Zbigniew "Bish" Turlej, PhD, a physicist and business analyst, whose healthy skepticism kept me grounded. I thank Professor David Brée, PhD, for his diligent cooperation throughout the entire project and his thoughtful comments and feedback, and Professor Andrzej Blikle for inspiration, especially drawn from his book *Total Quality Management* (TQM). Many thanks also to my son, Tom Praszkier, for his professional help in preparing the photos. And finally, thanks to Helen Taylor for her editorial skills and significant comments and suggestions, which have added value to the content of this publication.

The book is assigned to the Robert B. Zajonc Institute for Social Studies, University of Warsaw. It is supported by a grant for Regulatory Social Impact from the Polish Committee for Scientific Research [DEC-2011/02/A/HS6/00231].

Characters

(In the order of appearance)

Ramesh Kumar
Elie Abou Saab
Michel Babadjidé
Dagmara Bienkowska
David Kuria
Siriky Ky
Steve Bigari
Frank Escoubès
Mary Gordon
Bill Gore
Chris Rufer
Ricardo Semler
Krzysztof (Chris) Czyżewski
Dr. Yehudah Paz
Jos de Blok
Shannon Dosemagen
Tomasz Sadowski
Ahmed Edilbi
Teresa Ogrodzińska
Nijole Arbaciauskiene

Introduction

> A leader is best when people barely know he exists; when his work
> is done, his aim fulfilled, they will say: we did it ourselves. Lao Tzu

Leadership sometimes appears magical. Some leaders are able to harness enormous complexity and turn chaos into order with seemingly little effort. They can compel the homeless and the marginalized to take ownership of an initiative to improve their own lives, becoming trainers and leaders in combating poverty and developing a construction industry for the poor. Using simple rules, bottom-up development, and horizontal communication, they can turn a small group effort into a multibillion-dollar international company, with no top-down management whatsoever. They allow employees to relax in hammocks during working hours, and still their firm has skyrocketing market results. They believe the ultimate goal isn't money, but rather making people happy about their lives, and yet they still build leading companies in their field that remain profitable despite market ups and downs. Such leaders enable interactions in a seemingly chaotic way, yielding bottom-up dynamics and empowering individuals and groups. They may act atypically, appearing to others as "unreasonable people" (Elkington & Hartigan, 2008) or as Malcolm Gladwell's (2011) "outliers," as they find new ways to innovate and spearhead novel solutions.

Their leadership makes a large impact through small investments and, viewed traditionally, appears to make "something out of nothing." However, from the complexity perspective, this type of leadership isn't "magical" at all. To understand it, we must grasp the ways in which it uses small impulses to trigger big changes and creates a participatory environment that supports human development, engagement, creativity, and the emergence of added value.

This book examines the leadership that enables and empowers others to coparticipate, cocreate, and feel the joy of creativity. It does so in four ways: (1) through advancing the concepts of leadership in general and specifically the concept of Empowering Leadership; (2) by analyzing the nuts and bolts of complexity, as well as the mechanisms of social influence and creativity involved in facilitating leadership; (3) by presenting an illustrated portfolio of diverse examples and case studies; and, finally, (4) by establishing practical guidelines for development, e.g., how to enhance creativity or analyze future scenarios in a complex and unpredictable environment. (Yes, "future scenarios" in an "unpredictable world" sounds like an oxymoron, but in these pages you will see ways to circumvent this paradox.) On the one hand, this book is academic, and on the other, well suited for practical use. It tackles practical "how-to" questions and examines the conceptual backbone and underlying mechanisms of the method.

And if we're spying the future through a keyhole, this book's arrival couldn't be more timely. Not only is the phenomenon of leadership becoming a hot topic,[1] there is also a growing interest in the leadership of the future. How will leadership look in 2020 or 2030? How should we prepare to face the future challenges? Senior executives around the globe, when asked about major future trends, mentioned the rise of complex challenges and the innovation revolution.[2] Others indicate the importance of giving individuals greater control over their professional environment, in order to help them feel more empowered.[3] Yet another survey confirmed that the core quality of the future leader is to be able to communicate with empathy to create optimism, clarity, and certainty in uncertain times.[4] It will be shown here that most of those intuitions about the future are indeed justified.

As we dive in, an important caveat is that this book doesn't promote one kind of leadership over another. The goal is to demonstrate a certain approach, namely, Empowering Leadership, knowing that a diverse palette of different styles of successful management exists to suit different situations. For example, at one time there was a heated discussion around the management at Wal-Mart (top-down, low salaries, etc.).[5] The response was that yes, but through that Wal-Mart introduces jobs to places where there is high unemployment, and that their products are sold at lower prices than in other supermarkets, enabling poor people to purchase more than they could otherwise.

---

[1] As indicated by 510 million Google returns (May 2016); also see: McNamara (2010).
[2] Criswell & Martin (2007).
[3] According to 2020 Vision: Future Trends in Leadership & Management, Institute of Leadership & Management: www.i-l-m.com/~/media/ILM%20Website/Documents/research-reports/future-trends/ilm-research-reports-future-trends%20pdf.ashx; retrieved February 24, 2017.
[4] PCW (2008). How Leadership Must Change to Meet the Future. PriceWaterHouseCoopers: www.pwc.com/us/en/people-management/assets/future-leadership-change.pdf.
[5] See: www.nybooks.com/articles/2005/04/28/working-for-wal-mart-an-exchange/.

The title *Empowering Leadership of Tomorrow* suggests a forward-looking stance and springs from conclusions reached in previous studies, in which we analyzed social entrepreneurship. The insight then was that Social Entrepreneurs are introducing a form of Empowering Leadership (Praszkier & Nowak, 2012). Following those studies I identified the Empowering approach in other fields, especially in business (Praszkier, 2015). The idea for this book was conceived when I realized that Empowering Leadership isn't merely relevant to "running businesses" or "pursuing social missions." It also engenders a certain creed that informs the way we interact with people, approach problems, build trust and cooperation, rear children, care for the disabled, etc.

The book's structure merges theory with practice and is based on a blend of literature analysis, academic studies, and practical experience. Much of the latter is derived from my experience with Ashoka: Innovators for the Public, an international association of leading public entrepreneurs and innovators.[6] As a second-opinion reviewer, I had in-depth conversations with more than one hundred innovators from around the world – candidates for the Ashoka Fellowship. Moreover, I interviewed several business executives to understand better the bottom-up leadership model introduced in their companies. These conversations were a cardinal experience, immensely enriching my knowledge drawn from articles, books, and Web sites.

And, yes, I wear two hats: As an academician and researcher, I study change dynamics (those attributes that make change durable and irreversible), and as a practitioner, I'm involved in supporting social and business innovators in the field. I thoroughly enjoy these face-to-face meetings and draw inspiration from these gifted individuals. A third hat I wear is that of author: I've written and cowritten several articles, books, and book chapters.

The primary goal of this book is to introduce the phenomenon of Empowering Leadership (EL), incorporating the premise of complexity theory. Another aim relates to the way leadership in general is defined; each section's introduction will include a review of definitions of leadership in general, related to the particular section's content.

Moreover, there are several conceptual tracks sustained and explored throughout the book. For example, it seems crucial to understand the mechanisms of *social influence* used by leaders (intentionally or not). Therefore, the classical approach to social influence is introduced in Chapter 3, and the concept is expanded upon in Chapter 4 to include the dynamic approach.

---

[6] www.ashoka.org.

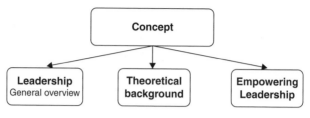

Figure 1. The concept.

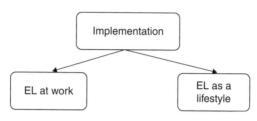

Figure 2. The implementation.

In the same vein, the concept of *charisma* arises in Chapter 2 and is continued in Chapter 4. *Creativity*, which is pivotal for this kind of leadership, comes along in Chapters 7 and 10, and is elaborated upon in Chapter 14. And *chaos* and *complexity*, both central to this analysis, are introduced in Chapter 5 and continued throughout the book. This structure reveals the unfolding logic of the phenomenon of Empowering Leadership and calls out its foundational psychological and sociological mechanisms.

The book is divided into three parts: **Concept** presents the theory of leadership, the social influence mechanisms, nuts, and bolts of creativity and the new kind of Empowering Leadership (see Figure 1).

Implementation includes multiple case studies from the business and social arenas and presents EL as a personal creed or lifestyle(see Figure 2).

Future outlines possible ways of predicting and planning in the complex universe, where matters are basically unpredictable; it also sketches some ideas for EL education (see Figure 3).

Taking a closer look at the structure, Section 1 concludes with an analysis of the mechanisms of social and psychological influence – a vehicle enabling leaders to attract and affect others (Chapter 3). These mechanisms are illustrated with examples of Social Entrepreneurs' very specific kind of influence. We look at individuals who demonstrate the kind of leadership

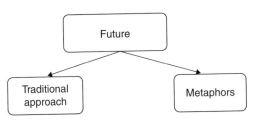

Figure 3. The future.

where passion for the mission leads to an immense, durable, and systemic social impact with low investment that empowers people, communities, and societies, thereby making them independent of their leader.

Section 2 advances us to the beginning of the twenty-first century and an analysis of leadership through the lens of complexity theory. We also see how complexity theory applies to the "magic" of getting "something out of nothing," with case studies of some large social movements that affected the world (e.g., the Gandhi, Civil Rights, and Polish Underground Solidarity movements). As creativity is pivotal for EL, Chapter 7 presents an in-depth analysis of the phenomenon of creativity, demonstrating its neuroscience and social and psychological determinants. The section concludes with an analysis of the horizontal and transversal communication that underlies the "chaos-into-order" processes.

Both Sections 1 and 2 pave the way for introducing, in Section 3, the concept of Empowering Leadership (EL), i.e., enabling bottom-up, participative processes – a kind of leadership that, by fostering horizontal communication, facilitates the process of emergence (economic and/or social), and at the same time, empowers participants, often to the level of partnership. In this section we also look at several case studies of successful businesses in which the employees, traditionally perceived as subordinates, are called and act as "associates" or "partners."

Harnessing chaos into order requires some specific preconditions presented in Chapter 10. Section 3 concludes with a review of diverse case studies of successful implementations of empowering leadership in business and in the social sector.

At this point new questions arise: Is EL merely a way of running business? Or, may it also be a creed or lifestyle? Are there some specific personality traits supporting EL? In Section 4 we suggest that, yes, there is a specific lifestyle and there are some personality characteristics associated with EL, and that they also manifest outside the work environment.

The claim that EL requires specific personality traits is examined in Chapter 13. Prior to reviewing the real-life implications of EL, we delve into the mechanisms and techniques enhancing creativity, as creativity seems to be an important driver for the empowering approach (Chapter 14). We look at how to augment creativity; what boosts serendipity, i.e., the casual, unplanned tendency to generate novel ideas; whether creativity makes one happy; and, if it does, then what are the mechanisms responsible for this?

Section 4 concludes with a review of real-life situations in which EL may manifest itself, including child rearing, education, counseling and coaching, and caring for people with special needs and for the aging (Chapter 15).

Section 5 deals with anticipating possible future scenarios. The question is how, in the world of complexity and unpredictability, can one predict the future? The traditional approach (e.g., through computer simulations) is presented in Chapter 16. Some nontraditional techniques are introduced in Chapter 17, enabling exploration of the future through simulations that are easy for readers at various levels of education and experience to adopt. Simulations (e.g., Live Action Role-Playing (LARP) Games, metaphors, dancing, and imagining) are delineated as gateways for understanding possible future scenarios.

Finally, the Précis draws all the strings together and introduces an Empowering Leadership model, highlighting the inevitably Empowering spirit.

PART I

Concept

SECTION I

Leadership

Where should we begin our exploration of the phenomenon of leadership? Should we start with tribal societies or go back even further to Paleolithic times? During that era, some eleven thousand years ago, there evolved a shared leadership model (Hart, 2006; Sveiby, 2010) that's still viable today (Pearce & Conger, 2003; Carson *et al.*, 2007). Or maybe we should start much later, when the tribal societies, such as the Melanesian and Polynesian communities, evolved the Big Man paradigm. To become a Big Man took a series of acts that elevated a common citizen to a standing far above his peers and attracted a loyal following (Douglas, 1979). This is another model that returns in the nineteenth century as the Great Man Theory. It describes highly influential heroes who, because of their personal charisma, intelligence, wisdom, or political skill, were able to exercise their power (Carlyle, 1988).

Charisma as a leadership trait[1] was resurrected by one of the founders of sociology, Max Weber[2] (1978). Elsewhere in this book we'll introduce an alternative to Great Man charisma: mission-based charisma, which springs from personal passion for a cause or path.

We could also begin our examination of leadership in Hellenistic times, hailing Socrates, who, in 400 BC, taught dialectics, the Socratic method of following a line of questioning or dialogue between an idea and something the idea isn't in order to substantiate or disprove it (Hope, 2000; Bruner, 2002; Tucker, 2007). Socrates is also credited with saying that true knowledge exists in knowing that you know nothing, a view frequently reflected in current notions of business leadership (Lindenmayer, 2013). Or, maybe we should start with the Roman Emperor Marcus Aurelius (second century AD), who suggested that the leaders should carry themselves with *gravitas*, a Latin word for dignity, impressiveness, seriousness, influence, weight, and

---

[1] or, as defined by wiki, a charm-based personality trait
[2] A well-known German sociologist, between the 19th and 20th centuries

9

presence. Certainly these traits must be critical for contemporary business leaders (Goyder, 2014).

Leadership has been part of the human experience for centuries and even millennia. In the Hellenistic era we started reflecting on this phenomenon and in the mid-twentieth century we started researching it. The first significant and comprehensive research seems to have been carried out in the 1960s, at Ohio State and Michigan Universities, mostly focused on leaders' behavior. This period seems the best departure point for our journey.

Prior to departure, we should briefly review baseline definitions of leadership. These will shift and grow throughout the book as we introduce new concepts.

Defining Leadership, First Round

Leadership has ancient roots and evolutionary origins that we've likely shared with animals for millennia (Van Vugt, 2006; King *et al.,* 2009; Van Vugt & Ahuja, 2011). Why animals? Most animals must decide, for example, when and where to forage or rest, when to leave a pasturage, and how to react to other animals (Van Vugt & Ahuja, 2011). Interestingly, some twentieth-century definitions of leadership can be applied both to traditional human working relationships and to the role of herd leaders. Here are two exemplary definitions that fit both: (1) Leaders should have an ability to organize participants and focus their attention on problems the leader considers significant (Cyert, 1990); and (2) leadership is a process of arranging a situation so that various members of a group, including the leader, can achieve common goals with maximum economy and a minimum of time and work (Bellows, 1959).

At the end of the twentieth century, the focus shifted to a specific relationship described as "influence," for example, that leadership is an influence relationship among leaders and followers who intend to implement real changes that reflect their mutual purposes (Rost, 1993). In the twenty-first century this "influencing" relationship has been further highlighted. Leadership today is seen as an *extraordinary* influence that is found in a person or a group (Robinson, 2010). Leadership is thus defined as a *process* of *social influence*, in which one person can enlist the aid and support of others for the accomplishment of a common task (Chemers, 1997, 2000; see also: Hersey *et al.,* 2001; Northouse, 2010; Kruse, 2013). In Chapter 3 we'll delve more deeply into the phenomenon of social influence.

An Ethical Caveat Prior to Taking Off

Influencing others has an ethical side. Ethical leadership not only is a value per se, but may also generate better financial returns, as some hold, for example, the Human Impact & Profit indexed portfolio, or HIP[3] (Herman, 2010).

Ethical leadership involves respect for ethical beliefs and values and for the dignity and rights of others (Watts, 2008). It's related to concepts such as trust, honesty, consideration, charisma, and fairness (Brown *et al.*, 2005). Ethical leadership is expressed through the leader as a person (i.e., self-knowledge, discipline, etc.), through leader–follower relationships, and through the ways in which leadership is performed (e.g., the extent to which the leader commands and controls; Ciulla, 2004). Northouse (2010) names several characteristics of ethical leaders, including respecting and serving others, showing justice, manifesting honesty, and building communities.

The ability to build a climate of trust is another important component of ethical leadership. The more people feel they're trusted, the more innovative they become; trust helps develop collaborative goals and roles (Kuper, 2006; Kouzes & Posner, 2008).

[3] HIP's way of evaluating the social and human impact of business ventures

CHAPTER I

Traditional Delineations of Kinds of Leadership

I planned to begin our journey with the Ohio State and North Michigan State University studies (1950s and 1960s), but I can't resist starting two decades earlier, with the father of social psychology, Kurt Lewin. He, together with his colleagues, developed in the 1930s a structure for identifying three basic kinds of leadership (Lewin *et al.*, 1939) still mentioned in contemporary sociological studies (e.g., Macionis, 2010). These three styles are:

- Autocratic (directive, authoritarian): characterized by a centralized authority dictating work methods, making unilateral decisions, and limiting employees' participation. This style is probably most appropriate when high-level coordination is needed, with no time for debate, e.g., in an emergency, conflict, or war.

- Democratic (participative): characterized by involving employees in the decision-making process, delegating authority, encouraging participation in deciding on work methods and goals, and using feedback as an opportunity to coach employees. The leader includes and involves others, although final decisions may be made using an autocratic approach or deciding by consensus. This style is applicable to most situations in business, education, the social sector, parenting, etc.

- Laissez-faire:; a free-style form characterized by giving employees liberty to ask questions, make decisions, and complete their work as they see fit. In this case leadership limits itself to providing materials and answering questions. This is seen as the most feeble leadership style, though it has proved effective in some exceptional therapeutic situations, e.g., the Summerhill school for problem children (Neil, 1977).

Lewin (2004)[1] also introduced the basic challenge for the leaders: maintaining the permanence of change. It's easy to disrupt the existing status

---

[1] A collection of Lewin's articles from the 1930s.

quo, but the real art and knowledge occur in making change durable. Lewin also introduced a theoretical framework for the study of leadership, but it wasn't until twenty years later, with the Ohio and Michigan studies, that a new era of research began.

The Ohio State University Studies

In the 1950s and 1960s, when the United States experienced its longest uninterrupted period of economic expansion in history, it became important for businesses in the United States to understand better what behaviors make a leader successful. The Ohio State University launched a study in which subordinates from various companies appraised their leaders for the number of times they engaged in certain types of behavior. These behaviors indicated the degree to which the leaders defined and structured their roles and the roles of their subordinates, with an eye toward achieving the goals of the group. The subordinates were asked to complete a Leadership Behavior Description Questionnaire (LBDQ, 1,800 questions) and its abbreviated version (LBDQ-XII, 150 questions). These questionnaires are still used today (Fleishman, 1953; Halpin & Winer, 1957; Stodgill et al., 1962).

The study found two types of behavior to be critical to success:

- Initiating structure: a task-oriented behavior, facilitating goal accomplishment (e.g., organizing work, giving structure, defining roles, scheduling) and
- Consideration structure: a relationship-focused behavior (e.g., building camaraderie, respect, trust)

The studies showed that these two types of behavior were distinct and independent of one another: The leader could demonstrate either high or low task-oriented behavior and, at the same time, have either a high or low focus on relationships (Rodrigue, 2013). In subsequent studies researchers tried to determine which of the two contributes more to effective leadership, but concluded that it depends on the context in which the leaders lead.

North Michigan State University Studies

Simultaneously, facing the same questions regarding a leader's behavior, Rensis Likert and his group of social researchers from the North Michigan

State University carried out similar studies, once again relying upon the perceptions of only one source (subordinates) completing a questionnaire on the features of a successful leader. The Michigan studies added Participative Leadership to the Ohio measures, identifying three types of leader behavior:

- Task-oriented behavior: planning, coordinating, and overseeing their subordinates' execution of tasks. The emphasis here was on production and technical aspects of the job. The leader looked at subordinates or employees as tools to accomplish the goals of the organization.
- Relationship-oriented behavior: not only concentrating on the task, but also on the relationship with subordinates. This kind of leader took a more considerate, helpful, and supportive approach with subordinates, including helping them with their careers and personal problems. He or she recognized effort with intrinsic as well as extrinsic rewards, thanking people for their work. Preferring a more general, hands-off approach to supervision rather than close control, he or she set goals and provided guidelines, but then gave subordinates plenty of leeway as to how the goals should be achieved.
- Participative leadership: the leader facilitated rather than directed, guiding the conversation and helping to resolve differences, and working to build a cohesive team to achieve team results, rather than focusing on individuals. For example, he or she might use team meetings to share ideas and involve the team in group decisions and the problem-solving process. Being responsible for results, he or she might make final decisions that take recommendations from the team into account (Likert, 1961; 1967).

Both the Ohio and Michigan studies asked subordinates in various companies to identify the features of a successful leader; both studies identified basic leadership categories relevant even today. However, they imagined the leader as someone who solidly and continuously performs in a certain style, independent of external conditions. In reality, conditions may change, and the question arose as to whether and, if so, how, leadership styles adapt to new circumstances. In response to this question there arose the Contingency Theory of Leadership.

Contingency Theory of Leadership

The contingency theory of leadership was conceived in the 1960s by Fred Fiedler (1967), who was probably the first management theorist to say that leadership effectiveness depends on the situation. His contingency theory holds that situational factors interact with leader traits and behavior to influence leadership effectiveness. There are no ideal and fixed leadership behaviors. Both task-oriented and relationship-oriented leaders can be effective if their orientation fits the situation.

Interestingly, to operationalize the study, Fiedler developed the Least Preferred Coworker (LPC) theory, in which leaders are asked to think of the coworker they like least.— someone with whom they would rather not work. Then, they're asked to rate some personal characteristics of this person, such as how friendly, nice, and cooperative he or she is. This process identifies two basic types of leaders:

- Those who, although they don't enjoy working with someone, can still describe that person in positive terms. These leaders scored high on the LPC scale; their ability to separate their personal feelings about a person and their ability to work with him or her, in Fiedler's theory, demonstrates a people-oriented approach.
- Those who don't want to work with someone and also actively dislike him or her would have a low LPC score and are seen as task-oriented leaders.

The LPC scale is still used as a tool to delve deeper into an understanding of leader–coworker relationships (Northouse, 2010).

The Situational Leadership Theory (SLT)

The Ohio and Michigan studies were focused on leaders and how they were perceived by their subordinates. However, there was also a growing interest in the role of employees and the way they influence a leader's approach; the focus shifted from the leader per se to include the role of coworkers.

In the 1970s and early 1980s, a model was developed that held that employees' readiness (defined as a combination of their competence and commitment levels) is the key factor determining the appropriate style of leadership. Situational Leadership Theory (SLT), as it was called, demonstrated that effective leadership should adjust not only to the task, job, or function that needs to be accomplished, but also to the person or group that is being influenced (Hersey *et al.*, 2012; Blanchard *et al.*, 1985).

Path-Goal Theory of Leadership (PGTL)

Some questions naturally arose, such as, What motivates employees? And, how does a leader's behavior relate to this motivation? In the 1960s and

1970s, researchers developed the Path–Goal Leadership Theory (PGTL), which claimed that the effectiveness of a leader's behavior is dependent not only on performance but also on subordinates' satisfaction and motivation (House, 1971). Based on the expectancy theory of motivation (Vroom, 1964) and the conviction that it's critical to maintain an adequate perception of how following a particular *path* will lead to a particular *goal* (Evans, 1970), PGTL holds that employees are motivated when they expect that their effort will lead to high performance, when these achievements are rewarded, and when the rewards are valuable to them. The leader's main job is to make sure that all three of these conditions exist.

Similar to Contingency and Situational theories, the PGTL theory assumes that leaders are flexible and can change their style as the situation requires, on the basis of the changing environment and their followers' characteristics.

Kaizen

Interestingly, at about the same time these studies were taking place (since 1950s) the Japanese economy was developing from scratch and skyrocketing toward the relatively high level of innovation and competitiveness it would achieve in the 1980s. The core philosophy and practice that perpetuated that growth was Kaizen – meaning "continuous improvement." Kaizen refers to diverse activities that continuously improve all functions and involve all employees at all levels (Imai, 1986).

It's intriguing to see how Japanese authors have compared the Western approach with Kaizen. For example *effect* in Kaizen's understanding is *long-term* and *undramatic*, whereas the Western cognition of effect is *short-term* and *dramatic*. Similarly, comparison of the notion of *pace* reveals opposite interpretations: *small steps* in Kaizen vs. *big steps* in the West. Time frame also differed – *continuous* and *incremental* (Kaizen) and *intermittent* (West) – as well as involvement: *everybody* (Kaizen) vs. the selection of a few *champions* (West) (Imai, 1986, fig. 2.1, p. 24). Kaizen is a continuous daily process going beyond productivity improvement. When done correctly, it humanizes the workplace and teaches people to experiment (Lairaia *et al.*, 1999, p. 26).

The Kaizen philosophy and methods spread across the world (Hannam, 1993). They're still recommended as a contemporary way to enhance achievements in business (Miller *et al.*, 2013) and beyond, e.g., losing weight or quitting smoking (Maurer, 2014).

It seems important to acknowledge that in the late twentieth and early twenty-first centuries, the analysis of leadership has greatly advanced.

While some scholars have focused on the dynamics of change (Senge, 1990; Senge *et al.*, 1999), and, more so, the acceleration of change (Drucker, 1995, 1999), others have highlighted stability as key to constructive leadership, based on the Roman notion of gravitas: "The absolute essential aspect of gravitas to success in leadership [–] would be [–] ability, as 'pilot of the plane,' to handle turbulence. Stability is the essence of gravitas" (Goyder, 2014). The ability to "handle turbulence" is indeed critical, especially given the rising manifestation of atypical and unpredictable Black Swans that cause abrupt change in the markets and in social life, best illustrated by the Black Swans Theory (Taleb, 2010). But instead of pushing for change or advocating for stability, it's critical that we strike a balance between the two. This leads to homeostatic analysis and to the concept of attractors, the first harbinger of complexity theory (see Chapter 5).

Chapter Coda

- Defining leadership, first round
- The first delineation of kinds of leadership was introduced in the 1930s by Kurt Lewin, who saw autocratic, democratic, and laissez-faire styles
- The Ohio and Michigan studies in the 1950s and 1960s found that there are basically three kinds of leadership: 1) initiating structure (Ohio) or task-oriented behavior (Michigan) – meaning task-oriented leadership; 2) consideration structure (Ohio) or relationship-oriented behavior (Michigan) – meaning a focus on relationships; and 3) participative leadership (Michigan) – meaning that the leader participates as a team member in various activities
- Contingent and Situational Leadership
- Path–Goal Leadership Theory (PGTL)
- Kaizen: inspiration from Japan

CHAPTER 2

Contemporary Views on Leadership

The leadership models we've discussed so far fall into two basic types:

- Autocratic, directive, authoritarian (Lewin et al., 1939); initiating structure (Ohio studies); and task-oriented behavior (Michigan studies)
- Democratic, participative (Lewin), consideration structure (Ohio), relationship-oriented behavior (Michigan)

Recently these styles were reframed and delineated as transactional and transformational (Bono & Judge, 2003; Burns, 2003; Judge & Piccolo, 2004; Bass & Riggio, 2006).

Transactional Leadership

Transactional leaders elicit cooperation by establishing exchanges of information with followers and then monitoring the relationship. They don't take into account the needs of their subordinates, but they're influential because their subordinates are convinced that it's in their own best interest to do as they're told (Northouse, 2010).

There are two basic components of transactional leadership (Judge & Piccolo, 2004):

- Contingent reward, understood as the degree to which the leader sets up constructive transactions or exchanges. The leader clarifies expectations and establishes the rewards for meeting them.
- Management by exception, defined as the degree to which the leader takes corrective action on the basis of the results of leader–follower transactions. More active leaders monitor their followers' behavior, anticipate problems, and take corrective actions before the behavior creates serious problems. Passive leaders wait until the behavior of the follower has created problems before taking action.

Transformational Leadership

Transformational leaders (Bono & Judge, 2003; Judge & Piccolo, 2004; Bass & Riggio, 2006) or *transforming leaders* (e.g., Burns, 2003) garner support by inspiring followers to identify with a vision that reaches beyond their own immediate self-interest. They stimulate and inspire followers to achieve sometimes-extraordinary outcomes and, in the process, develop their own leadership capacities (Bass & Riggio, 2006). It was recently documented that transformational leaders create a psychological climate conducive to organizational change and organizational creativity (Allen *et al.*, 2013).

Four components of transformational leadership have been identified (Bass, 1985; Judge and Piccolo, 2004; Bass & Riggio, 2006; Burns, 2003; Northouse, 2010):

- The first is called idealized influence, which basically refers to charisma. Charismatic leaders display conviction and appeal to followers on an emotional level. Because their style tends to be so spirited and energetic, they generate admiration, respect, and trust. Followers see them as having extraordinary capabilities, persistence, and determination and, therefore, often identify them as role models.

Charisma can be compelling, but it's not without its detractors. It's been criticized as a "false" leadership trait (Solomon, 2014) and also reframed as *socialized charismatic leadership* in order to take away its individualistic façade (Brown *et al.*, 2005; see more on charisma in Chapters 3 and 4).

- The second component, called *inspirational motivation*, is understood as the articulation of a clear, appealing, and inspiring vision. Leaders who use inspirational motivation challenge followers to meet higher standards, communicate optimism about future goal attainment, and provide meaning for the task at hand (Bass, 1985; Judge & Piccolo, 2004; Bass & Riggio, 2006; Northouse, 2010).
- The third, *intellectual stimulation*, inspires followers' creativity by questioning assumptions and challenging the existing status quo. The transformational leader challenges routines, takes risks, and solicits followers' ideas.
- The fourth is *individual consideration*, which means attending to and supporting the individual needs of followers.

Laissez-Faire

There is also a *laissez-faire* leadership style characterized as avoidance or absence of leadership. It is, by definition, the most passive. According to nearly all researchers, it's usually the most ineffective leadership style (Bass & Riggio, *ibid*).

In both the transactional and transformative models, the leader is perceived to be dominant and, in some situations, even charismatic, gathering followers by dint of personality and charm (Conger & Kanungo, 1998). While it's important to develop leadership qualities in those "below" (Bass and Riggio, *ibid*), this delineation in and of itself suggests that a structure in which there are those *above* and those *below* exists and that, presumably, newly developed leaders will replicate the "above–below" relationships.

Following is a review of approaches that counter the "above–below" structure, sharing leadership across the group or organization. Interestingly, the ideas of *participative leadership* were formulated as early as the 1970s (Vroom & Yetton, 1973).

At the beginning of Section 1, we reviewed some definitions of leadership, most of which were based on the mechanism of the individual's (leader's) *influence*. Here we present a different understanding of influence – that of the group. (The phenomenon of influence will be examined further in Chapter 3.)

Shared Leadership

Shared Leadership (SL) is a dynamic, interactive process among individuals and groups with the objective to lead one another. This process often involves peer-to-peer, or lateral, influence and at other times involves upward or downward hierarchical influence (Pearce & Conger, 2002). "Shared leadership only exists to the extent that the team actively engages in the leadership process" (Pearce & Conger, *idem*, p 12). Leadership is distributed among team members rather than focused on a single designated leader. A team does well when it relies on leadership provided by the team as a whole rather than looking to a single individual to lead it (Carson *et al.*, 2007).

The team in this approach can be viewed as a potential source of leadership (Mayo *et al.*, 2003). For support and analysis of the SL perspective, the social-networks approach seems a helpful conceptual framework (Mayo *et al.*, *ibid*). It also offers helpful insight in advance of our forthcoming discussion of complexity-oriented leadership.

Distributed Leadership

Similarly, Distributed Leadership (DL) is characterized as an emergent property of a group or network of interacting individuals open to shifting the boundaries of leadership and having varieties of expertise distributed across many individuals, instead of the few (Bennett *et al.*, 2003; Bolden, 2011).

Conventional constructs of leadership rarely accommodate change, especially to new patterns of interdependence and coordination, which give rise to a distributed approach to leadership (Gronn, 2002). DL has altered the idea of solo leadership (Gronn, 2009). It has been applied in educational and public sectors, as many schools have restructured their leadership teams to meet the needs of their workforce changes. Schools engage with complex collaborative arrangements, and DL requires team members to cross multiple types of boundaries and share ideas and insights (Harris & Spillane, 2008).

DL, by drawing attention to the large number of actors involved in leadership and the importance of organizational processes in shaping their engagements, makes a significant contribution to the ways in which leadership is accomplished in sectors such as higher education (Gosling *et al.*, 2009).

Leaderful Organizations

Shared and Distributed Leadership both have a practical implication: building Leaderful Organizations (LOs) in which everyone participates in the leadership, both collectively and concurrently, challenges the conventional view of leadership as "being out in front." It offers a true mutual model that transforms leadership from an individual property into a new paradigm that redefines leadership as collective practice (Raelin, 2003, 2005, 2011).

The idea of a LO is probably best characterized by Richard Ian "Ric" Charlesworth, M.D.,[1] who was a captain of the Australian hockey team and a member of the Australian team that won the World Cup in 1986. His LO story began when he became head coach of the Australian women's hockey team, which, under his leadership, won almost every top hockey contest in the world, including the Champion's Trophy, the World Cup, the Olympics, and the Commonwealth Games.

As a coach Charlesworth took a revolutionary approach to building winning organizations by developing a leaderful hockey team. He says that

---

[1] Interview by Varghese, S. (2009). Building "Leaderful" Teams. *Forbes*, retrieved February 24, 2017 from: www.forbes.com/2009/11/23/charlesworth-hierarchy-leaderful-leadership-ceonetwork-managing .html.

a single leader can generate only a certain number of ideas and concentrate on only a limited number of topics, while a critical mass of leaders allows for more possibilities and more solutions and ideas to be filtered by the group. With more leaders one is likely to come up with better answers. Moreover, having multiple leaders ensures that all feel they have a say in the decision-making process. In other words, the basis of a leaderful team is giving opportunities to everyone to contribute something significant.

Versatile Leadership

Leadership requires opposing strengths (e.g., the ability to listen, but also to take forceful action), and most leaders have a natural tendency to over-develop one strength at the expense of its counterpart. Moreover, while leaders are often advised to identify and build their strengths, a strength taken to an extreme can become a weakness. The resulting imbalance diminishes a leader's effectiveness. Yet the downside of "overdoing" is often obscured because its problematic aspects aren't immediately obvious. Going to extremes to meet challenges is part of the job. But leaders who resist such asymmetry may increase their versatility and their impact, say Robert Kaplan and Robert Kaiser (2006), the originators of the Versatile Leadership (VL) concept.

Versatility is the ability to understand and adapt to differences in communication preferences in order to make others more open and receptive, creating more effective and productive relationships. It's a skill that can be learned, and people who have it find it far easier to work with others toward shared organizational goals (Leimbach, 2009; Roth & Leimbach, 2015).

In that way, versatility is characteristic of both good leadership and good communication. Some say that companies can experience measurable improvements in performance when the team becomes versatile, i.e., people learn to adapt to others' social styles (Leimbach, 2009).

From the perspective of Empowering Leadership, as presented in this book (Section 3), versatility could be perceived as a characteristic of empathetic communication.

Creative Leadership

Creative leadership probably isn't an academically acknowledged kind of leadership, especially considering that any of the leadership styles discussed here can be performed in a more or less creative way. However, creative leadership has been of interest since the 1950s and as such is worth mentioning (see, for example, Bellows, 1959).

Creative leadership is proposed to be a core leadership competence (Puccio *et al.*, 2010) and is suggested as an important way of breaching barriers (Rickards & Moger, 2000). Predicting future trends, Min Basadur (2004) claims that the most effective leaders of the twenty-first century will help individuals and teams to drive change through applied creativity that includes continuously discovering and defining new problems, solving those problems, and implementing the new solutions.

In Chapter 7 we will delve more deeply into the essence of creativity and, in Chapter 14, how it may be augmented.

Transforming Buffaloes into Geese

The expression that best describes this book's core complexity narrative is Transforming Buffaloes into Geese.

In the analogy buffaloes represent the old leadership style. A herd will not act without the guidance of the head buffalo, even standing idly by to be slaughtered if the lead buffalo is killed first (Belasco & Stayer, 1993).

Geese represent the new and recommended leadership paradigm. A flock of geese has many leaders flying together in a "V" formation. They continuously exchange information on gravity, geographical directions, etc. There's no hierarchy. Their high-level, elegant "V" formation, sometimes sustained for thousands of miles, appears out of the unsystematic interaction of birds "on the lower level" (Reynolds, 1987). One study has shown that birds flying in "V" formation strategically position themselves in aerodynamically optimal positions and experience positive aerodynamic interactions that maximize "upwash" (good air) capture. They precisely time the flapping of their wings and adjust their position to make the best of the subtle effects of air turbulence; each bird takes advantage of upwash thrown up by the wings of the flyer in front while avoiding lift-sapping "downwash" (Portugal et al, 2014).

The metaphor of the self-managed flock of equally informed and involved geese becomes a recommendation for future teamwork, especially when a team needs to adapt to accelerating changes (Belasco & Stayer, *ibid*). It's worth adding that to be able to synchronize with others in the flock, the birds must, by some mechanism, "tune into" the others, mostly through empathy and the Mirror Neurons System (MNS) (Praszkier, 2014).

Later in this book we'll analyze the formation of a new order on a higher level out of seemingly chaotic interactions of elements on the lower level, as well as the empathetic mechanisms enabling better synchronization.

Authentic Leadership

Authentic leaders acquire their legitimacy through having honest relationship with followers who value their leaders' input and see them as open and ethical. By building trust and generating enthusiastic support from their followers, authentic leaders are able to improve individual and team performance (Gardner *et al.,* 2011). As we'll see later, leaders who typically exemplify authentic leadership are Social Entrepreneurs.

Chapter Coda

- Presenting Transactional and Transformational Kinds of Leadership
- Reviewing Shared and Distributed Leadership, and the Concept of Leaderful Organizations.
- Presenting Versatile Leadership, which holds that one should harmoniously develop all skills, instead of concentrating on one, specific skill
- Buffalo and Geese approach
- First step into the concept of creativity through presenting the ideas on Creative Leadership
- Authentic Leadership as a sneak peek at the leadership of Social Entrepreneurs

CHAPTER 3

Leadership and Social Influence

When we introduced leadership styles at the beginning of Section 1, we noted that leadership involves a process of *social influence*, in which one person is able to enlist the aid and support of others in the accomplishment of a common task. How does this process work? Let's take a closer look at the different ways leaders can garner support from their followers and whether that influence is based on *external control* (e.g., differential power, reward and punishment), *manipulation* (e.g., flattery), or *interpersonal coordination* (e.g., conformity) (Nowak *et al.*, 2003).

Obedience and Persuasion

Followers may adapt to a leader's ideas in numerous ways. One superficial way is through *obedience to authority*. This mechanism is most likely to occur within autocratic, directive, and authoritarian leadership styles, where the leader's core interest is to impose desirable behavior.

Several experiments have shown that people tend to obey someone solely because they perceive him or her to be an authority (Milgram, 2009; Martin & Hewstone, 2007). People justify their behavior by assigning responsibility to the authority, rather than taking it themselves. Moreover, they might obey orders even when the actions ordered are against their own ethical standards. The famous Milgram experiment in the 1960s, repeated many times within different societies, consistently showed the willingness of study subjects to obey an authority figure who instructed them to perform acts conflicting with their own personal ethical standards. Most subjects were obedient, even when they believed they were causing serious injury and distress by administering apparently dangerous electric shocks to people. In fact, no one was actually harmed (Milgram, 1963), but evidence of individuals inflicting real torture at the instruction of another abounds, even today.

This sort of "blind" obedience is often fleeting, and in the absence of authority, the imposed and ethically unsavory behavior may diminish or

26

cease. Furthermore, behaving under the pressure of an authority against one's own ethics may inflict severe mental harm. Milgram's experiments have been criticized as being highly unethical. Subjects suffered loss of dignity, shattered self-esteem, and loss of trust in authority in general, even when authorities they encountered later appeared rational (Baumrind, 1964).

Persuasion, on the other hand, is a deliberate and nonmanipulative attempt to influence others' beliefs, attitudes, intentions, motivations, or behaviors, as opposed to exercising authority. It may also be symbolic, using words, images, sounds, etc. (Wood, 2000; Gass & Seiter, 2013; Petty *et al.*, 2003), to earn subordinates' cooperation through various means.

Compliance, Entrapment, and Manipulation

The use of authority or persuasion may lead, at the very least, to *compliance*, meaning adaptation regardless of whether or not one agrees with the leader, as long as one's dissenting opinions are kept private. In other words compliance is about adjusting one's behavior (but not necessarily one's mind). Several studies have documented that greater external pressure generally leads to greater compliance with the wishes of the experimenter (Freedman & Fraser, 1966).

Another method of persuasion that can result in a high degree of adaptation is *entrapment*. This occurs when people can be persuaded to obey easy commands first and then feel compelled to obey more and more difficult commands, also known as the *foot-in-the-door phenomenon* (FITD). Studies have shown that carrying out an unpalatable but small request increased the likelihood that the subject would agree to a similar but even less palatable request made by the same person (Freedman & Fraser, *ibid*). The FITD phenomenon, if applied on purpose, is simply *manipulation*, understood as exerting devious influence over a person for one's own advantage (Braiker, 2004; Cialdini & Goldstein, 2004; Maxwell, 2013).

The FITD technique is often used in sales to entrap new clients. However, used purposely by leaders against their subordinates, it is pure manipulation (Freedman & Fraser, *ibid*). These tactics might work, often effectively, but they can also be destructive, exposing people to negative feelings and reinforcing dependency, helplessness, and victimization (Braiker, 2004).[1]

---

[1] Some kinds of manipulation may be less destructive, e.g., ingratiation: a psychological technique in which an individual attempts to become more attractive or likeable to the target (Jones, 1964).

In return, these negative feelings can limit subordinates' effectiveness as a source of information or innovation (Maxwell, 2013).

Self-Persuasion, Conformity, and Cognitive Dissonance

A more sophisticated method of adaptation is *self-persuasion*. In this case, people are not coerced. Rather, remaining free to choose, they build up internal justifications for obedience. Leaders influence self-persuasion indirectly, by placing people in situations where they are motivated to persuade themselves to change their own attitudes or behavior (Aronson, 1999). This seems a more "advanced" adaptation then mere obedience, as it involves modifications within the *internal* cognitive system, rather than *external* imposition. This form of adaptation is called *conformity*, which, as opposed to *compliance*, involves a change not only in behavior, but also in beliefs or thinking, in order to align with others or to align with normative standards (Deutsch & Gerard, 1955).

What, actually, makes people change their beliefs and thinking? How does the conformity mechanism work? When people's actions conflict with their prior beliefs or attitudes, they often change these beliefs or attitudes to be more consistent with their own actions. Making a new choice that isn't consistent with these prior beliefs or attitudes kindles *cognitive dissonance*, which is then reduced through rationalization: i.e., the prior beliefs are changed to be more consistent with the actions. The formulation of cognitive dissonance concept is considered to be one of the most influential theories in psychology (Festinger, 1957; Festinger *et al.*, 2009).

Leaders may (intentionally or otherwise) use the power of the situational context that influences the individual's cognitive structures and, in that way, societal mind-sets. *Consistency* in cognition is one of the basic human drives acted out when people incorporate a new behavior into a self-image they desire to be cohesive. The new situational context prompts restructuring and achieving consistency on a new level; situational context influences cognitive structures, so that the person ends up incorporating the new behavior into a cohesive self-image (Bem, 1967). If one begins an action, one will develop cognition that justifies this action intellectually, and the new cognitive structures will promote new attitudes and behaviors. For example, the purchase of a particular brand of automobile leads to the reading of advertisements or articles in praise of the brand purchased.

This sheds more light on the FITD phenomenon as well as on the process of conforming: One has to restructure internal beliefs in order to reduce the apparent cognitive dissonance and reach a state of internal cohesiveness on this new level. Most people want to perceive themselves as *consistent* (Mischel, 1969, 1973).

Majority Influence and the Asch Experiment

Another form of social influence is *majority influence,* in which the opinion of the majority sways the minority. The best illustration of this is the famous Asch experiment. In this study researchers gathered a group of seven to nine individuals in a classroom to take part in what appeared to be a simple experiment in visual discrimination. The task was simple: Participants were asked to say which of three lines of very different lengths was equal in length to a visually presented standard line. All but one of the participants were covert experiment assistants who each selected the same, noticeably wrong line. The subject was the last to choose and chose the same wrong line as the others. There were 123 subjects in this and similar tests. In most cases (75 percent) the subjects choose the wrong line in conformity with the assistants. This shows the power of the pressure of the majority. Even if they are making obvious wrong choices, most people tend to conform to the majority's false opinions (Asch, 1956; McLeod, 2008).

Deutsch & Gerard (1955) hold that there are basically two psychological needs that lead humans to conform to the expectations of others: the need to be right (so-called *informational social influence*) and the need to be liked (so-called *normative social influence*). Those needs were apparently in conflict during the Asch experiment; the subjects must have been torn between a belief that they knew the right answer and acceptance of the others' consensus around another answer. Fortunately, 25 percent never conformed to the assistants' choice and, instead, held to their own conviction.

Minority Influence

Minority influence takes place when members of a minority group persuade a majority to accept their beliefs or behavior (Gardikiotis, 2011). This occurs when a small group or an individual acts as an agent of social change, by questioning established societal perceptions and proposing alternative ideas that challenge existing social norms. Results of minority influence are generally observable only after a period of time, as a tendency within the majority to accept the views expressed by the minority (McLeod, 2007).

In this vein, some researchers have modeled the "diffusion of innovations,"[2] which led them to the "bubbles theory" (Vallacher & Nowak, 2007), in which "bubbles of new" appear and radiate in the "sea of old." This process is similar to the phenomenon of phase transitions in physics (Nowak & Vallacher, 2005), as when water, at a temperature of 212°F, transforms into gas. In this scenario, one first observes a small nucleus of bubbles, which connect together, grow in size, and become large, full-blown bubbles that eventually break the surface. Using bubbles as a metaphor for dynamical change, one can say that the bubbles are forerunners of the new state (metaphorical gas), becoming visible while the old state (liquid) can still be observed. Similarly, in societies undergoing rapid transition, we can find islands of the new reality intermixed with the old one. As change progresses, the islands of "new" gradually expand at the expense of the "old." Under this model, interacting groups, rather than isolated individuals, are subject to change.

Bubble leaders are of central importance, especially at the beginning of these minority-driven transitions. They sow the seeds of the "new" and help the minority withstand the pressure of the majority during early stages of change. They can also foster connections among isolated clusters of "new" that can influence of the propagation of the idea (Nowak& Vallacher, 2005; Vallacher & Nowak, 2007).

Identification and Internalization

On a higher level of leadership, the earlier mentioned mechanisms of executing authority, i.e., obedience, manipulation, compliance, and conformity, would not be satisfactory. Democratic, participative, relationship-oriented, shared, distributed, or transformational leadership would gain buy in from followers by earning their *identification* with the leader's vision and/or objectives.

Identification with a leader happens when people are influenced by a leader who is liked and respected (Kelman, 1958). Research has shown that people predicting job satisfaction and high performance highlight identification with the leader as a significant factor for intellectual stimulation and personal recognition (Hobman *et al.,* 2011).

Moreover, it was shown in Chapter 2 that transformational leadership is positively associated with personal identification with the leader, which

---

[2] The title of Everett Rogers' book is *Diffusion of Innovations* (Rogers 2003).

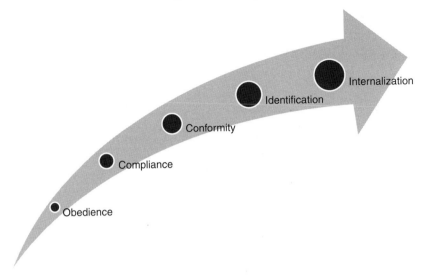

Figure 4. Levels of adaptation.

supports followers' ability to innovate and willingness to commit to the organization. Vice versa, limited personal identification between leaders and followers can have a negative effect on the leader's effectiveness and stifle innovation and commitment to the success of organization (Zhu *et al.*, 2013).

Probably the highest level of adaptation or acceptance is *internalization*, which happens when people adopt a belief or behavior both publicly and privately, without any internal conflict (Kelman, *ibid*) (see Figure 4). Through internalization people incorporate within themselves new values or attitudes and, in that way, become truly committed and loyal partners in pursuing desirable goals.

Charisma, Part 1

Personality-based charisma, characterized as a compelling attractiveness or charm that can inspire devotion in others, was introduced into the literature by one of the founders of sociology, Max Weber (1978),[3] and advanced by Robert Tucker (1968) and Stanley Stark (1977).

---

[3] Original printing in 1947.

The charismatic leader's inspiration, vision, and risk taking can help bring about radical change, especially in organizations trying to move out of lethargy (Conger, 1989). Charisma seen as a "magical gift" possessed by leaders makes their followers strongly identify with the leaders. The transformational leader, in contrast, inspires followers to pursue organizational goals instead of self-interests. Moreover, a transformational leader can operate without charisma and effectively influence team members using inspiration, intellectual stimulation, and individual consideration (Barbuto, 1997). And in fact, as mentioned in Chapter 2, charisma is perceived as a debatable leadership characteristic, being either criticized as a "false" leadership trait (Solomon, 2014) or reframed as socialized charismatic leadership (Brown *et al.*, 2005).

In Chapter 4 we will introduce an alternative known as mission-based charisma, associated with the mission and passion for pursuing this mission.

Chapter Coda

- Authoritarian leaders may use obedience to authority and persuasion as instruments for influencing their followers.
- This, however, is a lower-level social influence, invoking adaptation mechanisms such as obedience to authority and compliance.
- Medium-level social influence is achieved by instigating self-persuasion and conformity.
- Higher-level social influence comes through identification and internalization, when people modify their own internal cognitive structures and adopt their leader's vision as their own.

CHAPTER 4

Example
The Specific Social Influence of Social Entrepreneurs

At the upper end of the spectrum of social influence are social entrepreneurs (Gentile, 2002; Leadbeater, 1997; Steyaert & Hjorth, 2006; Brinckerhoff, 2000; Martin, 2007). In the past decade social entrepreneurship has made a popular name for itself as a "new phenomenon" that is reshaping the way we think about social-value creation (Mair & Marti, 2006). The term "social entrepreneur" has also spread rapidly through the nonprofit sector, sparking the interest of major foundations and private funders (Kramer, 2005). Moreover, two social entrepreneurs have been awarded the Nobel Prize in peace: Mohammad Yunus in 2006 (banking for the poor and microcredits)[1] and Kailash Satyarthi in 2014 (Global March against Child Labor).[2]

Ashoka: Innovators for the Public,[3] was set up in 1980, to identify, select, and empower leading social entrepreneurs. The Ashoka founder and CEO Bill Drayton believes that all social entrepreneurs have a powerful, system-changing idea and that they "envisage a systemic change, identifying the jujitsu points that allow them to tip the whole society into the new path and then persist and persist until the job is done" (Drayton, 2002, p. 123).

Social entrepreneurs are a rich source of new and creative ideas on how to solve pressing social problems. Such ideas, imbued with distinguished ethical fiber, have impact that is far-reaching (Drayton, 2000; Hammonds, 2005; Bornstein, 1998, 2004). Social entrepreneurs usually redefine and introduce new solutions to many areas of human need, such as health, the environment, and youth development (Drayton, 2004). The three thousand Ashoka Fellows are the world's leading social entrepreneurs; they are

[1] Ashoka Academy Member, see: www.ashoka.org/press/3798.
[2] Ashoka Fellow, see: www.ashoka.org/fellow/kailash-satyarthi.
[3] www.ashoka.org.

33

changing or have changed the existing patterns of society (interview with Bill Drayton; Koo, 2013).

These leaders have addressed, mostly with extraordinary success, seemingly insurmountable and unsolvable social problems. In so doing, they've not only managed to motive the players critical to a solution and influence people's mind-sets; they've also had an enormous effect on the social landscape. They often trigger a bottom-up process of change, involving and empowering groups or societies to take upon themselves actions necessary for solving their social problems (Praszkier & Nowak, 2012,). Peter Drucker noted that social entrepreneurs change the performance capacity of society,[4] meaning that their impact far exceeds their specific areas of involvement or control.

Social entrepreneurs, in particular Ashoka Fellows, aim to bring about change not only in the way something is being done but also in the minds of those involved in the doing. Social influence that leads to mind-set modification requires that a whole of society see new potential for change. Leading social entrepreneurs are mass recruiters and facilitators of local change makers, who in turn become local role models for change making. Encouraging local change makers provides local persuasive leadership (interview with Bill Drayton; Hartnell, 2015). Social entrepreneurship also involves cooperation critical for building social capital. Drayton (2013) calls this "collaborative entrepreneurship." Given the remarkable results these leaders have achieved, it seems a worthy exercise to take a closer look at the ways social entrepreneurs work.

The Unique Influence of Social Entrepreneurs

Since 2004, I've been a second opinion interviewer for Ashoka Fellow nominees.[5] During my second-opinion interviews, I was usually struck by the candidate's captivating presence and often sensed a magical mixture of optimism, confidence, and commitment. For example, while talking to Ramesh Kumar.

---

[4] Interview with Peter Drucker; Gendron, 1966.
[5] Since 2000 the author has been doing second-opinion reviews for the Ashoka Fellowship, for example, in Canada (eight times), Uganda (three times), Nepal (three times), Pakistan (five times), the USA (twice), India (three times), Nigeria (twice), Thailand (three times), Senegal (three times), Egypt (twice), and Burkina Faso (once), Bangladesh (once), Mexico (once), and Indonesia (once).

Ramesh Kumar from India

I was entranced by his idea of introducing valuable, affordable, high-quality houses into the most disadvantaged rural areas. He did this by creating an innovative process of microfinancing to be used for building houses in sections. Each section requires a separate loan, which is much smaller than a loan needed to finance an entire house. The process is adopted by a community, which guarantees the loans. Kumar is also concerned with sanitation in these houses, so he's provided hygiene education and installed toilets.

Tracing back to the source of Kumar's social commitment, I found that his father, from whom he inherited his social passion and yen for connecting people from all walks of life, was his strongest role model. He was also active in the Boy Scouts and, working for a bank after graduation, traveled across the country building self-help groups. Being creative and committed, he advanced in his company, while remaining dedicated to the idea of empowering people at the bottom of the social pyramid.

I sensed the same sort of "magical emanation" talking to Elie Abou Saab.

Elie Abou Saab from Lebanon

Saab is reversing the passivity of citizens (especially in societies with low or nonexistent civic engagement) by creating a new culture that empowers and engages citizens in the effort to defend their rights and hold governments accountable. To achieve this, he finds neutral, nonpolitical areas where people can take action to address grievances in a nonconfrontational way.[6]

Saab's idea was to focus on roadway potholes, which the authorities had completely neglected. He launched a well-designed and vibrant platform where people could report holes on the street, upload photos, and follow the authorities' response. He also initiated a competition for reporting the largest and (ironically) "nicest" hole of the month, which proved very efficient in calling the authorities to account and prompting action. Saab's work has created a feedback loop in which people enjoy the positive results they see and get more involved in civic engagement.

During his school days Saab took part in outdoor activities and was always engaged in social work, including work with the Red Cross. After graduation he launched his own multimedia and e-business company,

---

[6] See: www.ashoka.org/fellow/elie-abou-saab.

becoming a successful business entrepreneur, and remained involved in the Red Cross as a first aid instructor. Always active, expressing himself passionately, finding solutions to insurmountable problems, being successful both in business and in the social arena, Saab created a unique aura that draws people to him and commands their attention wherever he goes.

Similarly, it's impossible to ignore Michel Babadjidé.

Michel Babadjidé from Benin

Benin is increasing organic food production by blending traditional agropastoral practices with the most modern farming techniques. His inclusive approach helps farmers in all economic strata, including the poorest and the most advanced, make their farming practices more profitable. Through his work he is reversing the food importing trend to one of exporting and stemming the migration of youth to cities.

As a young boy Babadjidé spent much of his time with animals, discovering that we need to care for their health the same way we care for people's health. This drove him to become a veterinary surgeon (though he could have chosen to become a high-earning doctor for people). He invented several new ways of breeding livestock and, in so doing, met with some resistance. Colleagues, universities, and scientists rejected his practice of breeding different species together. Denigrated and despised, Babadjidé was reviled by his peers and the Ministry of Livestock and banned from all seminars and benefits. But this didn't stop him. He took every opportunity to promote his concept and ultimately became one of the most honored and respected experts in the field. His work created significant innovations in animal husbandry in Benin and the region and provided valued educational opportunities to university students.

After meeting all of these remarkable leaders, I was compelled to identify what it was, exactly, that they radiated. One exploratory track was to delve into the personality traits of social entrepreneurs; another was to pin down the social influence approach they use; and a third was to identify any specific mission-oriented charisma they manifest.

The world is changeable, it's worth a try! I first thought that the source of these leaders' captivating presence would be found embedded in personality traits specific to social entrepreneurs. It's likely that the Ashoka Fellows represent the most comprehensive body of social entrepreneurs in the world (Bornstein, 2004), so we selected them as our research cohort.

Candidates are elected to Ashoka Fellowship through a strict multilevel process[7] focused on the criteria that, according to Ashoka, define social entrepreneurs (Drayton, 2002, 2005; Hammonds, 2005). These criteria include:

- Having a new idea for solving a critical social problem
- Being creative
- Having an entrepreneurial personality
- Envisioning the broad social impact of the idea
- Possessing an unquestionable ethical standard[8]

For the purpose of our research, we treated these criteria as independent variables. The main question was whether or not individuals elected under this set of criteria also share other personality traits, which would become our dependent variables.

We found in our study that the personality traits that significantly differentiated social activists, including social entrepreneurs, from a random sample of the society were (Praszkier *et al.*, 2009; Praszkier & Nowak, 2012):

- Trust
- Optimism
- Cooperation
- Involvement in social networks
- Adversity coping mechanisms
- Risk-taking
- Belief in the malleability of people and the world[9]

The last two traits, risk-taking and belief in the malleability of people and the world, also differentiated social entrepreneurs (Ashoka Fellows) from social activists (non–Ashoka Fellows). This means that the profile of a social entrepreneur (and the message he or she implicitly conveys) is not only of someone who is trusting, optimistic, and ready to cooperate; has a broad personal support network; and is eager to overcome obstacles; it's also of someone who strongly believes that it's worth taking great risks in order to create change and that bringing about necessary change in people is feasible.

---

[7] See: www.ashoka.org/sites/ashoka/files/Ashoka%20Search%20and%20Selection%20Process.jpg.
[8] See also: www.ashoka.org/support/criteria.
[9] Following Professor Carol Dweck's theory related to the belief in the changeability of people and the world (Dweck, 2000, 2006).

Specific Energy, Passion, and Optimism

Because they have energy specific to their cause, optimism in their ability to achieve their goal, and passionate involvement in their work, social entrepreneurs are a contagious source of energy that radiates commitment and a heightened level of motivation. Indeed, those who have had the opportunity to talk to social entrepreneurs usually say that it was a unique and powerful experience in which the entrepreneurs exuded passion, commitment, and energy. Also, some studies have confirmed that energy is a key personality trait that supports leadership (Kirkpatick & Locke, 1991; Schneidr, 2007). From a corporate perspective, energy is one of the five personality traits employers value most. It rates second (78 percent) behind professionalism (86 percent), followed by confidence (61 percent), self-monitoring (58 percent) and intellectual curiosity (57 percent) (Casserly, 2012).

Passion is another critical component of the "magic" of social entrepreneurs' influence. Bill Drayton says that social entrepreneurs usually won't sleep until they find solutions.

One important caveat here: Being possessed by an idea shouldn't mean being obsessed. Passion is defined as a strong inclination toward a self-defining activity that one likes or even loves (Vallerand, 2008). But there are two types of passion, obsessive and harmonious, and only the latter is constructive (Vallerand, *ibid*).

Passion produces not only pleasure but often hardship as well, especially if one can't stop thinking about how to solve the onslaught of problems that continually present themselves. This fixation may draw one's thoughts away from social or even family life and, as a result, may even endanger relationships. Being passionate means balancing on the line between the present reality and the future (solutions, plans, and innovations). To remain balanced one should take real breaks and periods of total withdrawal. Resetting one's mind, even for a short time, helps one return to planning with more strength.

Social Entrepreneurs' Authentic Leadership

Talking to social entrepreneurs arouses an awareness of their deep and authentic engagement. Milway (2014) framed it that "they come from a place of deep authenticity." Their deep commitment usually derives from early life experience and is a logical and authentic rationale behind their professional trajectory.[10] There is no doubt that social entrepreneurs fall under the definition of Authentic Leadership.

Short Distance–Long Distance

It seems it's also important for social entrepreneurs to have both short- and long-distance perspectives. The short-distance perspective enables the initial taxi and takeoff, or launch, whereas the long-distance perspective enables the climb to cruising altitude, the long flight, and the successful landing: in other words, the long haul to scale (Deiglmeier, 2013). This is especially true, given that the secondary consequences of change can be more important than the initial change; Everett Rogers (2003) holds that it is not change per se that matters; it's the consequences of that initial change that play a crucial role in the way transformation proliferates over time.

Social entrepreneurs (Ashoka Fellows) seem to master both. All three of the men mentioned earlier (Ramesh Kumar, Elie Abou Saab, and Michel Babadjidé) started with a small-scale, local pilot project and when, through probes and trials, they had refined their models, they scaled up, with a vision of how to help those most in need and a strategy (often instinctual) to win the buy in of key players, build sustainability, etc.

Mission-Oriented Charisma, Part 2

Social entrepreneurs' outstanding impact on the world around them wouldn't be possible without a special kind of social influence. They eschew control through obedience to authority or manipulation and avoid top-down, persuasive forms of social influence, yet they still have a significant effect on the mind-sets and attitudes of people and groups. So how do they do it? The results of our analysis suggest that they use a specific *Mission-Oriented Charisma.*

"Mission-oriented" means that it isn't necessarily personality-based (as indicated by Weber). Instead, it's a specific radiating power associated with the particular mission being pursued and passion behind the pursuit. Influence is achieved by summoning people to join in a movement for change and in coleading such a movement (Tucker, 1968). It's this form of

---

[10] Interviewing candidates to the Ashoka Fellowship involves tracing down this logical life path, even to the early family days and inspirations from important figures.

charisma that enables social entrepreneurs to initiate and pursue possible avenues of action (Edles & Appelrouth, 2014).

Concluding, it seems that social entrepreneurs demonstrate a specific kind of social influence. This calls for reflection on the definition of leadership, which we'll begin in Section 2.

Chapter Coda

- An overview of the phenomenon of Social Entrepreneurship and the uniqueness of the Ashoka Fellows' approach
- Social entrepreneurs' exert social influence through:
  - Specific personality traits, especially the conviction that everything is changeable
  - Specific energy and optimism
  - Authentic kind of leadership
  - Short-term and long-term perspectives
  - Unique kind of charisma

Complexity and Networks

This section introduces the concept of complexity (Chapter 5); illustrates its successful application in business and within large, peaceful social movements (Chapter 6); presents the essence of creativity (Chapter 7), and looks at aspects of efficient and vibrant networks that harness its power (Chapter 8).

Continuing from Section 1, we begin with new definitions of leadership styles.

Defining Leadership, Second Round

Leadership, as defined in Section 1, focused participants' attention on significant problems, arranged a situation to achieve common goals, and established a relationship of influence. That definition doesn't cover activities within new styles of shared, distributed, and creative leadership, and it especially doesn't reflect the leadership styles of social entrepreneurs. Perhaps a more inclusive definition, following Kouzes & Posner (2008), is that leadership is a process of creating a way for people to contribute to making something extraordinary happen. (And certainly, social entrepreneurs are leaders passionate about making something extraordinary happen.) This definition suggests that leadership "creates a way for people to contribute," rather than "influences people," and along these lines, opens up an avenue for bottom-up leadership. It also asserts that the purpose of leadership isn't simply to achieve a task but to make a difference in the world. This characterization is the gateway for our complexity-based definition of leadership, which will be described in Chapter 9.

CHAPTER 5

Complexity
What Does It Mean?

Insights into complexity leadership started as early as the 1990s, when Waddock & Post (1991) noted that social entrepreneurs recognize the complexity of social problems and use their understanding to become catalysts in the change process – agents that engender significant changes with surprisingly limited resources.

In common parlance and even in thesauri, "complex" is often considered synonymous with "complicated" or "compound," and "complexity" synonymous with "multiplicity." However, "complexity" has a completely different meaning in complexity theory.

One cannot comprehend the potential of groups, communities, or societies by analyzing individuals separately. Even if all the possible tests and interviews were applied to each individual, one wouldn't be able to predict the possible dynamics of a group consisting of those individuals. For example, a group of loosely associated individuals can at some point become an organized group, quite unexpectedly. During the Tahir Square protests in Egypt (February 2011), the Christians organized themselves to protect Muslim prayers, and the Muslims protected a Christian mass.[1] This unpredictability is also visible in nature, in the phenomenon of sound waves traveling through air, for example. Even with a meticulous analysis of every single air particle, one would never conclude that when such particles were collected together they would propagate waves. Similarly, could an ornithologist tell from studying many single birds that, together, they can form an elegant V-shaped flock? Indeed, mysterious potential is embedded in the free interaction of molecules, animals, and people.

---

[1] See: MailOnline report of February 2011 at: www.dailymail.co.uk/news/article-1353330/Egypt-protests-Christians-join-hands-protect-Muslims-pray-Cairo-protests.html and Daily News at www.nydailynews.com/news/world/muslims-return-favor-join-hands-christian-protesters-mass-cairo-tahrir-square-article-1.137961; retrieved February 24, 2017.

Generally, complexity theory is considered to be any of the various branches of mathematics, physics, computer science, or other fields concerned with the emergence of order and structure in complex and apparently chaotic systems.[2] A narrower definition fitting the business and social arena is that *complexity science is the study of the phenomena that emerge from a collection of interacting objects or agents* (Johnson, 2009); this definition has several implications. Let's take a closer look at the cardinal characteristics of the term.

Dimensions of Complexity

Collection of Interacting Objects

The definition of complexity mentions a collection of *freely interacting objects*, as opposed to an orderly top-down structure. In network theory, complexity arises from the connections among components of a system. What might that look like in business? Let's consider an example.

Gore (W. L. Gore & Associates) is a $3 billion high-tech firm[3] founded by Bill and Vieve Gore in 1958. Currently the company has more than ten thousand "employees" (known as "associates") located in thirty countries worldwide. On average a plant has about three hundred employees. This eliminates the need for "the usual layers of middle and upper management, because in groups that small, informal, personal relationships are more effective" (Gladwell, 2002); in other words, there's no need for management levels or organization charts (Hegar, 2012).

Associates experience a great deal of freedom, but they also have much more responsibility to be self-driven and self-initiated. Chaos becomes part of the firm's culture: "Some days things are chaotic. You have teams coming together, storming and forming and building relationships" (free interactions), says one of the associates (Manz *et al.,* 2009; Hamel, 2010a: interview with Gore's CEO, Terri Kelly). Associates cannot be forced to make commitments. All associates strive to make a big contribution to the enterprise, so they're looking for opportunities that will leverage their strengths and that they're passionate about (Hamel, 2010a).

The company has no traditional organizational charts, no chains of command, and only a few predetermined channels of communication.

---

[2] See: http://dictionary.reference.com/browse/complexity+theory; according to *The American Heritage Science Dictionary*, 2002.
[3] See: www.gore-tex.com/remote/Satellite/home; retrieved February 24, 2017.

Associates are encouraged to communicate directly with each other and are accountable to fellow members and team up in order to pursue innovations. Teams organize themselves around opportunities and leaders emerge. This corporate structure has proven to be a significant contributor to associate satisfaction and retention. Leaders are most often elected from within their own team, not appointed from above (Reingold, 2007). They may also emerge naturally, by demonstrating special knowledge, skill, or experience that advances a business objective.[4] The leader doesn't make individual decisions, but rather acts as the representative of the team. (Typically ten people compose a basic management unit.) Information may flow freely in all directions, and people-to-people communication is the norm. Individuals and self-managed teams go directly to anyone in the organization to get what they need to do their task successfully (Hamel, 2010b).

Managed that way Gore remains successful in its marketplace and stays on the lists of best companies to work for and best managed companies (Gladwell, *ibid*). The company was also selected in 2015 as third in the list of the World's Best Multinational Workplaces. We'll take a closer look at W. L. Gore & Associates in Chapter 11.

Complex systems are characterized, inter alia, by the existence of many strongly interdependent "variables" with multiple inputs contributing to observed outputs (Kastens *et al.,* 2009). From this perspective Gore management structure enables the "collection of interacting objects" to communicate freely and generate some "phenomena emerging" from these interactions, i.e., new groups or leaders, novel products, and market innovations. Let's survey this fascinating phenomenon of *emergence*, which happens in the "absence of any sort of 'invisible hand' or 'central controller'" (Johnson, 2009, p. 15).

Emergence

Émile Durkheim (1984)[5] was probably one of the first sociologists to notice the importance of the appearance of new phenomena resulting from the interaction of discrete elements. He asserted that the main object of sociology is to study social facts. Although Durkheim never used the term "emergence," most of his key theoretical concepts, such as social facts,

---

[4] From Gore Web site: www.gore.com/en_xx/aboutus/culture/; retrieved February 24, 2017.
[5] Durkheim's doctoral dissertation titled "*The Division of Labor in the Society*" was written in 1893; the English translation under the same title was first published in 1933.

dynamic density, social milieu, social substratum, and sui generis, were actually other ways to express this idea.

Emergence is defined as the arising of novel and coherent structures, patterns, and properties during the process of self-organization in complex systems (Goldstein, 1999). Both social facts and collective representations are emergent social phenomena and both are sui generis properties of a social system emerging from the association of individuals (Sawyer, 2007).

Certain phenomena (on a higher level) emerge from these (lower-level) interactions. The process of interactions among low-level elements sometimes reaches a turning point beyond which they transform into completely new, higher-level, irreversible phenomena (Gladwell, 2002). The movement from low-level rules to higher-level phenomena is called *emergence* (Johnson, 2002; Nowak, 2004).

Consider, for example, how a pile of sand takes shape. As grains of sand are spilled on top of one another, the pile "automatically" forms a conical shape, which is our "emergent entity." New sand, even if spilled on the top in a chaotic way, slides down, building up the shape of a cone. The elegant sand cone is an emergent phenomenon that appears out of the interactions between grains of sand and gravity (Bedau & Humphreys, 2008a). Another example: The elegant V-shaped flock that suddenly appears out of a randomly assembled gathering of birds could be characterized as an *emergent phenomenon*. Birds are not hierarchic, and the formation of the higher-level V shape appears out of the free interaction of birds "on the lower level" (Reynolds, 1987). There is no "invisible hand" or "central controller," though the V shape of a flock can persist for thousands of miles (with single birds intuitively interchanging their positions).

Blend of Upward, Downward, and Horizontal Causations

As described, at Gore, numerous teams spring up to support new products or projects throughout the company. These emergent teams develop and thrive to accomplish the required work and may eventually dissolve if appropriate. The organization operates without "managers," but with many leaders, who emerge on the basis of their knowledge, skill, enthusiasm, track record, and ability to attract followers (Manz *et al.*, 2009).

This means that the results result from upward causation, complementing the traditional downward flow. It's worth mentioning that the ability of subordinates in traditional companies to have upward influence is seen as an essential ingredient of organizational effectiveness (Schilit & Locke, 1982).

An illustrative example of upward and downward causations arises from the analysis of social emergence, especially from R. Keith Sawyer's (2007) concept of five levels of social emergence:

- The first is the individual level, which consists of individual intentions, memories, personalities, and cognitive processes.
- The second is the interaction level, which involves patterns of discourse, symbolic interaction, collaboration, and negotiation.
- The third is the ephemeral-emergent level, at which some emergent manifestations may appear, though they are still unstable; there may arise some common topics, frames of interactions, structures for participation, and some relative roles and statuses. However, at this point conditions can be easily reversed.
- The fourth is the stable-emergent level, at which there arise group structures, new language (group jargon, catchphrases), and conversational routines. These elements are the base for final and irreversible emergence.
- And finally, the fifth is the social-structure level, where written texts (procedures, laws, and regulations), cultural and technological novelties, and systems of the society emerge.

Sawyer (*ibid*) proposes the simultaneous coexistence of a variety of upward and downward causations between levels. In addition to these, there is a stream of horizontal causation, where workers on the same level, from the same or different departments, inspire each other with new ideas.

Enabling diverse directions of causation (Tourish & Robson, 2003; Tourish, 2005; Érdi, 2008) creates an environment where, from unorganized interactions on the lower level, there emerge structural changes and new concepts on the higher level. This is especially so if there are multiple feedback loops involved.

Feedback Loops

Complex systems are characterized by multiple feedback loops in which there isn't one easily identifiable thread of causation, such as A leads to B, B causes C, C influences D. On the contrary, there are multiple feedback loops among A, B, and C, which together lead to complex results (Johnson S., 2002; Miller & Page, 2007; Johnson N., 2009; Praszkier & Nowak, 2012). Those feedback loops may be self-reinforcing and so trigger a chain of change, taking the system into a new state, from which it cannot return to its original state.

Feedback loops not only accelerate but also may dampen change (Kastens *et al.,* 2009). Let's take, for example, a disadvantaged, stagnant rural community and an NGO project sent there to enliven this community. To energize people the NGO organizes a series of events, such as dancing festivals or tournaments. They deliver entertainment, but the change they produce originates outside (is *exogenous*). People seem happy to participate in the events, but they passively wait for the NGO to continue the activities. When the NGO's relevant grant expires, they withdraw, leaving the people disappointed and feeling as if they've been abandoned. This increases the level of frustration. The people interact, sharing their feelings of helplessness and irritation, and the feedback loops among various community members and groups foster aggression, until protests turn violent and the situation becomes destabilized.

In this case there were no preconditions secured for the change to become *endogenous* and, as such, to empower people. In contrast, the example that follows is one in which the change emerges through bottom-up initiatives (endogenous change), and where the feedback loops lead to positive dynamics. To assert the positive flow some preconditions are inevitable. (This will be discussed in Chapter 10.)

Chaos May Be a Source for New Order

Generally speaking, contexts that set the stage for the emergence of new ideas include networks of interaction, complex patterns of conflicting constraints, patterns of tension, interdependent relationships, rules of action, direct and indirect feedback loops, and rapidly changing environmental demands (Uh-Bien *et al.,* 2007, p. 307) – in other words, chaos.

Indeed, complexity examples suggest that chaos may be the source of new order (Fisher, *ibid*; Érdi, *ibid*; Mitchel, 2009; Strogatz, 2003) and, as such, may have a positive connotation. The chaotic sprinkling of sand turns into a perfect sand cone; ants' anarchy transitions into a perfect swarm; an audience's cacophonous clapping becomes rhythmic applause. For better illustration let's consider a hypothetical example of a disadvantaged, underfinanced community (e.g., the inner city).

In an underdeveloped inner-city area, at some moment in time, a group of young scouts starts cleaning the streets. Independently, someone designates a clean space for a kindergarten, and other young adults plan a baseball square. Elsewhere, a group of women form a choir, and others open a gym. All those initiatives are bottom-up, isolated, and chaotic. However, remaining isolated in the adverse ambience they may blur over time.

Eventually, the activists involved might consider ways to work together to form a more nurturing and safer environment. Scout leaders might meet with the kindergarten principal and the baseball coach, also inviting the choir director and the fitness advocates. Deliberating on how to increase the safety and quality of their neighborhood, they create a proud-of-our-community club, which, in turn, attracts many other dwellers to various community actions and promotes this new approach to community enhancement. People organize themselves, setting new safety, health, and prosperity rules. At some point the community becomes a neat, desirable location with skyrocketing housing prices. Through a feedback loop, this compels the dwellers to maintain higher standards, affecting their mindsets, as they begin to identify with their new status.

In a chaotic, uncared for, and unwanted community there appear, unexpectedly, "bubbles of new in the sea of old" (Nowak & Vallacher, 2005) and through mechanisms described as minority influence, those bubbles connect and influence the majority. Chaos, previously understood as a threat, becomes a "primordial soup" of emerging bubbles of a new order. It's a challenge for leaders to accept and harness chaos (see: Axelrod & Cohen, 2000; Eoyang & Holladay, 2013) and, in that way, to master *chaordic*[6] processes, which in business may mean, for example, unstructured interactions among employees.

One caveat to all of this is that not all chaotic situations sow the seeds of new-order creation. Sometimes the system may drift into self-destruction, as we are seeing in some Middle Eastern countries. This bifurcation – chaos-into-order or chaos-into-destruction – is apparently determined by specific control parameters. In the case of the sand cone, for example, a determinate condition could be the absence of wind. In the case of a business, it could be an attractive vision, trust in the team, or belief that the procedures hold promise for market success. In the social field, some necessary preconditions may relate to passion and commitment to the mission and, as we found in our research, social capital (more on preconditions in Chapter 10).

Discontinuous Processes with Sudden Leaps

We typically perceive business and social arenas as continuous processes – everything evolves, one step logically leads to another, etc. Yes, there are

---

[6] An abbreviation from "chaos" and "order," a term coined by Dee Hock (2000), the founder and long-term CEO of Visa International.

some upheavals (prices fall more rapidly than expected, some goods unexpectedly become fashionable, new information technologies totally shatter the old ways of marketing), but we usually understand that these events are unavoidable properties of the natural flow and that, ultimately, everything evolves along a continuous trajectory.

On the other hand, if we agree on the process of emergence (especially from-chaos-to-order), we should also agree that sudden leaps and discontinuities should be expected and accounted for. At the Gore enterprise, "chaotic" discussions might unexpectedly generate innovation, which might spread rapidly through the market. The chaotic group of birds might suddenly take off and form a V-shaped flock, establishing in seconds a new, harmonious order. In other words, new phenomena on a higher level often emerge as a rapid and often unexpected jump. Sometimes they're happy accidents. See, for example, Malcolm Gladwell's "Tipping Point" tale about Hush Puppies shoes, which suddenly exploded in popularity, without any deliberate marketing (Gladwell, 2002, pp. 4–5).

Discontinuous processes with sudden leaps from one state to another may be illustrated using the phenomenon of phase transitions in physics, as when water, at a temperature of 212°F, transforms into gas or, at 32°F, into ice (Nowak & Vallacher, 2005; Érdi, 2008). Such fields as ecology, economics, and urban studies would greatly benefit from a paradigm shift that incorporates possible discontinuities (Holling *et al.*, 2008).

It was Joseph Schumpeter, the father of the concept of entrepreneurship, who in the 1940s held that the function of entrepreneurs is to revolutionize the pattern of production and to introduce a "gale of creative destruction" (Schumpeter, 2016).[7] He simply prompted discontinuities.

Unpredictability

It was impossible to predict that Hush Puppies shoes would become a must-have on a global scale, especially since no significant capital was invested in their promotion. And while we know that at some point migration will occur, we can't predict when a chaotic and noisy group of birds will take off, forming an elegant flock and flying in that emergent order for thousands of miles.

Observing the scouts, chorus, kindergarten, and other groups in the disadvantaged community, we might see some progress, but we won't be

---

[7] First printing in 1942.

able to predict whether it will reach Malcolm Gladwell's "tipping point" and "leap" into its new form as a well-cared-for, high-profile community.

Unpredictability is an intrinsic feature of emergence (Goldstein, 1999; Bedau & Humphreys, 2008b). However, there are ways to predict the future when dealing with complex systems, including simulation of various scenarios (see Chapter 16).

Force Field, Homeostasis, and Attractors

Kurt Lewin, a psychologist also trained as a biologist, held that prior to taking any action one should analyze the factors (forces) that influence a given social situation (Lewin, 2004 – articles published in the 1940s). He viewed social processes as resulting from the interplay of counteracting social forces. The configuration of the forces can be defined as a *force field* where most forces have their counterforces. Stable social systems are at the points of balance where the force is equal to the counterforce.

This perspective provides the foundation for understanding how social change can be achieved. One must first see the situation as a whole, then analyze the mosaic of social forces that aggregate to maintain the current balance of the social field, and finally draw out which forces will drive the desired change (Lewin called them *locomotion* or *helping forces*) and which will interfere with *barriers* or *hindering forces*. Interestingly, Lewin, as early as the 1940s, was describing nothing other than the dynamics of *homeostasis*.

Complex systems must be in a state of homeostasis in order to maintain stability. On the other hand, a complex system must evolve by adapting to modifications of its environment. Otherwise, outside forces will soon destabilize and destroy it (de Rosnay, 1997).

To change and evolve, a leader who "is inspired to alter an unpleasant equilibrium" should create a new, stable equilibrium, one that provides a meaningfully higher level of satisfaction for the participants in the system. "The new equilibrium is permanent, because it first survives and then stabilizes, even though some aspects of the original equilibrium may persist" (Martin & Osberg, 2007, pp. 33–34).

Most complex systems have a characteristic equilibrium. In a natural way, over time and independent of actions taken, the systems will have a tendency to drift back toward this stable state. This is called the *attractor*, because it "attracts" the system (Vallacher & Nowak, 2007; Nowak & Vallacher, 1998a). An *attractor* refers to a subset of potential states to which a system's behavior converges over time. Metaphorically, it "attracts" the system's behavior, so that even very different starting states tend to evolve toward the subset of states that are called "the attractor" (Vallacher *et al.,* 2010). For example, storms may repeatedly damage an anthill, yet the ants, without any control or driving force, will meticulously rebuild it. Some authors mention the importance of identifying *levers* for initiating the change dynamics and for further scale-up (Deiglmeier, 2013). Those levers are, from the complexity perspective, *alternative attractors*, which become the kernel of a new homeostasis.

Many social actions that were successful in the short term have failed in the long term, because no matter what is done, the system tends to revert to its initial attractor. Within the social field short-term actions meant to enliven flagging communities often create visible change only temporarily, as the embedded *attractor* eventually causes the community to revert to its initial state. Therefore, directly confronting the system's natural tendency usually fails; what succeeds is moving the system to the vicinity of an alternative positive attractor (Praszkier & Nowak, 2012) or circumventing any negative ones (Praszkier *et al.,* 2010). This might seem to be a daunting challenge, but in truth, it may require only a very small and low-cost impulse.

Small Impulses Initiate Big Change

Imagine that you're on a raft, drifting on the North Atlantic current, somewhere west of Ireland. At some point the raft is about to reach a big bifurcation (fission): One stream of the current flows northwest, and the other heads northeast. At some point a small breeze could either push your raft toward the east, and you would land in the Norwegian fiords, or it could give you a tiny nudge toward the west, and you would find yourself in the Labrador Sea. One small impulse or event could determine your destination.

Dr. Edward N. Lorenz, a meteorologist, discovered and coined the famous insight called the *butterfly effect*. It revealed that very small variations at the initial stage had a huge effect distant in time and space. His breakthrough presentation[8] was titled "Predictability: Does the Flap of a Butterfly's Wings in Brazil Set Off a Tornado in Texas?" (Érdi, 2008). The image of a butterfly's flutter causing a tornado thousands of miles away became a popular metaphor for the notion that, in complex situations,

---

[8] Delivered at a meeting of the American Association for the Advancement of Science in 1972.

small impulses can have major impacts, often at a distant point, making them hard to predict (see: Gleick, 2008, pp. 12–31).

A complex environment with multiple feedback loops and the interaction of downward, upward, and horizontal causations may be prone to immense changes initiated by very small impulses. Through small initial investments or innovations, an *autocatalytic* process may get started. Interconnected and interrelated people may become carriers of novelties that spread rapidly, like a disease. The process is based on multiple communications, and at some point, one more connection could initiate the launching impulse.

To illustrate how a small impulse can trigger a big change, let's look at another story of social entrepreneurship in action.

Dagmara Bienkowska from Poland

This project took place in Zegocina, an economically and socially disadvantaged region of southern Poland. Several top-down attempts to address the society's plight had failed. People were frustrated by and resistant to outside experts, who had little knowledge of the community. The inhabitants felt powerless, and their hopelessness was compounded by distrust, aggression, and lowered self-esteem. As the problems became intractable, the society split into several isolated and conflicting groups, pitting youth against senior citizens, and so on.

Dagmara Bienkowska[9] started her intervention in Zegocina by learning about the community from within. She lived there for a month, staying with local families, eating local food, sharing stories and lifestyle, and spending time with youth groups. She soon realized that there were positive, though latent, potentials, such as a strong identification with the region and dreams for its development.

After gaining a better understanding of the social fiber, Bienkowska finally decided to involve one of the marginalized groups, the bullying youth. While sharing a beer she said that the traditional food she had been eating since her arrival was delicious, and she suggested they visit the senior citizens (another marginalized group) and gather from them some recipes of regional dishes. This worked out perfectly, as the senior citizens were more than eager to share their traditional recipes, and the young people felt that they were doing something new and worthwhile.

---

[9] See: www.ashoka.org/fellow/dagmara-bienkowska.

(Dagmara discovered the youths' latent desire for doing something "good" while socializing with them.) The image of local bullies and senior citizens working on a project together, something that was previously inconceivable, was intriguing. The local authorities saw this as an opportunity and proceeded to print an unedited edition of the "Cookbook of Zegocina County," distributing it at conferences as a first local product that the community could be proud of. The second edition was published professionally. It sold out, and proceeds from sales were channeled into community educational projects.

One small impulse generated a success that transformed the youth group into a major entrepreneurial force, as they saw that trust and cooperation yielded an immense payback. Soon after, they launched several new ventures, triggering an entrepreneurial movement among other community members. For instance, during a time of national disaster, when the region was heavily affected by floods, it turned out that the Zegocina community was the best organized and best equipped to cope with the disaster. Capitalizing on this development, a Zegocina Flood Book was published and sold as a manual for other communities on how to cope with natural disasters. The proceeds from sales again were channeled into the community's social projects. Eventually, through their bottom-up approach, Zegocina County experienced unforeseen economic development, surpassing that of all their neighboring communities.

To summarize, a very small impulse – the suggestion to assemble recipes – triggered an autocatalytic process of change, based on the community's dormant potentials. Dagmara built an alternative attractor around the cookbook, which, over time, deepened while the old negative one (inertia, frustration, hopelessness) diminished naturally, without direct confrontation of the community's existing problems.

This example serves as an important hint for future leaders. As with complexity, small impulses such as small, smart investments or small initial successes, may have an immense impact, while big changes, such as huge outside investments may produce minimal effect and may actually dampen the process (e.g., people waiting for the big investor to solve problems and hence, becoming less entrepreneurial).

The Power of Simple Rules

Many highly complex phenomena, such as self-organization and pattern formation, that are observed at the level of the system can be explained by simple rules. These simple rules can, for example, reproduce the shapes of plants and shells through simple interactions of nearby cells (Meinhart, 2003; Wolfram, 2002). Simple rules are thus at the core of complexity theory (Waldrop, 1992; Holland, 1999; Kaufman, 1995; Johnson, 2002).

The intelligent ant swarm isn't orchestrated by any kind of leader; the queen is there only to reproduce. Instead, ants search for food, following a set of genetically determined behaviors (Dubakov, 2009):

1   Travel randomly in search of food.
2   If you find food, take it to the nest, laying down an odor trail on the way.
3   Signal to other ants the discovery of food, which encourages them to search for it.

The newly recruited ants will follow the odor trail directly to the food source; moreover, each newly arrived ant will reinforce the odor trail for the next comers.

In Chapter 11 we'll look at a company that used two simple rules to become a leader in its field. Morning Star is the top tomato processing company in the world, with industrial sales of approximately $350 million. It began with two rules called The Morning Star Colleague Principles. The first was that people shouldn't use force or coercion against others, and the second was that people should honor the commitments they make to others. Those two rules initiated a culture of self-management. There are no bosses other than peer groups, no vertical structure, and no top-down control. All processes are based on peer-to-peer accountability, planning, and innovating. The self-management idea was so successful that the company launched the Morning Star Self-Management Institute,[10] studying and disseminating the idea.

The message here for future leaders is that to facilitate complex processes one needs only simple rules. Moreover, complicated rules may hinder the flow of necessary activity. Let's take the example of applause after a concert. If a leader wanted to organize clapping in unison, she or he could either impose a complicated procedure of top-down control (sections managed by section officers who control whether everyone is clapping rhythmically, following a predetermined script) or enable a self-directed activity. With simple direction, the applause automatically becomes synchronized into rhythmic beats created by people adjusting their clapping to each other's. In the first case the rules and structures are complicated and do not lead

---

[10] See: www.self-managementinstitute.org/.

to order. The rules controlling the latter are simple: be empathetic and synchronize with your neighbors (Praszkier, 2014). In seconds the entire audience finds and maintains its synchronized rhythm.

Groups can use simple rules to powerful effect, but so can individuals. Some see simple rules as tools to achieve our most pressing personal and professional objectives, from overcoming insomnia to becoming a smarter investor (Sull & Eisenhardt, 2015).

The "Fractals Syndrome"

As stated, within their structure, leaves and shells replicate the same pattern. So do snowflakes; the same pattern is visible at each level of magnification (Johnson, 2009). Zoom in to uncover a finer, previously invisible, new structure and no new detail appears. The same pattern repeats over and over. These self-similar patterns, known as fractals, are self-organized replications of simple rules on many levels.[11]

How do fractals apply to groups and organizations? Humans have a tendency to follow the behavior of others, especially in situations in which they don't know how to behave. This tendency to imitate others is called modeling (Bandura, 1976). There have been studies documenting that group members may behave as if they share a common basic assumption: Under some conditions, each individual reproduces the group dynamics on a different scale. In particular, the chaotic behavior of the group is reflected in each member (Dal Forno & Merlone, 2013). This means that a general organizational ethos may be reproduced on many levels of the organization. In the case of Gore, the general idea of participation, partnership, and freedom of exploration is reflected on the global level, in the more than thirty countries where they operate; at the team level; and at the level of individuals who, through social-influence mechanisms, have internalized the same values. This kind of self-replication on many levels is here called "the fractals syndrome."

Complex Adaptive Systems

Within the well-observed world of animals, collective behavior, such as intelligent swarms of insects or V-shaped flocks of birds, often emerges from a set of simple rules for causing the interaction between neighbors

---

[11] An exemplary illustration of fractals is provided by the Fractal Foundation at: http://fractal foundation.org/fractivities/WhatIsaFractal-1pager.pdf, retrieved April 5, 2016.

(Fisher, 2009). The complex, adaptive, and efficient swarm is, in our understanding, the emergent phenomenon, which, "in the absence of any sort of invisible hand or central controller," appears out of chaotic interactions among ants.

The basic units of analysis in complexity theory are ant-swarm-like Complex Adaptive Systems (CAS). CAS are networks of interacting, interdependent agents who are bonded in a cooperative dynamic by something common. They are changeable structures with multiple overlapping hierarchies, and like the individuals that compose them, CAS are linked with one another in a dynamic, interactive network (Uhl-Bien *et al.*, 2007, p. 299). CAS are dynamic systems able to adapt to and evolve with a changing environment (Chan, 2001).

We've determined that chaos may be a source of new order. In Complex Adaptive Systems this new order, if based on free interactions of agents on the lower level, may become the seeds (bubbles) of a new order.

Social Influence in the Complex Systems

How does the universe of complexity look from the perspective of the social influence theory? It seems it's based more on minority than majority influence, especially when seen through the lens of "bubbles theory." However, the overall application of simple rules regarding communication and sharing may also generate a majority-influence mechanism, especially for the newcomers.

At Gore, where leadership has been taken to a whole new level, the organization relies heavily on the advantages of teamwork and consists of both established teams and teams that emerge on the basis of need. Members of the organization can interact directly with everyone else in the work system without having to go through a chain of command. This creates a tipping point of mutual inspirations. Numerous teams spring up to support new products or projects throughout the company. These emergent teams develop, thrive, and eventually dissolve as appropriate, to accomplish the required work. The organization operates without "managers" but with lots of leaders who emerge on the basis of their knowledge, skill, enthusiasm, track record, and ability to attract followers. Social relationships, shared responsibility and influence, and teamwork are of special importance (Manz *et al.*, 2009, p. 240).

This sort of complex universe may foster individuals' identification with the firm's paradigm and internalization of its values. And, as we've learned, identification and internalization are the highest-level social influence mechanisms.

Chapter Coda

- Section 2 starts with an advanced definition of leadership
- Eleven pivotal dimensions of complexity are explained and illustrated through examples of business and social activities:
  1 Collection of interacting objects
  2 Emergence
  3 Blend of upward, downward, and horizontal causations
  4 Feedback loops
  5 Chaos
  6 Discontinuity
  7 Unpredictability
  8 Force field, homeostasis, and attractors
  9 Small impulses initiating big change
  10 The power of simple rules
  11 Complex Adaptive Systems
- Social influence mechanisms in complex systems are delineated: minority and majority influence, identification, and internalization

CHAPTER 6

Something Out of Nothing
Big Social Movements Harnessing Chaos into Order

Now that we've presented a theoretical delineation of complexity, it may be supportive to see complexity in action. Our illustrations are taken from big peaceful social movements that succeeded and changed the world. By "social movement" we mean nonpolitical and noneconomic movements supported by people who took responsibility and initiated bottom-up actions in a manner best described by Martin Luther King Jr. (2001, p. 189) when he said, "We are caught in an inescapable network of mutuality, tied in a single garment of destiny. Whatever affects one directly, affects all indirectly."[1]

Such actions, studied by New Social Movement theorists, are usually centered around a big idea that emphasizes social issues and culture as both the arena for and the means of protest. They are accomplished through the use of social relations, symbols, and identities based in the culture, rather than by economic production (Buechler, 1995, 1999, 2011; Scott, 1990). The backbone of these New Social Movements is a network that develops different or even new kinds of identity, e.g., "resistance identity" or "project identity" (Castells, 2010). Jürgen Habermas (1985) complements this picture with his concept of "communicative action": the phenomenon of widespread public participation, sharing of information, reaching consensus through public dialogue rather than exercise of power, and avoiding empowerment of experts and bureaucrats, which sheds light on the way people in these social movements communicate, interact, exercise trust, and cooperate. Habermas replaces the technical expert with the reflective planner. Although he didn't use the term "social capital," his writings clearly relate to the process of building it (Bolton, 2005), especially when he talks about "communicative action" designed to promote cooperation and common understanding in

---

[1] Letter from Birmingham Jail, written on April 16, 1963.

a group, as opposed to "strategic action," designed simply to achieve the group's goals (Habermas, *ibid*).

We look now at two such social movements: the civil rights movement in the United States and the underground Solidarity movement in Poland.

The Civil Rights Movement in the United States

The American civil rights movement of the 1950s and 1960s clearly meets the definition of a New Social Movement. It highlighted racial segregation and succeeded in generating greater equality by forcing alterations in the law and bringing about immense change in the American and global social arenas. The civil rights movement was based on multiple civic initiatives, such as the "Club from Nowhere" (founded by Georgia Gilmore, a midwife from Montgomery), which raised money, baked cakes and sold food to beauty parlors, and used the profits to support the movement. (It's worth mentioning that collective cake baking in small groups created what's known in social network analysis as "small worlds," self-organizing a communication structure from the bottom up). The Club from Nowhere especially supported the Montgomery bus boycott (Williams 2002). Instead of riding buses, boycotters self-organized a system of carpools in which car owners volunteered their vehicles or themselves to drive people to various destinations. The boycott was successful; King himself said "a miracle had taken place" (Martin Luther King Jr., 2001). Georgia Gilmore later commented that she was glad it was a success and "nobody didn't get killed"; also that the boycott revealed that they had a lot of white friends they didn't realize were really and truly interested (Williams, 2002).

Authors studying the civil rights movement describe the emergence of bottom-up initiatives, in which trust, contacts, solidarity, and rituals develop and solidify (Andrews, 2004; Morris, 2006). Moreover, this new culture spread through the networks, mobilizing and giving the movement "structural proximity." People and groups who had previously been distant, in terms of knowing about, being influenced by, and being able to communicate with one another, were now close to one another (McAdam, 1999).

Polish Underground Solidarity Movement

A more recent example is the Polish Solidarity movement, which in the 1980s[2] successfully united the majority of Polish working people and

---

[2] Accurately: from December 13, 1981, when martial law was imposed, until June 4, 1989, when the

converted the society into a Gandhi-like, nonviolent operation. While enduring many hardships engendered by the imposition of martial law, the movement overthrew the totalitarian regime, setting in motion the wheels of freedom in other Central and Eastern European countries, e.g., East Germany and the fall of the Berlin Wall (Ash, 2002; Kenney, 2001, 2008; Kubik, 1994; Osa, 2003).

So what was it that enabled this essentially leaderless, decentralized, and unorganized movement (the original Solidarity leaders were either in prison or in hiding) to become so utterly powerful, widespread, and efficient, with 10 million of a population of 40 million participating (Brown, 2003)? It's an intriguing question, especially given that it came to fruition within a structure that was unconventional and erratic, with new groups constantly emerging and dissolving. The answer is social networks. Created ad hoc by civil society, despite the absence of a technical means of communication,[3] these networks skillfully connected the entire society and enabled both local and national coordination. In the absence of any top-down management, solidarity activists set up a secret technical unit that regularly published and widely disseminated illegally printed materials, without the availability of printing presses or chemical ingredients for printing ink. They supported educational services underground. They held clandestine, illegal art exhibits and home-based theatrical performances with actors who were banned from, or boycotted, the public stage. And they executed well-orchestrated national demonstrations of civil disobedience. For example, in big cities, people effectively boycotted the government-sponsored TV news. Each evening, at exactly 7:30 p.m., when the broadcast began, people left their homes to take walks around their neighborhoods, socializing with other families along the way, until 8:00 p.m. sharp, when the nightly news ended and everybody returned home for dinner. The police were helpless to stop the "protest," given that no one was verbally or physically confronting the regime. However, the collective action taking place at a specific time made a powerful impact and sent a strong, albeit sub rosa, message.

---

first free election took place. Prior to the martial law, the protests achieved a legal period for the Solidarity trade union (after the iconic Lech Walesa's jump over the shipyard fence); a treaty was signed in August 1980, and the legal period of Solidarity lasted until December 1981.

[3] The profound peaceful social transition phenomenon unfolded in an environment totally devoid of ICT (information and communications technology), with all communication media shut down or highly controlled: The entire telephone network was turned off, the mail was heavily censored, and all broadcast media were banned except for a few official propaganda sources; train travel was severely restricted and required special permission; and on the roads private cars were searched at frequent checkpoints.

Additionally, the movement developed an uncanny ability to experiment with whatever was available on the market. For example, the technical section found a way to make printing ink by mixing cleaning agents and boot polish and a way to build portable printing equipment that could fit into a backpack. Manuals on how to fabricate the equipment were disseminated, and, consequently, thousands of small publishing units were tasked with the ongoing job of printing and disseminating illegal newsletters and magazines and banned books.[4] Brown (2003) shows that it was the strength of this private sphere, and the social cohesion resulting from it, that enabled people to constitute a civil society so rapidly. The rich variety of flourishing independent social organizations, e.g., discussion clubs, political forums, illegal educational activities, and home theaters, countered the totalitarian system's attempts to control the public sphere and, ironically, empowered the civic sphere as a whole.

To be sure, there was a heavy police presence, but for the most part, the Solidarity movement survived their arrests and physical assaults. How was this possible? Does the answer lie in the shared determination to stand up for freedom, without the use of violence? According to Osa (2003, p. 179), "In authoritarian systems, networks must play an additional role: Social networks must substitute for media when a society lacks a free press. Since information is the basic currency for social action … government authorities move quickly to cut telephone and telex lines, jam radio broadcasts, and shut down post offices."

In the case of Solidarity, many of the important undertakings were organized ad hoc, using personal and professional networks (Friszke, 2006). One example of this took place in Gdańsk:[5] B. H., one of the activists,[6] was asked during the martial law period by one of the underground leaders[7] to organize an illegal broadcast, *Radio Solidarity*, without any detailed instructions of how to do it. He was told, "Just do it; you will know how." B. H. developed his own plan and assembled a team. He would write the news then have a female friend read and record it and make copies of the recording on three separate tapes. He would

---

[4] An oral narrative recounts an incident when the secret police identified one of the backpackers and created a trap near the house where he was suspected of printing illegally. The Solidarity network (namely, some local activists without any top-down leadership) spontaneously and agilely reacted by putting a few dozen walking backpackers on the nearby streets. This confused the police and allowed the real printing agent to escape.

[5] The region where Solidarity was born in August 1980.

[6] Interviewed during the field-preparation phase of my research.

[7] Lech Kaczynski, later, in the mid-2000s, the president of Poland.

then board a crowded train, where another person (whom he barely knew) would take the tapes out of his pocket and place them in three portable tape recorders, all of which were stored in different suitcases, together with homemade broadcasting equipment. Finally, the suitcases were placed on three roofs in different areas and set to play at the time of the official TV news, in effect jamming the audio track of the regime's propaganda. After the broadcast, a different team not known to B. H. (except for a loose connection with its leader) would observe whether the police detected the suitcases. If the coast was clear, they would collect them for further use.

This is just one example of "do-it-yourself" initiatives. Here is a sampling of quotations from interviews with former Solidarity activists[8] showing bottom-up organizing techniques:

> When there were no leaders,[9] nobody to assemble around, we simply started to undertake several actions with my neighbor, just to demonstrate that Solidarity exists. – (male, thirty-three,[10] blue-collar)
>
> We organized ourselves spontaneously, based on people's ideas, especially at the beginning when there were no coordinated plans and when the leaders were interned, though people wanted to do something. And we did, exposing ourselves to danger. (female, thirty-two, physical rehabilitation technician)
>
> The Solidarity members organized themselves bottom-up as a reaction to the attempt to deprive us of the minimal independence we achieved before; it looked like social self-organizing. (female, thirty-six, teacher)
>
> My underground activity derived from my values and beliefs and, at the beginning, was totally spontaneous; nobody pushed or talked me into it. (female, thirty-one, librarian)

One of the Solidarity ex-leaders (male, twenty-seven, blue collar, Walesa's deputy, remaining in hiding) commented on his role in leadership:

> The top-down leadership was limited to maintaining boundaries; one of them was to keep the movement peaceful (some hotheads wanted to dig up guns buried after the Second World War); the other essential goal was to keep the relief aid to families of arrested activists out of other illegal endangerments. This meant, for example, that in relief places no illegal printing be allowed. Relief to families was a priority, and we didn't want to endanger it through other actions.

---

[8] The author conducted these in 2011 in two cities among the former Solidarity activists

[9] Referring to most leaders having been arrested when martial law was imposed on December 13, 1981; a few remained in hiding.

[10] Age at the time of underground activity.

Peaceful Social Movements and Complexity

Both the civil rights movement in the United States. and the Solidarity movement in Poland were based on people's commitment to a big, compelling idea and executed through multiple spontaneous interactions among people "at the lower level," which aggregated into the emergent phenomena of well-oiled and successful national movements at a higher level.

In both movements there was a blend of upward, downward, and horizontal causations (especially manifested in a desire for cooperation with and openness to others) and multiple feedback loops between spontaneous actions and higher-level results, occurring in discontinuous leaps, such as the leap from a bottom-up system of self-help carpools to the widespread success of the bus boycott. Small impulses, such as Solidarity's family walks during the TV news, aggregated into a big change. And the rules were simple indeed: reach out with your initiatives, organize yourself, and keep your "eyes on the prize."[11]

Obviously, there have been other similar efforts, such as Mahatma Gandhi's movement leading, in the beginning of the twentieth century, to the liberation of the Indian subcontinent. One of the drivers of the Gandhi movement was *satyagraha*,[12] a philosophy and practice generally known as nonviolence or civil resistance (Gandhi, 2001; Brown, 2008). On an individual level it involved a life committed to truth, chastity, and hard work. In terms of action, *satyagraha* employed nonviolent measures to influence an opponent and, rather than force him into submission, convert him. Gandhi believed (correctly, as history revealed) that the individual *satyagrahas* will aggregate into an undefeated people's movement (Shridharani, 1973). His movement had global impact on other efforts to organize.

These movements and others like them harnessed chaos through the use of social networks to create immense change. Empowering Leadership uses these same techniques to foster progress from the bottom up. We'll look at examples of this in Section 3.

Chapter Coda

- New Social Movements theory is presented
- The example of bottom-up initiatives of the civil rights movement

---

[11] "Eyes on the Prize": The title of the civil rights movement leading song; also the name of an American TV documentary about the civil rights movement.
[12] A term coined by Mahatma Gandhi, loosely translated as "insistence on truth" or "truth force."

- The case study of the bottom-up formation of the Polish Solidarity underground movement
- Those movements are reviewed from the complexity theory perspective
- Finally, the Gandhi movement is mentioned

CHAPTER 7

Creativity
What It Is and How It Works

Creativity is a divine madness, a gift from the gods. Plato
No great genius was without a mixture of insanity. Aristotle
(via Seneca)

In Chapter 4 we saw that creativity is a crucial part of social entrepreneurship. Here we'll look at the essence of creativity, and in Chapter 14 we'll
review methods for its enhancement. Let's start with a telling example of
creativity in action:

David Kuria

A young architect in Kenya[1] was ostracized both by his peers and by his
family for spending days and nights in the Kiberia slums. He was search-
ing for a way to address the problem of sanitation in these poverty-stricken
areas, which were at great risk of an epidemic. Kuria was determined to
overcome the slum dwellers' apparently insurmountable resistance to sanitary disposal of human waste. For largely historical reasons they continued to place it in plastic bags and deposit it anywhere outdoors. Many
top-down governmental and international efforts to solve this problem
failed, and much money had been wasted, as the predominant attractor
of neglecting the issue of sanitation countered all short-lived, top-down
initiatives.

Instead of designing neat rows of bungalows, as his peer architects would
commonly do, Kuria realized that he needed to find a creative rather than
obvious solution to this intransigent problem. He understood that the
only way was to make the slum dwellers see the issue as something that
was theirs to solve, not something that needed a solution imposed from
the outside.

---

[1] See: www.ashoka.org/fellow/david-kuria and http://ecotact.org.

Kuria found an innovative way to create a mind shift that circumvented the conflict (Praszkier *et al.,* 2010), by engaging the community and convincing them to care for the sanitation. He formed small groups and initiated regular meetings, during which the dwellers drew illustrations of their own ideal toilets, discussing their sketches with each other and gradually identifying with their drawings.

Kuria used the groups' drawings to create an architectural project that became a dream goal for the dwellers. During a meeting of all the groups' participants, he demonstrated the project and asked whether they wanted to proceed. This was met with an enthusiastic "Let's do it." With minimal initial investments, using pro bono labor courtesy of the residents themselves and scrap materials, the slum dwellers built their own dream toilets, cared for them, and protected them from being vandalized. They used funds raised from advertisements placed in the toilets to maintain them and implemented cooking facilities that used biogas obtained from human waste. As a result, the area became a focal point for the community, which was proud of its cleanliness. The trend toward sanitary waste disposal grew and spread, and Kuria continues to share his bottom-up approach to sanitation issues with many other places in the world. He has reported that innovating against all odds was a source of immense personal satisfaction, and in a feedback loop, it motivated him to pursue further exploration and innovation.

What is the source of this feeling of happiness associated with creativity? "Lost in Antarctica or confined to a prison cell, some individuals succeed in transforming their harrowing conditions into a manageable and even enjoyable struggle, whereas most others would succumb to the ordeal" (Csikszentmihályi, 1991, p. 90). What generates this joy of innovating? Is it solely emotional satisfaction?

Creativity in general is vivid, easily recognized in the innovations and solutions it generates, and most often admired. A popular example is the apocryphal story about a truck stuck in the tunnel. Experts argued whether to cut off the top of the truck or blow up the roof of the tunnel, until finally a young kid asked, "Why don't we simply deflate the tires and, thus, lower the truck?"

In this book we'll consider creativity as a continuous state of mind and a specific kind of drive that can be maintained through reinforcing mechanisms (Flaherty, 2005) – what makes people like David Kuria remain in this specific state of creative drive and what reinforcing mechanisms are involved?

But first, let's look at the phenomenon of creativity.

What Is Creativity?

Some define creativity as a specific process resulting in a novel work that is accepted as tenable or useful or satisfying by a group at some point in time (Stein, 1953, 1974; Amabile, 1996; Sternberg & Lubart, 2004). However, most authors perceive creativity as a capacity of the human mind – an ability to generate ideas that are new, surprising, and valuable (Boden, 2004, 2013). This capacity was highlighted by Findlay & Lumsden (1988), who see creativity as a constellation of personality and intellectual traits demonstrated by individuals who spend a significant amount of time engaged in the creative process.

The essence of creative cognitive processing is seen as *divergent thinking,* i.e., the ability to generate novel ideas by exploring many possible solutions, as opposed to *convergent thinking,* which follows a particular set of logical steps to arrive at one solution, which in some cases is viewed as a "correct" solution (Guilford, 1950; Runco, 2007). In that vein, creativity may also be seen as an ability to retrieve and connect disparate concepts stored in long-term memory.

Some refer metaphorically to the creative act as "quantum leap thinking" analogous to an electron changing its orbit while generating or absorbing a quantum of energy (Mapes, 2003). Following this path we may perceive the creative act as a sort of eruption following a sudden association of concepts retrieved from either short- or long-term memory. We will later see that this experience may feel pleasant.

State of Mind

What does "being creative" mean? Fundamentally, it supposes continual output of multiple creative acts and implies being confident, independent, risk-taking, intuitive, and flexible, as well as demonstrating the courage to dare to differ, to make waves, to challenge traditions, and to "bend a few rules" (Davis, 1993).

Some creative individuals possess an abundance of enthusiasm and curiosity and have broad interests, while others have a tolerance for complexity and ambiguity and an attraction to the mysterious. To be considered a creative thinker, one must be able to work with incomplete ideas, where relevant facts are missing, rules are cloudy, and "correct" procedures are nonexistent (Davis, *ibid*).

Creative people are alike in one respect: They all love what they do. It isn't the hope of achieving fame or making money that drives them. Rather, it's the opportunity to do the work that they enjoy doing (Csikszentmihalyi, 1997). This indicates that creativity is a truly joyful experience.

Creativity through the Lens of Complexity Theory

Divergent thinking that connects disparate concepts – a hallmark of creativity – is also apropos of the complexity theory. Out of several connections (from long- and short-term memory) there appears a sudden "jump," which some perceive as analogous to a "quantum leap" (Mapes, 2003). Discussing the complexity theory, we mentioned that free associations (chaotic connections of elements) may lead to a "discontinuous process with sudden jumps" generating emergent phenomena. In that vein, creative acts may be defined as the combination of previously unrelated structures put together in such a way that you get more from the *emergent whole* than you have put in (Koestler, 2009).

Arthur Koestler, one of the important writers on conceptualization, indicated that there are "Three Domains of Creativity" (the title of his essay). The first domain is artistic creativity, which he called the "ah" reaction. The second is scientific creativity, called the "aha!" reaction. The third is comic inspiration, called the "haha" reaction (Koestler, 2009).

As for the third ("haha" reaction), Koestler posits that humor is the domain of creative activity where a *stimulus on a high level of complexity* (laughter) produces a massive and sharply defined *response on the lower level of physiological reflexes* (release of *endorphin*), which in turn provides a burst of energy and an impetus to creativity. In that way, the "haha" reaction influences the "aha" reaction of creation (Koestler, 1964, 2009). This could be seen as "downward causation," one of the features of complexity, which is blended with "upward causations" (free associations generating a "jump" into higher-level emergent phenomena).

Joyful Experience

Professor Mihaly Csikszentmihályi's (1997) analysis of ninety-one videotaped interviews illustrated that the reason creativity is so fascinating is that creative people live more fully than others. Creative people love what they do. It is not the hope of achieving fame or making money that drives them; rather, it is the opportunity to do the work that they enjoy doing (Csikszentmihalyi, 1997, p. 107).

> When creative people were asked to choose from a list the best description of how they feel when doing whatever they enjoy doing most – reading,

climbing mountains, playing chess, whatever – the answer most frequently chosen was "designing or discovering something new. ... it seems perfectly reasonable that ... some people ... enjoy discovering and creating above all else. (Csikszentmihalyi, 1997, p. 108)

If this creative act is so pleasant, then it's no wonder that some individuals become addicted to being creative, constantly indulging in self-induced joyful experiences of innovation. The truly fascinating question is whether it works in reverse, and Koestler is right in saying that joy stimulates creativity. We would agree that it does.

How Our Brain Becomes Creative

So, if creativity produces all of these desirable results, how can we train ourselves to have more of it? How does our brain stay flexible in order to overcome routine thought patterns and generate new associations and novel ideas? It may seem that, over the course of a lifetime, the opposite is more likely to occur: that the older we are, the more rigid our thinking tends to be.

It starts when we're young. The baby experiments with movements and reactions, learning by trial and error. Imagine, for example, the baby reaching for a toy. How many different muscles in the arm and shoulder must be coordinated in that simple act? The movement is at the beginning quite clumsy, becoming more precise with time. Each act involves multiple neuronal connections, and in the baby's case, they are newly established and unstable. However, over time, when the movement is repeated, there develops a neurological "movement memory" that becomes routine. This simply means that a solid track of neuronal connections is being established and entrenched. These patterns serve us by eliminating the need to experiment with each activity over and over again, but they also make us use fixed neuropaths, which may cause rigidity.

Previously, it was believed that this rigidity of thought was an inevitable part of aging. However, contemporary neuroscience discovered the phenomenon of brain plasticity, which enables flexibility despite old, proven neuronal pathways.

Brain Plasticity

Although plasticity is greatest during childhood, the adult brain retains a capacity for functional and structural reorganization that had been underestimated earlier (Johansson, 2004). The word *plasticity* suggests pliability and malleability. It can be defined as the capacity of neurons and neural circuits in the brain to change structurally and functionally in response to new experience. This property is fundamental to the adaptability of our behavior, learning and memory processes, brain development, and brain repair (Sale *et al.*, 2014).

Brain plasticity can also be conceptualized as nature's invention to overcome limitations of the genome and adapt to a changing environment. As such, plasticity is an intrinsic property of the brain from birth to death, enabling the nervous system to escape the restrictions of its own genome and thus adapt to environmental pressures, physiologic changes, and experiences (Pascual-Leone *et al.*, 2005, 2011). Simply put, plasticity is the brain's ability to rewire itself (Johansson, 2004).

Neuroplasticity became a hot topic when two popular books were published: *How to Think Like Leonardo da Vinci* (Gelb, 2000) and *The Brain That Changes Itself* (Doidge, 2007). Each featured case studies of people whose mental limitations or brain damage was previously thought to be unalterable and how their conditions – once thought hopeless – and their lives were transformed through the mechanisms of neuroplasticity.

All contemporary studies support the view that the human brain is much more plastic than had been believed twenty years ago (Jäncke, 2009). Fortunately, experience can shape brain physiology and brain anatomy (Chaney, 2007).

There are three kinds of plasticity of the brain. The kind that has been known for some time, especially in rehabilitation, is *functional compensatory plasticity*, where parts of the brain take over when, for some reason, the other parts aren't functioning well (Shelton, 2013). This is particularly important for aging people (see Chapter 15). The most recently discovered form of plasticity is *neurogenesis plasticity*, where stem cells can reproduce fully functioning brain cells. The third, and for us the most important, kind of plasticity is *synaptic plasticity*, evidenced by the appearance of new neuronal paths.

New Neuronal Connections and the Role of Neurotransmitters

Recent research shows that for both neurogenic and synaptic plasticity dopamine plays a critical role. It influences the formation of new neurons deep in the center of the adult brain (Shelton, 2013) and serves as one of the basic neurotransmitters.

Neurotransmitters and the Role of Dopamine

The brain provides neuronal connections in two ways. The first is through direct synaptic bonding and the second is through special *neurohormones*, which serve as *neurotransmitters*, connecting more distant synapses.

There are several neurotransmitters, e.g., serotonin, epinephrine (also known as adrenaline), norepinephrine (noradrenaline), endorphin, and dopamine. We're especially interested in those that contribute to creativity by making it a joyful experience. For example, *dopamine* helps control the brain's reward and pleasure centers (Beversdorf, 2013; Flaherty, 2005; Chermahini & Hommel, 2010) and *endorphins* are endogenous opioid peptides that provide pleasure and euphoria (Hawkes, 1992; Stoppler, 2014).

Dopamine

Dopamine influences the formation of new neurons deep in the center of the adult brain. Once formed, they move to areas of the brain associated with higher brain functions, thus playing a critical role while enhancing brain plasticity (Shelton, 2013). Dopamine also influences novelty seeking and creative drive (Flaherty, 2005). It's associated with pleasure (Sprouse-Blum *et al.*, 2010) and is considered a factor contributing to a divergent mind (Kaufman, 2010).

Dopamine helps control the brain's reward and pleasure centers. The brain transmits representations of reward to the dopamine system, thus initiating further similarly motivated behavior (Ballard *et al.*, 2011). In that way it mediates reward-seeking activity ranging from gambling and cocaine addiction to the appreciation of beautiful faces and music (Flaherty, 2005; Aharon *et al.*, 2001; Breiter *et al.*, 2001).

Conversely, a deficiency in dopamine influences various diseases, such as Parkinson's disease, in which case dopamine therapy is often prescribed to increase dopamine levels in the brain. In the treatment of artistic patients with Parkinson's, achieving a proper balance in the level of dopamine helps increase creativity (Kulisevsky *et al.*, 2009).

Endorphin

Endorphin (an abbreviation for *endogenous morphine*) serves as a brain-controlled painkiller (MacLean Jr. *et al.*, 1985; Sprouse-Blum *et al.*, 2010; Stoppler, 2014; Scheve, 2014); it also delivers the feeling of pleasure and even euphoria (Stoppler, 2014).

Its effects are similar to codeine's or morphine's, but aren't addictive. Several human activities are rewarded with pleasure stemming from the endorphinergic system in the brain, especially sex and some intense and prolonged forms of exercise, where endorphins can decrease muscle pain (Hawkes, 1992; Stoppler, 2014). As such the endorphin plays a role in a mental reward system that may cause a habit of exercising (Boecker *et al.*, 2008; Hockenbury & Hockenbury, 2011).

The Magic Feedback Loop: Creativity Delivers Joy and Joy Enhances Creativity

It's worth mentioning that endorphin's effect lasts only for a short time, delivering a brief but noticeable "kick" of pleasure, while dopamine gives a longer-lasting feeling of joy (Rusu, 2013). In that vein, creative individuals are both rewarded short-term and invited to continue the "creative drive" for a more sustained "high."

David Kuria reported that inventing the idea of slum dwellers sketching their dream toilets delivered a sort of a "kick" of happiness. However, wishing to maintain this state of joy, he launched many similar national and global sanitation programs based on endogenous dynamics, each of which was a challenge whose completion was rewarded by immense satisfaction. There is no doubt that solving apparently insurmountable problems and achieving mission-impossible goals is a source of satisfaction per se. But, there's more to it: The neuroscience of the human being is constructed in an intelligent way. Innovations are based on launching new neuronal connections, which are constructed to a great extent by neurotransmitters. Those neurotransmitters, in a feedback loop, provide more ecstasy.

And there is yet another feedback loop: As stated, joy augments creativity. In that way some people sustain creativity, as innovations deliver more satisfaction and satisfaction triggers more innovations. As Alice Flaherty (2005, p. 147) has elegantly stated, "Dopamine influences novelty seeking and creative drive."

We'll look at ways to enhance creativity in Chapter 14.

Chapter Coda

- Example of creativity demonstrated by a social entrepreneur
- Various delineations of creativity and the definition chosen for this book, referring to a specific creative state of mind
- Creativity seen through the lens of complexity theory
- The neuroscience of brain plasticity
- The role of neurotransmitters – hormones providing new neuronal connections and contributing to the joyful aspect of creativity

CHAPTER 8

Efficient Networks

There indeed is something magical in the potential of groups and networks. Individual elements don't contain the information on the what would happen if they would be grouped together.

For example, if the world's best physicists and chemists meticulously analyzed individual air particles, they would never discover that, if grouped together, those particles propagate sound waves.

Networks are an essential component of human life. In Chapter 6 we mentioned the importance of networks in social and business transformations. In business multiple Web sites promote networking as the single most important marketing tactic an individual or organization can use to accelerate and sustain success.[1] Under some conditions networks also have the power to augment innovation. For example, Maria Nieto and Lluis Santamaría (2007) found that the most novel developments result from collaborative networks comprising different types of partners. In this chapter, we'll delve into the aspects of networks that enhance creativity.

The word "network" has become a catchword used to describe any loosely associated group of individuals, but there's much more to it than that. The structure of a given network – who interacts with whom, how frequently, and on what terms – has a major bearing on the flow of information and resources through it. The well-developed science of networks considers the ways people are connected. For example, Social Networks Analysis (SNA) enables quantitative examination of such characteristics as *density*, *closeness* or *structural cohesion*, and many more parameters, all critical to determining the characteristics of the overall network.[2]

It's important to analyze different kinds of networks and the properties that support transformation and, from a more general perspective, enable

---

[1] Strategic Business Networks at www.strategicbusinessnetwork.com/about/importance; see also: www .girlsguidetopm.com/2014/07/6-reasons-why-networking-is-important/; retrieved February 24, 2017.
[2] See for example: Degenne & Forsé (1999).

complex chaos-to-order processes, especially in business and in the social arena. This paves the way to understanding the challenges future leaders will face and the acumen they'll need to master networks and the ability to make them productive, nimble, and agile.

In the following we'll consider the properties of networks that support and augment creativity and social capital. Metaphorically, this chapter reveals "the structure of the magic,"[3] which casts spells on social networks to make them efficient and vibrant, augmenting creativity and enhancing social capital.

Vertical, Horizontal (Lateral), and Diagonal (Transversal) Communication

It seems obvious that the structure of an organization should enable communication in three distinct directions: downward, upward, and horizontal (Lunenburg, 2010). The two fundamental processes of communication are vertical and horizontal (Welch, 1980), and the dominant form of communication in most organizations is vertical; commands and control travel from the top down, and reports or complaints move from the bottom up (see Figure 5).

Vertical communication has several disadvantages: Information is often filtered as it moves up and down the chain of command, and managers receiving a request directed to upper management may decide that the request isn't valid and slow, change, or halt its progress.[4]

Horizontal or lateral communication is the flow of information across departmental boundaries (Bovee & Thill, 2011) or across functional areas at a given level of an organization. People at the same level communicate freely without going through multiple organizational levels (Papa *et al.*, 2007).

Given horizontal elasticity, members communicating this way within an organization have an easier time with "problem solving and information sharing across different work groups and task coordination between departments or project teams." The use of horizontal (lateral) communication in the workplace "can also enhance morale and provide a means for resolving conflicts" (Papa *et al., idem*, p. 56). Moreover, horizontal communication

---

[3] After Bandler & Grinder's book about communication in psychotherapy titled *The Structure of Magic.*
[4] See Linda Ray's article in Chron: http://smallbusiness.chron.com/vertical-communication-organization-20985.html Retrieved February 27, 2016.

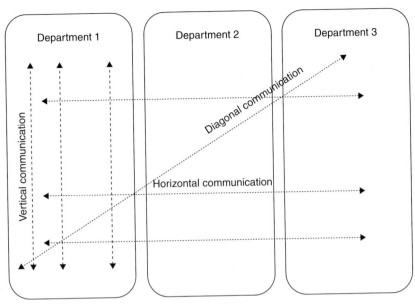

Figure 5. Vertical, horizontal, and diagonal communication.

is very important for promoting understanding and coordination among various people and departments and for quicker communication in the organization.[5]

Serendipity and Networks (Creativity, Continued)

Horizontal properties of social networks may also boost the propensity for generating unexpected ideas. This seems especially intriguing given that many big discoveries were made by chance, e.g., Velcro, penicillin, X-rays, Teflon, and dynamite (Roberts, 1989). Other important discoveries made by accident include Newton's theory of gravitation and the Big Bang theory of the creation of the universe.

Fortuitous discoveries, happenstance, pleasant surprises, these are all examples of *serendipity*. The word "serendipity" is based on an old Persian fairy tale, in which the heroes continuously make unexpected discoveries.[6]

---

[5] Retrieved February 26, 2016 from Business Communication: http://bizcommunicationcoach.com/what-is-horizontal-communication-in-business-importance/.

[6] The fairy tale "Three Princes of Serendip" is about the travels of princes from Serendip, who made a series of accidental discoveries. The word "serendipity" was coined in the mid-eighteenth century

As the art of making unsought findings (Andel, 1994), serendipity is a desirable phenomenon that indicates creativity and generation of new ideas. It also plays a central role in finding interdisciplinary discoveries (Darbellay *et al.*, 2014). If we value novelty and new ideas, we will invariably trend toward greater serendipity over time (Lindsay, 2014).

Serendipity is so valued in Silicon Valley that they started engineering it. Admittedly, that sounds like an oxymoron. (How one can engineer something that is by definition accidental?) But new findings indicate that there are tangible paths for augmenting serendipity. Serendipity isn't magic. Rather, it's a state of mind and a property of social networks, which means that it can be measured, analyzed, and engineered (Lindsay, 2014). Some say that serendipity arises from both nonpurposive conditions, e.g., from the environment, and from purposive strategies, e.g., from intentional knowledge acquisition (Foster & Ford, 2003).

Here are some examples:

Between 1974 and 2005, U.S. Big Pharma noted a significant increase of management resources with a parallel decline in its patents. The offices were traditional and the workplaces stable. During more or less the same time (1997–2012), the French company Paris Jussieu[7] was thriving. They published fifty-five thousand scientific papers during this time. Also, Paris Jussieu employees were three to five times more likely to collaborate with their peers and did so nearly four to six times more often (as measured by citations).

What was the core driver for Paris Jussieu doing their best work ever while other companies struggled? Retrofitting. During this time, Jussieu's offices relocated labs several times, moving and reorganizing staff in random groups, as a result of ongoing asbestos removal. People who didn't know each other met at the new locations and eagerly discussed their work, inspired each other, and collaborated (Lindsay, 2015).

In another example, when Yahoo instituted a work-from-home policy for employees in 2013, the result was a decline in productivity. When Marissa Mayer became CEO, she reversed the policy, claiming that working solo couldn't compete with lingering meetings around the coffee machine and the unexpected inspiration that can result. Some of the best decisions and insights arise from hallway and cafeteria discussions, meeting new people, and impromptu team meetings. In fact, to increase serendipity Yahoo

by Horace Walpole, who mentioned that the phenomenon of accidental discoveries may be called *serendipity* (see wiki: https://en.wikipedia.org/wiki/Serendipity)

[7] The largest medical research complex in France of a similar pharmaceutical profile

commissioned a new campus expressly designed to maximize casual collisions among the workforce. Likewise, Facebook hired the famous architect Frank Gehry to build a space that would keep thousands of people in close proximity, to encourage collaboration (Lindsay, 2015).

Researchers have followed these experiences, attempting to document whether, indeed, random encounters and meeting in groups enhance serendipity. For example, Arizona State University used sensors and surveys to study creativity within teams. The exploratory study indicated that movement and face-to-face interaction between the team members might be a significant indicator for enhancing creativity. Participants felt most creative on days spent in motion meeting people, as opposed to working for long stretches at their desks (Tripathi & Burleson, 2012).

MIT Media Lab's Human Dynamics Laboratory used "sociometric badges" to measure workers' movements, speech, and conversation partners. The discovery was that employees who ate at cafeteria tables designed for twelve people were more productive than those at tables for four, because there were more chances for conversations within larger social networks. It was shown that these collegial lunches, along with random encounters during coffee breaks, can boost individual productivity by as much as 25 percent. In his conclusion, the MIT researcher Ethan Zuckerman said that the greatest threats to serendipity are our ingrained biases and cognitive limits; we intrinsically want more known knowns, not unknown unknowns (Baber *et al.*, 2015).

Following this path, Lindsay (2015) defined serendipity as the process through which we *discover unknown unknowns*; it is based on an emergent property of social networks, instead of sheer luck.

As seen in these examples, horizontal networks may play a significant role in boosting serendipity and "idea-bubbling" creativity.

Networks Supporting Social Capital

In our previous research we documented that Social Entrepreneurs build social capital, which not only supports the long-term sustainability of their projects but also empowers people and societies (Praszkier *et al.*, 2009; Praszkier & Nowak, 2012). This has been best formulated by Peter Drucker: "The social entrepreneur changes the performance capacity of society" (interview by Gendron, 1966, p. 37).

Social capital is a driving force for the development of societies. Communities with strong social capital are more successful in combating poverty, resolving conflicts, and taking advantage of new opportunities

(Woolcock & Narayan, 2000; Maskell, 2000). Social capital is also a vital ingredient in economic development around the world (Putnam, 1993). Social capital (i.e., trust among entrepreneurs, employees, suppliers, and customers) is the essential underpinning for creating business networks that lead to sustainable economic growth and success (Neace, 1999). And social interaction, a manifestation of the structural dimension of social capital, has a significant effect on product innovation (Tsai & Ghoshal, 1998).

So in essence, social networks enhance social capital and are a prerequisite for endogenous dynamics (Chapter 10) and for becoming an Empowerer (Chapter 13). Let's look at the role they play.

Burt's Concept of the Role of Structural Holes

Social capital generated by social networks is a critical element in business strategy, as markets, organizations, and careers become increasingly more dependent on informal relationships. Almost everything that happens in a firm flows through informal networks built by coordination, cooperation, friendship, gossip, knowledge, and trust (Burt, 2011).

Opinion and behavior are more homogeneous within groups and clusters than between them. Accordingly, people connected across and between groups are more familiar with alternative ways of thinking and behaving. Some of them are at the edge of small-knit circles, i.e., close to networks' *structural holes*, connected not only to their own circle, but also to other clusters. Hence, they become brokers for exchange between groups.

Brokerage across the structural holes between groups provides the ability to see options otherwise hidden, which is the mechanism by which brokerage enhances social capital. The between-group brokers are more likely to express ideas, less likely to have ideas dismissed, and more likely to have ideas evaluated as valuable (Burt, 2005; see Figure 6).

Putnam (2000) introduced the concepts of *bridging* and *bonding* social capital. The former is creating connections across diverse social groups, and the latter is doing so only among homogeneous groups. Each mode serves an important purpose, as the bridging links groups with the outer world, whereas bonding builds internal connectivity. In that way *bridging* social capital is more a function of brokerage across structural holes than *bonding* social capital, which prompts closure within a network.

The two leading network mechanisms (*brokerage* and *closure*) can be joined in a productive way within a more general model of social capital. Structural holes are the source of value added, but network closure

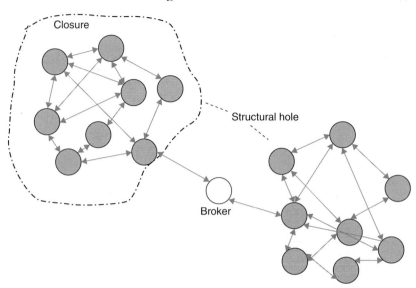

Figure 6. Structural holes, brokerage, and closure.

(bonding social capital) can be essential to realizing the values available in the holes (Burt, 2000).

Brokerage is the activity of people who live at the intersection of social worlds and can see and develop good ideas. Closure is the tightening coordination of a closed network of people. Ronald Burt's *Brokerage and Closure* explores how these elements work together to define social capital, showing how, in the business world, reputation replaces authority, and reward is associated with achieving competitive advantage in a social order in continuous disequilibrium (Burt, 2011).

It's important to add that Burt found that managers who straddled holes between teams and domains consistently produced better ideas (creativity!) than those inside their respective circles and distant from structural holes (Burt, 2005).

Granovetter's Strength of Weak Ties

To weave the connections among members of one's close-knit circles, as well as between those circles and diverse social strata, requires a variety of bonds – some strong, such as those between family members, friends,

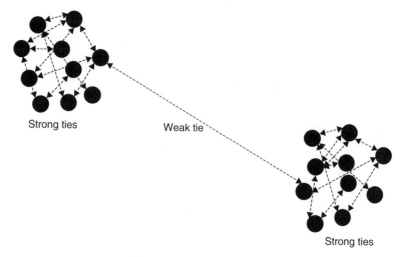

Figure 7. Strong and weak ties.

long-term professional colleagues, or neighbors, and some weak, such as recently formed liaisons or representatives of different and distant groups.

Research carried out in the 1960s, by Mark Granovetter, revealed that the connections that proved most effective in conducting a job search were not close friends but distant acquaintances. Granovetter's later studies confirmed that not only did weak ties result in greater job opportunities, but also that those who found jobs through strong ties were far more likely to have had a period of unemployment between jobs than those using weak ties (who held their jobs for a longer time (1983, 1995).

This discovery led to the concept of *the strength of weak ties* (Granovetter, 1973; Barabási, 2003).[8] Granovetter holds that a weak tie becomes a crucial bridge between two densely knit clusters of close friends. One member of a group of close friends having a weak relationship with a member of another close-knit group connects all members of both groups. Hence, the significance of weak ties is that they are far more likely than strong ones to bridge the gap between groups (see Figure 7).

Moreover, lack of weak ties deprives close-knit group members of information from distant parts of the social system and confines them to the provincial news and views of their close friends. They are thus isolated

---

[8] Granovetter defines the strength of a tie as a combination of four indicators: its longevity, its emotional intensity, the intimacy quotient, and the reciprocal services.

from the latest ideas and trends. One possible consequence of this is that they will find themselves at a disadvantage in the labor market, where time is of the essence when it comes to seizing opportunities for advancement. They'll also be poorly integrated into political or other goal-oriented movements (Granovetter, 1973, 1983, 1995). Social systems lacking weak ties will be fragmented and incoherent (Granovetter, 1983), as weak ties become a specific gateway for creating social capital, reaching far beyond isolated "small worlds." (The concept of small worlds is explained later in this chapter).

Strong ties, on the other hand, are relationships among people who work, live, or play together. They create a bonding type of social capital and engender a tendency for group members to think alike and reduce the diversity of ideas (Porter, 2007). However, they also provide a societal backbone, help maintain and transmit values and traditions, provide a sense of identity, and serve as reference points in case of disturbances (Praszkier, 2012). Strong ties naturally occur as a result of familial and community connections. Establishing weak ties requires cognitive flexibility and an ability to function in complex organizations. Weak ties not only provide access to heterogeneous resources but also enhance people's opportunity for mobility, augmenting their social capital (Granovetter, 1973, 1995; Lin, 2001). So it follows that a state of harmony between strong and weak links is most beneficial for fostering productivity and enhancing creativity (Praszkier, 2012). Striking this balance seems to be the Empowering Leader's compelling challenge.

The Role of Network Embeddedness

Our networks often interpenetrate one another. Some members of our family network are also part of our social cluster or members of our professional circle, some neighborhood networks cross with social ones, etc. This phenomenon is called *network embeddedness* and has been defined as the degree to which individuals or firms are enmeshed in a social network (a concept coined by Granovetter, 1985) or are located within a larger entity or context (Moody & White, 2003). The embedded nature of social behavior determines the way in which action is based in the existing social context (Aldrich & Zimmer, 1986; see Figure 8).

Individuals who are embedded in diverse networks are more likely to be innovative than those who rely on homogeneous ties (Ruef, 2002). However, the paradoxical nature of embeddedness is such that while an initial increase of relational ties leads to increased efficiency of action,

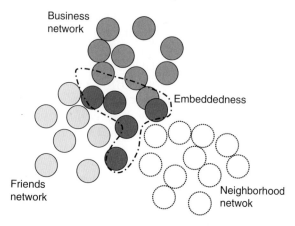

Figure 8. Network embeddedness.

when actors are too highly embedded, their effectiveness diminishes (Uzzi, 1996, 1997). This suggests that there should exist an optimal degree of embeddedness.

Networks' embeddedness provides connection and exchange among individual networks, otherwise isolated. The conjunction of networks creates a specific "exchange" of social capital, where ideas, values, and narratives pervade different clusters. By some, networks' embeddedness is seen as the core of the social network theory and social capital theory (e.g., Xin & Qin, 2011).

Random, Small Worlds, and Scale-Free Networks

Human social connectivity was initially (from the late 1950s to the mid-1970s) seen as myriad random connections. The nodes in the network were perceived as having a more or less similar number of connections (Barabási, 2003).

Following Granovetter's innovative concept, in the mid-1970s, theorists began to envision large networks as a universe full of *small worlds* densely interconnected through weak ties (Watts & Strogatz, 1998; Barabási, 2003). Small worlds often become close-knit circles cultivating a bonding type of social capital and, as Granovetter indicated (1973, 1983), often deplete their possible resources.

However, even a few extra links (weak ties) among clusters are sufficient to decrease the separation of small worlds and particular nodes drastically.

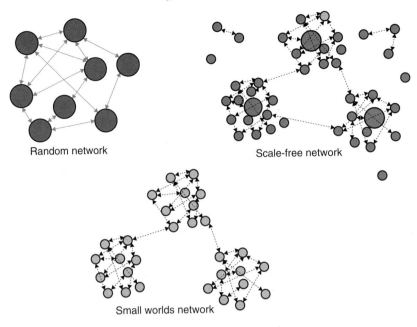

Figure 9. Three types of networks.

If only one individual from a close-knit circle has a weak relationship with someone from a distant small world, then, through that tiny relationship, all members of both small clusters are potentially interconnected.

The network was then envisioned as a universe of small worlds, connected through weak ties, playing the function of bridging social capital. If we return to Burt's theory, we see that inside the small worlds there exists a closure type of network mechanism, where the connected members provide brokerage across small worlds (bridging through structural holes; see Figure 9).

The small worlds concept was based on the belief that the degree (number of connections) of nodes was randomly distributed, i.e., that the number of connections per node is more or less close to a network's average connectivity. However, over time, it became clear that nodes with a high degree of connectivity as well as nodes with very few ties were both present in global human networks. The distribution (number of connections per node) is far from random, as extremely high-degree and low-degree nodes are equally possible. This sort of grid, called a *scale-free network*, indicates that there is no typical or average node.

Scale-free networks usually provide better coordination and flow of information and are resilient and impervious to failure, a property called *robustness* (Barabási, *ibid*). If, for example, some nodes become damaged, the flow of information is replaced by alternative paths, through weak connections, linking densely connected clusters through at least one of their participants.

A scale-free type of network, with several highly connected nodes, seems to be the best solution to secure the formation of social capital (of both the bonding and bridging kinds) and augment creativity, using horizontal (weak ties) connections and providing brokerage over structural holes.

Designing a social milieu for augmenting creativity and serendipity and for enhancing social capital may require leaders to manage scale-free networks with multiple brokerages via structural holes (i.e., among densely connected clusters) and build bridging social capital through weak and horizontal connections. This seems to be a specific art and requires a certain sagacity that will probably become part of the acumen of the leaders of tomorrow.

Chapter Coda

- The various types of communication were reviewed: horizontal, diagonal, and vertical.
- The concept of serendipity and the way to enhance creativity in networks were introduced.
- The ways social capital (bridging and bonding) can be built through the specific network structure were presented:
- Burt's concept of the role of structural holes,
- Granovetter's discovery of the power of weak ties,
- The role of networks' embeddedness,
- The various structures of large networks: random, small worlds, and scale-free.
- The leaders of tomorrow will have the sagacity to manage scale-free networks with brokerage across structural holes and weak ties providing bridging social capital.

Empowering Leadership

One of the inspirations for this book was an adventure I had, learning how simple desert stones were turned into development and community wealth, with absolutely no financial investment. It was in February 2012, when I visited Burkina Faso, a poor country even by West African standards, landlocked and suffering from recurring droughts. Traveling outside the capital, Ouagadougou, one sees mostly rocky desert with the occasional dwarfed tree. This barren landscape is typically viewed as useless, so I was thrilled to hear the story of how those gloomy stones became a source of income and community development. No surprise, I decided to visit Laogo, the site of this miracle, twenty miles from Ouagadougou.

Siriky Ky from Burkina Faso

Legend has it that Siriky Ky, a sculptor from Burkina Faso, once fell asleep in the desert and awoke with his head on a stone. As an artist his natural reaction was to carve the stone, and his excitement grew as he saw his sculpture emerge from the lifeless rock. Siriki Ky then invited a few of his Burkinabe friends to see his work, and each of them chose a stone to carve. Thrilled with the result, they invited a group of African colleagues, and again, each one of them chose a stone and turned it into a sculpture. This led to the idea of organizing an international annual symposium. The first one, in January 1989, was a gathering of eighteen sculptors from thirteen countries. Their primary motivation for getting together was their passion for art and enthusiasm for sharing their ideas and having fun together.

Since then sculptors from around the world, some of them well known, with works exhibited in the best museums, have been invited to attend each year to exchange ideas, have fun, and create in situ a piece of art from their choice of granite boulders that occur naturally in the area. The result is a huge park with hundreds of stone sculptures embedded in the natural environment, rather than placed in a museum. Tourists flock to see the

Figure 10. Sculpture Park in Laogo, Burkina Faso.

sculpture park, and a new surrounding infrastructure supports the community's burgeoning tourism business (see Figure 10).

One man with passion, with no other investments than his idea, a chisel, and a gavel, turned the desert into a blooming community. Upon seeing this transformation I had several reflections: First, that turning gloomy stones into growth levers is somewhat magical, and the most fascinating pursuit would be to explore the essence of such magic; second, that big results don't actually need large investments – they can originate from a very small impulse from the very bottom; third, that passion plus fun can be a perfect driver for creation of novel solutions; fourth, that it's critical to create an enabling environment for similar initiatives to arise and thrive; and finally, that there must be some kind of leadership focused on creating such an environment.

This section will look at this enabling and empowering sort of leadership. As stated earlier, the purpose here isn't to promote Empowering Leadership (EL) as the best style; there are many other leadership styles, each suited to its context. Instead, the intent is to delineate the EL approach as compelling in its own right, without undermining other methods of management.

Let's first then continue our reflection on the general definition of leadership.

Defining Leadership, Third Round

At the beginning of Section 2 we concluded that leadership is the process of creating a way for people to contribute in order to make something extraordinary happen (Kouzes & Posner, 2008). However, from the examples cited so far and the knowledge of complex systems and efficient networks, we understand that contemporary leadership aims at establishing durable processes, not at creating just one extraordinary "thing" or event. Moreover, it provides more than "a way for people to contribute"; it also enables them to identify with an idea and take coownership of it.

Elaborating on Kouzes & Pozner's definition, a new way to define leadership would be as a process of unleashing the capabilities of groups, communities, or societies and enabling them to identify and take coownership of the idea, pursue it, and make something extraordinary, i.e., a durable change process, happen.

A narrow category of this broad definition is called Empowering Leadership.

CHAPTER 9

Empowering Leadership

Prior to introducing Empowering Leadership, it would be useful to take a closer look at the descriptor, the phenomenon of Empowerment, and its three pivotal dimensions.

The Phenomenon of Empowerment

Empowerment is sometimes defined as a process of maximizing the contributions of others through recognition of their right to guide their own destiny (Manz & Sims, 1991; Page & Czuba, 1999), or as a process of significantly strengthening subordinates' beliefs in their own abilities (Conger, 1989). In other words, it's the capacity of individuals, groups, or communities to take control of their situation, exercise power, and achieve their own goals. Through empowerment people are able to help themselves and others to maximize the quality of their lives (Adams, 2008). Although some authors limit empowerment to an increased intrinsic task motivation (Thomas & Velthouse, 1990), here it will be understood as something much bigger. Using the complexity perspective we may define empowerment as creating an enabling environment for free interactions, participation, innovation, and taking coresponsibility, and, in lieu of this, enabling the process of emergence.

The value of empowerment seems obvious: on one hand, it leads to individual benefits, as people gain greater access to and control over resources (Zimmerman, 2000) and significantly strengthen their beliefs in their own abilities and self-efficacy (Conger, 1989). And on the other hand, it improves productivity (Conger, ibid; Stanley, 2005), enhancing knowledge sharing (Özbebek & Toplu, 2011) and team efficacy, both of which are positively related to performance (Srivastava et al., 2006).

One point we should clarify, however, is that we're talking about three dimensions of empowerment: the one who empowers others – let's call her or him the "Empowerer"; the process of empowerment; and the person being empowered – let's call her or him the "Empoweree." These dimensions can be described as follows:

- The Empowerer

Empowering others is sometimes defined as the ability to maximize the contributions of others through recognition of their right to guide their own destiny (Manz & Sims, 1991). However, "empowering others" sounds like an oxymoron: you are doing something for people "in need," sort of patronizing them – which is contradictory to "empowerment."

That's why some authors say that it isn't possible for a leader to "empower" someone to be accountable and make good decisions. It's the people who have to empower themselves. The leader's role is to create an enabling environment that encourages and supports the decision-making process, and to provide opportunities for people to make and act upon their own decisions. By doing this, the leader helps others reach an empowered state (Goldsmith, 2010).

This is a new form of leadership, designed to create and facilitate a milieu supporting people's self-reliance and self-leadership. This kind of leadership enables others to discover potential within themselves. Under this model the empowerer must be viewed not as "hero" but as "hero maker," and the spotlight must be not on the leader but on the achievements of the followers (Manz & Sims, 1991). In other words, a true empowerer isn't a center-stage sort of person. Instead, he or she plays a supporting role, helping others enjoy and celebrate their success. Remember the leadership definition at the beginning of this section? The leader enfranchises the capabilities of groups, communities, or societies and enables them to identify and take coownership of the idea and pursue it to make something extraordinary happen. Hence the motto from Lao Tsu at the beginning of this book: "A leader is best when people barely know he exists; when his work is done, his aim fulfilled, they will say: we did it all ourselves."

It's a tall order to remain in the shadows while others celebrate success that, to a great extent, you made happen, specifically by creating intentionally a supportive environment. So what motivates the Empowerer to choose this bold path? We'll reflect on this question later in this chapter and in Chapter 13.

- The process

Empowering is seen as an intentional, ongoing process, involving mutual respect, critical reflection, caring, and group participation, through which people gain greater access to and control over resources (Zimmerman, 2000).

The empowerment process comprises a series of experiences in which individuals learn to see a closer correspondence between their goals and a sense of how to achieve them and gain greater access to and control over resources. In short, it's about creating opportunities for community or group members to develop skills so they don't have to be dependent on others, e.g., professionals, experts, superiors (Zimmerman, 1995). Following that track, it's the participatory process that develops an "eco-identity," whereby participants become members of the community (Kelly, 1971, 2013).

Empowerment may be perceived as a "relational construct," which means that the power is seen as the core function of the dependence and/or interdependence of actors (Conger & Kanungo, 1988). In that vein, empowerment depends on the possibility of changing the power structure. If power can't be shifted – i.e., if it is inherent in positions or people – then empowerment isn't possible nor conceivable in any meaningful way (Page & Czuba, 1999).

Some authors mention quite technical methods of empowerment, such as developing self-leadership through reward, constructive reprimand, and teamwork (Manz & Sims, 1991). Others (e.g., Arnold *et al.*, 2000) have identified some related actions, including coaching, informing, leading by example, showing concern/interacting with the team, and participative decision making. As we understand it, the core method for empowerment is to create an environment supporting free interaction, sharing, inspiring others, and being inspired (often in horizontal relationships). It also entails weeding out the subordinate–superior terminology and enabling everyone to exercise leadership behavior, no matter what position he or she holds in the organizational flowchart (Clark, 2013).

- The Empoweree

Empowerment can be characterized as a property of the empoweree, either as an internalized attitude or as an observable behavior (Rappaport, 2013). Here we will focus on the first. As stated, through empowerment people significantly strengthen their beliefs in their own abilities and self-efficacy (Conger, 1989). This, per se, is meaningful as a value; it also has several impacts:

Empowerment is a "motivational construct" in the sense that power refers to an intrinsic need for self-determination (Deci, 1975) or a belief in personal self-efficacy (Bandura, 1976; Conger & Kanungo, 1988). Moreover, positive self-evaluation traits are related to psychological empowerment, which is positively associated with a broad range of employee outcomes, including job satisfaction, organizational commitment, and performance. Additionally, it is negatively associated with employee strain and turnover intentions (Seibert *et al.,* 2011).

This may be best illustrated with an example:

A company hires low-income workers, who frequently quit, generating a high turnover rate. The company incurs additional costs not only for educating new workers, especially since many of them do not speak adequate English, and also to cover the costs of mistakes and damage unavoidable in the initial employment period. Concurrently, employees who leave the company often collect unemployment benefits, and doing so put them and their families in a high-risk group.

Steve Bigari from the United States

It was at a McDonald's in the Denver area where a fast-rising, creative manager, Steve Bigari,[1] dug in his heels, determined to create an environment where employees would stay. Bigari was discouraged by his colleagues' stance that the low-income workers' high turnover was unchangeable and that it's traditional for McDonald's to budget extra money to cover related liabilities. Despite being pegged as a bit of a deviant by his peers, he looked for a solution. He said he was motivated by the reality that unemployment is damaging for people and their families; by his Italian/Catholic roots, which instilled a desire to do something to protect people from the vicious cycle of unemployment; and by a desire to reduce the company's costs.[2]

He first ascertained the circumstances that accompany losing a job and found out that the process usually starts with the employee calling in and saying that he can't come to work because, for example, his car won't start, or her child is sick. The manager who receives such a call more than once says, "This is the third time you've been out because something's happened. You're fired." Because low-income workers typically drive old cars that break down and often have trouble finding child care when their kids are sick, they're, as Bigari put it, "one call away from unemployment."

Bigari reversed this trend by modifying the way the workers were handled when they called in and reported problems. When someone called

---

[1] Steve Bigari was the only two-time recipient of McDonald's Ronald Award, an honor rewarding lifetime achievement in selfless community service.

[2] I interviewed him in June 2004 in the process of selection to the Ashoka Fellowship.

in saying he couldn't report to work because of some pressing issue, the call was transferred to the top manager. The manager, seeing the situation as a great opportunity to turn things around, would tell the employee that he was going to send someone right away to help fix the problem. As a bonus, the employee would be taught how to deal with such a problem in the future. In that way Bigari turned those situations into positive learning opportunities. He organized a system of local NGOs into "social-emergency systems" to train people to handle various crisis situations. But the most meaningful change was the radical reversal of the way managers responded to the calls.

Bigari, as an empowerer, created a positive environment (process) where low-income workers (empowerees) could thrive. They were appreciated and treated with dignity and, hence, became loyal and motivated for further development. Bigari's stories of empowerment – stories of employees "one call away from unemployment" who are now learning and contributing to the company's success and advancing in their own careers – are extremely touching. In addition, staff retention skyrocketed, and the company saved money that would have been spent on employee turnover.[3]

This example shows that empowering people not only makes them more self-reliant and motivated but can also benefit the company and create a win–win situation.

Empowering Leadership Defined

This seems to be an appropriate moment to merge the concepts of "empowerment" and "leadership," drawing on our knowledge of complexity (Chapter 5), and introduce Empowering Leadership (EL).

Applied EL is typically both value- and efficiency-driven. However, the value piece is tricky; while some authors mention the value orientation of empowerment (e.g., Zimmerman, 2000), concern over preserving people's dignity and enabling them to achieve their full potential is difficult to measure through research. (It can, however, be more easily assessed during live interviews.)

If we assert then that EL is based on both the drive to enhance efficiency and values concerning care for others, we find that, as in Bigari's case, the two motivations mutually reinforce each other, creating a win–win situation.

---

[3] Steve Bigari became an Ashoka Fellow, see: www.ashoka.org/fellow/steve-bigari

The general definition of leadership stated previously mentions a *process*. The leaders we've looked at are focused on far-reaching processes. They also rely on the potential of people and groups more than on the wisdom of experts. In other words, they embrace *endogenous* dynamics, and research tells us that *endogenous* leadership is much more effective than *exogenous* leadership (i.e., imposed from outside) (Rivas & Suttery, 2009).

Moreover, these leaders set off an *autocatalytic* process, where initial impulses, such as sparking bottom-up activities and horizontal communication, result in self-perpetuating dynamics.

Finally, as we've seen, they enable free interactions on the lower level, leading to the emergence of new qualities (e.g., innovations, market paradigm shift.) on the higher level. In doing so, they *harness complexity* and facilitate the *chaos-into-order emergence.*[4]

Summing up, Empowering Leadership may be defined as a process that is both value- and efficiency-driven, facilitating emergence through endogenous dynamics aimed at triggering the potential of individuals, groups, communities, or societies. Through this process people and groups identify with and take coownership of an idea to make something extraordinary (e.g., innovation) happen.

As we've seen, this process can generate amazing results, but preconditions are cardinal, as not all free interactions lead to desired outputs. Sometimes chaos leads to destruction. But with appropriate preconditions leaders can turn chaos into order and maximize the effects of empowering leadership.

Chapter Coda

- Introducing a new approach to the general definition of leadership
- The phenomenon of empowerment seen from the perspective of the Empowerer, the process of Empowerment, and the Empoweree.
- Defining Empowering Leadership.

---

[4] It is worth mentioning that the idea of leadership based on harnessing chaos was introduced as early as the 1990s by Youngblood (1997), who predicted a new breed of companies thriving on chaos.

CHAPTER 10

Preconditions for Endogenous Dynamics

Not all groups and networks generate constructive results. Leaving people free to explore and communicate isn't sufficient to guarantee that the system will thrive or, riskier still, that it won't collapse into destructive chaos. Something more is required.

I have been studying this "something more" for the last decade, interviewing social and business entrepreneurs, studying literature, and carrying out my own research. As a result, I have identified five chaos-to-order prerequisites. My conviction is that these are essential conditions for the success of the chaos-to-order process. Are they all that is required? I do not think so. I think a successful chaos-to-order process also needs a compelling mission and a convincing strategy. There will be more about the mission and vision in Chapters 11 and 12. Here, let us focus on the necessary preconditions.

"Complexity as a Way of Thinking"

This title is a citation from one of the titles of Axelrod & Cohen's book *Harnessing Complexity* (2000, p. 28). The authors maintain that in the emerging, complex universe people will be comfortable with perpetual novelty and ready for adaptations on many societal levels. They will value diversity and experimentation, and all of this will foster decentralized authority (p. 29).

This may come as a shock to many, as we have been trained to think in a linear way: A cause leads to a consequence. A leads to B, and B to C. In thinking about organizations, we envision charts with tidy boxes and arrows clearly illustrating a team's structure. But as we enter the emerging world of complexity science (Dooley, 2009), we must completely change our approach, envisioning multiple formal and informal connections and horizontal communications, hidden potential, latent tendencies, leverage points for initiating the chain of change, etc. (Praszkier, 2015).

Moreover, perceiving chaos as a potential source of higher order is often limited by our culture, which trains us to avoid chaos, which is understood as a source of disintegration and a synonym for "mess." On the other hand, chaos theory offers a unique perspective, which may improve our understanding of learning and development (Levin, F. M., 2000). In that vein, organizations are viewed as nonlinear dynamic systems with typical "chaos" properties, such as sensitivity to initial conditions (see the discussion of the butterfly effect, Chapter 5). Thietart and Forgues (1995) propose several indications of a constructive alignment with complexity theory organizations that align with complexity theory. They include:

- A constant balance of counteracting forces, which put organizations in a potentially chaotic situation[1]
- Resulting changes that are usually discrete, manifesting discontinuities and jumps
- Small changes that have big consequences
- Long-term consequences that are unpredictable in a linear "A to B" way[2]
- Identical patterns that can be found at different scales (see the discussion of "fractals syndrome," Chapter 5)
- Similar actions that do not lead to the same results; in other words, the rapidly changing context (internal and external) makes Heraclitus' saying "You can't step twice into the same river" analogous to contemporary reality.

This sort of complexity cognition requires a real shift in mind-set and a new psychological approach. There will be more about related personality traits in Chapter 13 and 15, but at this point, it is enough to say that complexity theory has also revolutionized our understanding of how the human brain works (Ibáñez, 2007), leading to the emergence of a new neuroscience (Skarda & Freeman, 1990). This revolution in our cognition and cognition of cognition may be a real leap forward.

Social Capital, Part 2

Relationship networks manifest extraordinary properties. Beyond the *human capital* (people) and the *financial* or *economic capital* (resources) is something intangible, lying under the surface *between* individuals. Remember the discussion in Chapter 8 about the capabilities of the few vs.

---

[1] The balance between counteracting forces was introduced in the 1940s by Kurt Lewin; see Chapter 5.
[2] Yes, predictable, though in nontraditional ways, e.g., through simulations; see Chapters 16 and 17.

the many? A single particle of air does not have the properties a group of particles manifests, e.g., the ability to propagate sound. And likewise, when people gather, their connections generate an added value not revealed by getting to know the individuals singly. This is called *social capital*.

Defining Social Capital

In the 1990s, Putnam defined social capital as referring to features of social organization, such as trust, norms, and networks, that can improve the efficiency of society by facilitating coordinated actions (Putmam, 1993). Several years later, he offered another definition, saying that social capital refers to connections among individuals – social networks and the norms of reciprocity and trustworthiness that arise from them.

Others define social capital as the aggregation of the actual or potential resources that are linked to the possession of a durable network, which consists of relationships of mutual acquaintance and recognition, more or less institutionalized. Social capital perceives social structures as resources that can be used by the actors to realize their interests (Bourdieu, 1986; Coleman, 1990). In simpler terms, social capital appears when a person's family, friends, and associates constitute an important asset, one that can be called on in a crisis or enjoyed for its own sake (Woolcock & Narayan, 2000); and this asset is based on cooperation among the members of a society, of a family, or of peer groups (Bourdieu, 2003).

Social Capital Helps

As mentioned in Chapter 7, there is consensus that despite the vague definition of social capital (Portes, 1998; Lin et al., 2001; Yang, 2007) it is predominantly perceived as an important value, both for individuals (Coleman, 1988; Brehm & Rahn, 1997; Burt, 1997, 2001; Adler & Kwon, 2002; Ellison et al., 2007) as well as for groups or societies (Woolcock & Narayan, 2000; Fine 2001; Praszkier et al., 2009). Moreover, many authors highlight its significance for community development and eco-nomic growth (Putnam, 1993; Neace, 1999; Maskell, 2000; Fukuyama 2001; Claridge, 2004).

Social capital is important for its effect on individuals and groups, i.e., the inclinations that arise from participating in social networks to do things for each other (norms of reciprocity). Putnam (2000) observed the correla-tion of a rise in crime rates and a decline in educational achievement in the United States, between the 1950s and the 1990s, with a reduction in social capital during the same time. Furthermore, at any one time, more positive features were to be found in states located closer to Canada, where measures of social capital were deemed higher.

Social capital helps make the difficult achievable (Coleman, 2000; Putnam & Gross, 2002). For example, it has been found to reduce turn-over rates (Krackhardt & Hanson, 1993) and facilitate entrepreneurship (Chong & Gibbons, 1997) and the formation of start-up companies (Walker *et al.,* 1997). In particular, social capital is a critical factor in the ability to sustain bottom-up mechanisms (Woolcock, 1998) essential to the introduction of social change (McAdam, 1999; Piven, 2008), such as efficiency in delivering high-quality health care (Carey, 2000; Edwards *et al.,* 2003) and in eradicating poverty in rural areas (e.g., in Bangladesh; Blair, 2005).

Social capital not only encompasses the institutionalized relationships among people, but also the shared values and understandings that enable individuals and groups to trust each other and work together. Mutual trust reinforces societal development (Fukuyama, 1996; Coleman, 2000; Bourdieu, 2003). Higher trust yields better societal outcomes, and these in turn, raise the level of mutual trust, which, in a feedback loop, positively influences further results (Putnam, 1993).

Trust and Cooperation – Pivots of Social Capital

Societal trust emerges through the aggregation of individual trust rela-tionships (Tyler, 2003; Cook *et al.* 2005). So social capital is sometimes also thought of as a property individuals possess as a consequence of their mutual trust with others, arising through bonds, bridges and links within various social networks. Social capital also produces positive outcomes at the individual level. For example, it empowers the individual to take some risk and explore new opportunities (Coleman, 1988; Brehm & Rahn, 1997); it also influences career success (Burt, 1992; Podolny & Baron, 1997; Gabbay & Zuckerman, 1998).

The other pivotal dimension of social capital is *cooperation* (Putnam, 1993; Knack & Keefer, 1997; Woolcock, 2004; da Silva, 2006; Bouma *et al.,* 2008). It takes mutual commitment and cooperation from all par-ties involved to build social capital (Adler & Kwon, 2002). The more that individuals are in regular contact with one another, the more likely they are to develop a "habit of cooperation" and act collectively (Wasko & Faraj, 2005). Cooperation is also seen as a value per se (Kenworthy, 1997; Maxwell, 2002).

Why Social Capital Is a Precondition

Why is social capital seen as an important precondition for securing chaos-to-order dynamics? The simple answer is that social capital, i.e., a network of trust and cooperation, is a pathway for exchange, mutual inspiration and support, as well as a springboard for value-added creation.

The more complex answer relates to our research focused on the methods used by social entrepreneurs while addressing pressing, though protracted and insurmountable problems. The research question posed was "How do these leaders achieve durable system-change with minimal investments?" The findings demonstrated that, regardless of the field or mission and prior to addressing their direct goals, they first build social capital. They often do that by circumventing the main conflict area and building alternative attractors that provide easy, fast, and enjoyable success, around which social capital then develops. Because it is based on endogenous dynamics, this social capital becomes a key force in the pursuit of the core mission while adding value by empowering people, communities, and societies in a general way and enabling them to cope successfully with other problems. Social capital mutually reinforces mission-related dynamics, and in a feedback loop, the mission empowers people and communities, further augmenting social capital (Praszkier & Nowak, 2012).[3] This indicates that social capital is a prerequisite for positive transformations.

Connectivity Spirit

"Networking" and "network effect" are popular terms these days, but if you ask how networking is done and how its effect is measured, the typical response is that there is a platform. A platform is a space for potential connections to occur, not the network per se. From my interviews it seems that the term "network effect" is sort of trendy; many leaders claim to have achieved "the network effect," though they have not even bothered to measure the network's properties such as *density*,[4] *closeness* of the nodes,[5] or, most importantly, *structural cohesion*;[6] nor do they identify the *structural holes*, so as to pin down the critical role of the "brokers" (Chapter 8).

---

[3] Peter Drucker, the business consulting expert, captured this social-value creation process saying that social entrepreneurs change the performance capacity of society (interview with P. Drucker, Gendron, 1966, p. 37).
[4] The number of existing connections divided by the number of potential connections.
[5] The average distance of a node from all the other nodes.
[6] Exposing the network's vulnerability to fragmentation into disconnected parts.

Figure 11. Frank Escoubès demonstrating his concept.

Example of a Productive Connectivity Platform

It may be helpful to introduce an example of filling a potential platform with a vibrant and productive network.

Frank Escoubès from Canada

The Imagination for People (I4P) project in Montreal (see Web site video)[7] attracts and stimulates cross-cutting cooperation among the public, social, and business sectors, as well as among individuals. The project founder Frank Escoubès' vision is to build and share ideas in order to create tomorrow's solutions. He creates channels for citizens to influence public and private policy focused on social innovation[8] (see Figures 11 and 12).

By fostering institution-to-institution, individual-to-individual, and individual-to-institution cooperation, the platform generates multiple value-added ideas and projects. I4P representatives continually operate online to encourage diverse and vital collaborations. The Orchestrator

---

[7] http://imaginationforpeople.org/en/, click "Watch the video."
[8] See: www.ashoka.org/fellow/frank-escoub%C3%A8s.

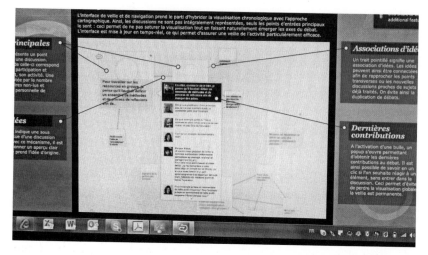

Figure 12. The I4P platform.

prompts and enables connections, the Catcher/Hunter captures information, and the Mapper maps the network and the field. In short, I4P is not merely "a platform," but a vibrant and complex network of connections and productive cooperation.

Teams Become Trendy Again

The team concept has also become popular. An article titled "Team Spirit" (*The Economist*, Schumpeter, 2016) states that teamwork is back in fashion. Companies are abandoning traditional structures and organizing employees into cross-disciplinary teams. These teams are gaining more power to run their own affairs and spending more time working with each other, instead of focusing on reporting upward. A network of teams is replacing the conventional hierarchy.

The article also mentions a breakthrough book, *Team of Teams*, written by General Stanley McChrystal, who led the Joint Special Operations Command in Iraq during the Persian Gulf Wars and was top commander of American forces in Afghanistan. During the battle, responding to the enemy's agile operations, he completely reshaped his army's structure, decentralizing authority and shifting to self-organizing teams. General McChrystal discarded centuries of conventional management wisdom and remade the task force, in the midst of the war, into a network that combined extremely transparent communication with decentralized decision-making authority (see: McChrystal, 2015).

But What Teams?

The same *Economist* article also mentions a Steelcase Global Report, "Engagement and the Global Workplace," from a new study of twelve thousand workers in seventeen countries. One of the key findings was that employees who have more choice and control over their work experience are more engaged.[9]

The team and network spirit is indeed a crucial gateway for building a chaos-to-order-enabling environment. However, spirit is not enough; we need to know what kind of networks and teams really work. In Chapter 8 we reviewed desirable properties of networks, including the role of structural holes brokerage, the power of weak ties, network embeddedness, and the outstanding properties of scale-free structures.

One might think that the more densely a network is connected, the better. However, some studies show that it is not so simple. We have seen that social capital grows with the increase of network density, but at a certain point, it starts dropping off (Borgatti *et al.*, 1998). In other words, if people in the network are connected with too many others, then the quality of their relationships (i.e., trust and readiness for cooperation) decreases. The real challenge (and art) is to find the right balance.

Also, teams are not always efficient. They perform well when, above all, a compelling purpose drives them (Hackman, 2002; Wageman *et al.*, 2008). And, surprisingly, participants' portfolios and IQs do not drive team efficiency.

Shedding Some New Light: Aristotle Project at Google

Aristotle, a recent four-year research project by Google, shed new light on what makes teams efficient. Through many probes and trials in diverse settings, the company discovered that the individual strength of participants, even the highest-scoring participants, has no influence on the team's performance. In other words, selecting the best of the best does not increase the team's capacity (Duhigg, 2016). What really matters

---

[9] For the report go to www.steelcase.com/blog/why-employee-engagement-matters/ and click Register for Report; retrieved February 24, 2017.

is, first, the psychological safety of the team members. People should feel comfortable and safe in the group, focusing not exclusively on the task, but also on the others by, for example, sharing personal information. Second, all members should speak for roughly the same amount of time in total, though they might speak for varying periods over time. These two features alone are sufficient to boost the group's performance, regardless of the qualities of its participants. This, again, confirms that potential embedded in group relationships doesn't always correlate with personal traits.

These findings have particular significance when we consider the role of empathy as another pivotal precondition.

Social Empathy

Empathy is seen as essential for successful business. "Some people think of empathy as a touchy-feely, "soft" skill. It is not. Empathy is a hard business skill that is absolutely critical to the bottom line. It is not about being nice. It is about "feeling someone else's pain" (Booth, 2015, p. 1). It provides the ability to connect with and relate to others; in that sense, the power of empathy is to break down barriers and open doors (Boyers, 2013). Empathy is not merely a foundation to build a business on; it is also a way to adapt when the market inevitably turns (Pomerenke, 2014).

What Is Empathy?

The idea of "feeling with" seems as old as civilization, or even older. For example, psalms thousands of years old are titled and refer to "Thinking and Feeling with God" (Piper, 2008).

Between the nineteenth and twentieth centuries, the concept of empathy was introduced by Theodor Lipps, who used the term *Einfühlung* (German: "feeling with"), which referred to the tendency of perceivers to project themselves onto the objects of perception and experience them as being "in" the object, so that they were "felt" as well as "seen" (Håkansson, 2003). The term *empathy* was coined during that period,[10] in the process of developing Lipp's Einfühlung ideas (Håkansson, *ibid*).

---

[10] By Edward Bradford Titchener.

Emotional and Cognitive Aspects of Empathy

"Feeling into" indicates that empathy is predominantly emotional. Indeed, many authors refer to empathy as an affective reaction. Saberi Roy (2010), for example, considers empathy an essential part of emotion (and, in a way, a specific emotion in and of itself), involving a feeling element of familiarity or connection and a bodily reaction of verbal or nonverbal communication. Empathy is conceptualized as feeling a vicarious emotion that is congruent with, but not necessarily identical to, the emotion of another person (Stotland, 1969; Hoffman, 1987; Barnett *et al.*, 1987).

As such, empathy involves sharing the perceived emotion of another – "feeling with" another (Eisenberg & Strayer, 1990). It is closely related to intuition and, like intuition, helps in the understanding of others. Empathy is thus described as recognizing other people's emotions through intuition and is marked by a feeling of connecting to the other person (Roy, *ibid*).

"Feeling into" is for some authors not descriptive enough. It is also important to understand the other. The cognitive aspects of empathy were introduced in the 1930s by Mead (1967) and Piaget (2008). Mead saw children's ability to role play as the key to their development through understanding others (Mead, *ibid*). Empathy as a cognitive function requires defocusing on oneself in order to imagine the feelings of the other (Håkansson, *ibid*; Piaget, *ibid*).

Empathy also helps to develop a more precise and direct estimate of others' plausible future actions and, as such, also serves as a driver at the epistemological level (De Vignemont & Singer, 2006). This sort of cognition is fundamental for leaders.

It seems that there is a tendency to integrate the affective and cognitive aspects of empathy and see it as a syndrome involving both (Davis, 1996; Ickes, 1997; Pavlovich & Krahnke, 2012). In that vein, Eisenberg (2002) defined empathy as "an affective response that stems from the apprehension or comprehension of another's emotional state or condition, and that is similar to what the other person is feeling or would be expected to feel" (p. 135).

All this leads to a conclusion that empathy is a connection between people, as we instinctively know what another person is feeling (Roy, *ibid*). Empathy enhances connectedness through the unconscious sharing of neuropathways that dissolve the sharp distinction between self and other (Pavlovich & Krahnke, *ibid*).

Empathetic connectedness is also perceived as *embodied simulation* (Gallese, 2005, 2009). The bodily (embodied) approach to intersubjectivity and interconnectivity is viewed as a relation between whole human bodies, which Gallese (2014) called "inter-corporeality."

Augmenting Empathy: The Example of Roots of Empathy

We can, undoubtedly, ingrain and enhance the capacity for empathy in small children. Empathy can be increased, for example, when we urge a child who is hogging all the toys to be more considerate of her playmates (De Waal, 2009). Studies revealed that empathy-enhancing programs in preschool children reduce bullying and aggressive behaviors in their later school careers. For example, consider Mary Gordon.

Mary Gordon from Canada

In her project, Roots of Empathy,[11] Mary Gordon discovered that if five- to seven-year-olds spend time with infants, their empathy, prosocial behaviors, and social competencies increase and keep them out of trouble later in their schooling (Gordon, 2005). In this program parents with infants from the school's neighborhood engage in a series of classroom meetings with the students. A Roots of Empathy Instructor guides the children as they observe the relationship between baby and parent, helping them understand the baby's intentions and emotions. Students are also allowed to touch and play with the baby (see Figures 13–15):

In this situation the baby, paradoxically, serves as "teacher" and catalyst, helping children, through experiential learning, identify and reflect on their own feelings and the feelings of others. Longitudinal research on the impact of the Roots of Empathy program (Berkowitz & Bier, 2007) documented that Roots of Empathy (ROE) children demonstrated a lasting

- Increase in social and emotional knowledge
- Decrease in aggression
- Increase in prosocial behavior (e.g., sharing, helping, and including)
- Increase in perceptions among ROE students of the classroom as a caring environment
- Increased understanding of infants and parenting

---

[11] See: www.ashoka.org/fellow/mary-gordon.

Figure 13. Roots of Empathy, younger class.

Roots of Empathy proved especially effective in significantly reducing aggressive behavior of bullying children, who became caring and pro-social. Gordon (2005) concludes that empathy can be efficiently taught at an early age.

Discovering the Neuroscience of Empathy

In an accidental discovery – a true manifestation of serendipity – the3 Italian researcher Vittorio Gallese in Parma was working in the early 1990s in a room with a macaque monkey with electrodes implanted in its brain. At lunchtime, as Gallese reached for his food, he noticed neurons begin to fire in the monkey's premotor cortex – the same area that showed activity when the animal made a similar gesture. This was a remarkable and quite unexpected discovery (Iacoboni, 2009; Society for Neuroscience, 2008). How was it possible that the monkey sat still, merely watching him, yet the animal's brain reacted as if it were reaching for food itself?

Figure 14. Roots of Empathy, older class.

Through his discovery Gallese identified mirror neurons, and researchers later found that their role was to mirror the action of the observed other. Initially named "empathy neurons" or "Dalai Lama neurons," as they seem to dissolve the barrier between self and others (Ramachandran & Oberman, 2006), they were ultimately called Mirror Neurons (MN). Mirror Neurons provided a framework for understanding many mental disabilities (Ramachandran, 2000) and a plausible neuropsychological explanation for complex forms of social cognition and interaction (Iacoboni, *idem*). As keys to understanding the neuroscience mechanisms that allow our brain to build a representation of what it sees in the world (Keysers, 2011), Mirror Neurons are definitely worth a closer look.

The accidental Parma discovery was later confirmed in many other experiments. For example, researchers found that certain cells in the human brain,[12] which normally fire when you poke the patient with a needle ("pain neurons"), will also fire when the patient watches another

---

[12] *Anterior cingulate* location.

Figure 15. Mary Gordon demonstrating the Roots of Empathy.

patient being poked (Ramachandran & Oberman, 2006). Various other studies, using different experimental methodologies and techniques, have documented that in the human brain there exists a mechanism that directly maps action, perception, and execution, defined as the Mirror Neuron System, MNS (Gallese, 2003, 2009). It has also been shown that when we passively observe the action of others, the brain is activated in the same areas[13] that are activated when we perform similar movements ourselves.

But human MNS goes beyond mere imitation of simple movements. It also plays a central role in imitation-based learning of complex skills, in the perception of communicative actions, and in the detection of action intentions (Gallese, 2009). Similarly, we now know that mirror neurons are involved in our capacity to share emotions and sensations with others (Gallese, 2003, 2006, 2009; De Vignemont & Singer, *idem*).

[13] E.g., premotor and posterior parietal.

MNs are involved in mirroring for both the integration and differentiation of perceptual and motor aspects of actions performed by self and others (Mukamel *et al.*, 2010; Keyserss & Gazzola, 2010). MNS also contributes to human communication, amplifying cognition of the speech of others and enhancing the ability to communicate, especially when encountering a foreign language (Hasson *et al.*, 2012; Stephens *et al.*, 2010). Moreover, MNS enables the observer to understand better the intention behind human behavior and the reason for the intention (Rizzolatti & Fabbri-Destro, 2008).

This mirroring may be seen as internally simulating others' action, so Gallese (2003, 2005, 2009) accounts for connectedness by *embodied simulation* – an implicit, automatic, and unconscious process that enables the observer to use his or her own resources to penetrate the world of the other without explicitly theorizing about it. Embodied simulation is understood as a basic functional mechanism by which our brain/body system models its contact with others. In that way, it constitutes a crucial functioning mechanism in social cognition.

Metaphorically speaking, through brain mirroring, "the other" becomes "self," as another's action is represented in our MNS as if we had taken the same action ourselves. The sharp distinction classically drawn between an individual and the other, at the level of acting and experiencing emotions, appears to be much more blurred at the level of the neural mechanisms mapping it. The gap between my own perspective and another's is bridged by the way intentional relations are mapped at the neural-body level (Gallese 2011).

Back to Empathy and Organizations

No wonder that some researches argue that empathy enhances connectedness through the unconscious sharing of neuropathways (which, we know, is an MNS) and that this process dissolves the barriers between self and other (Pavlovich & Krahnke, 2012) and facilitates the ability to find common ground for solution building.

Empathy also enhances sharing of coherence between individuals (Pavlovich & Krahnke, 2012); on a societal level it might facilitate social communication and create social coherence (De Vignemont & Singer, 2006). Through the positive emotional contagion, group members experience improved cooperation, decreased conflict, and increased task orientation (Barsade, 2002).

Creativity-Enabling Environment (Creativity, Continued)

Creativity was dissected in Chapter 7 and mentioned in Chapter 8, especially in the context of boosting serendipity. Serendipity was found to be enhanced by random encounters and meeting in groups, movements and face-to-face interactions among team members, and random meetings, e.g., around the coffee machine. Also it was mentioned that participants felt most creative on days spent "in motion" meeting people, not when working for long stretches at their desks.

In Chapter 14, we will do an in-depth analysis of methods to enhance creativity (e.g., metaphors, fun, and dance). At this point, however, let us look at the key role empathy plays in augmenting creativity. Business articles on the subject have stated that creative entrepreneurs who make a lasting impact often are not the most talented, but they are the most empathetic.[14] Research suggests that empathy is positively correlated with creativity and, interestingly, is inversely related to dogmatism (Carlozzi *et al.*, 1995). Researchers (Grant & Berry, 2011) also found that prosocial motivation (often based on empathy) strengthened the association between intrinsic motivation and creativity (documented in three studies, using both field and lab data).

All in all, an environment that enhances creativity should be rich with empathetic relationships, full of horizontal and random encounters, and alive with humor, joy, and dance, all of which advance individual and group creativity.

Chapter Coda

- The five central preconditions for the chaos-to-order processes are introduced:
- Complexity as a way of thinking
- Social capital – definitions and implications
- Connectivity spirit and what really works
- Empathy as a key driver for successful teamworking and cooperation; the definitions, some neuroscience of empathy, and implications
- Creativity-enabling environment

---

[14] See: http://99u.com/articles/24713/the-most-underrated-skill-for-creatives-empathy; retrieved February 26, 2017.

PART II

Implementations

Empowering Leadership in Action

Section 4 introduces Empowering Leadership in Action, demonstrating through diverse case studies how this kind of management operates within the context of business and the social arena and depicting EL as a lifestyle outside the workplace.

CHAPTER 11

Empowering Leadership in Business

There is probably no better field for illustrating innovations in management than business. Successful business people continuously look for ways to innovate in order to stay ahead of the curve. For example, in some cases artistic competence can be a source of inspiration and innovation for both individual managers and organizations as a whole. Artists are able to challenge organizational routines, stimulate new ideas, and open leaders' minds to think and behave differently (Boyle & Ottensmeyer, 2005). Language can also disrupt the status quo and spark new ideas – through haiku poems, for example. Institute of Business Consulting[1] declares that the traditional seventeen-syllable form of Japanese poetry is probably the most sublime expression of the state of mind. Set in three nonrhyming metrical units of five, seven, and five syllables, the haiku can express a company's philosophy.[2] And, in fact, there are some interesting collections of business haiku available.[3] Haiku are a kind of metaphor, providing distance and fun. We'll take a closer look at the way these tools enhance creativity in Chapter 14.

One of the more extreme ways companies innovate is to delegate complete power to the employees. Called a revolutionary cultural transformation by some, this approach can have a remarkable effect, as we will see in the examples of three companies: Gore, Morning Star, and Semco Partners.

[1] See: www.imcusa.org.
[2] See: www.imcusa.org/blogpost/356624/106336/Consulting-Haiku.
[3] See for example: www.haikupoemsandpoets.com/poems/business_haiku_poems; retrieved February 24, 2017.

Exploring a Community of Associates: The Gore Example

Bill Gore from the United States

W. L. Gore & Associates Inc. was founded in 1958 in Newark (Delaware) by Wilbert L. (Bill) and Genevieve (Vieve) Gore.[4] After a seventeen-year career as a chemical engineer with DuPont, Bill Gore left at the age of forty-five to launch his own business. He and his wife invested their life savings in the new company and started to produce a special polymer material called polytetrafluoroethylene (PTFE) in the basement of their home.

Bill Gore dreamed of having a company devoted to innovation, where imagination and initiative would flourish and people would be free to search and invent. However, at the time there were no written guidelines for creating an innovative working environment, so his challenge was to find completely novel solutions. One of his first concepts was that employees should be called "associates." Another was that they should all have a space free for contacting and cooperating with each other, enabling them to innovate within or outside the company.

In 2016, fifty-eight years after its founding, W. L. Gore & Associates Inc. had annual sales of more than $3 billion and more than ten thousand associates located in more than twenty-five countries. The company is still owned by members of the Gore family and the associates, following the founder's belief that private ownership reinforces a long-term perspective.

By using proprietary technologies with the versatile PTFE, Gore has created numerous products for electronic signal transmission, fabric laminates, and medical implants, as well as membrane, filtration, sealant, and fibers for use in diverse industries including the production of hydrogen-powered fuel cells. The company has pioneered fabrics for boots, shoes, headwear, gloves, and sleeping bags, some of which have been used for expeditions to the North and South Poles, for scaling Mount Everest, and as part of the space suits worn by NASA astronauts. Gore medical products, including synthetic vascular grafts and surgical meshes, have been implanted in more than 13 million patients, and more than 40 million innovative Gore medical devices have been adopted, saving and improving the quality of lives worldwide.

---

[4] Gore Web site: www.gore.com/en_xx/aboutus/fastfacts/index.html; retrieved February 24, 2017; interview with Gore associates Nicole Kochems and Michael Haag, March 18, 2016; Deutschman (2004); Hamel (2007); this is a continuation from the introduction to Gore in Chapter 5.

Figure 16. Gore team demonstrating their products.

Throughout its long history Gore has been granted more than two thousand patents in a wide range of fields, including electronics, medical devices, and polymer processing (see Figure 16).

It has been cited as the best workplace in several countries, including China, France, Germany, Italy, Korea, Spain, Sweden, and the United Kingdom, and included on the "Fast 50" list of the "Most Innovative Companies in the World" by *Fast Company* magazine in 2009. In 2016, Gore was once again nominated as a "Great Place to Work." It also ranked fourth in the "2016 Best Workplaces in Germany" competition.

Given these accomplishments, the company's use of EL is certainly worth a closer look.

Horizontal Connections Promoting Serendipity

Gore has a nonhierarchic structure, enabling every individual in the organization to connect easily with everyone else in the unit. Lines of communication are direct – person to person and team to team – and there are multiple nodes on the same level (resembling horizontal connections and scale-free structure, see Chapter 8). Also, associates report to their peers

Figure 17. One of the Gore teams.

rather than to the boss, which means that working groups have the power to self-organize and elect their own leaders.

As we've seen, this horizontal structure enhances serendipity and maximizes opportunities for personal and often impromptu interactions. Bill Gore saw that as the number of people in the business increased, associates inevitably felt less connected with one another and with the ultimate product, so he keeps the average size of company units below three hundred people. This enables interaction among research and development (R&D) personnel, salespeople, engineers, chemists, and machinists, who typically work in the same building. The proximity of different disciplines makes it easier to discuss issues directly, cuts time to market, and keeps everyone focused on the ultimate goal of satisfying customers. Teams are usually small in order to keep everyone connected and enhance interactions in a flat structure (see Figure 17).

Free to Innovate

To encourage the free flow of information and ideas further, Gore has also dispensed with traditional organizational charts and typical chains of command. Instead, associates communicate directly with each other and are accountable to fellow members. Teams organize themselves around business opportunities, and leaders emerge in a natural process. Associates are encouraged to innovate and team up to pursue innovations.

One of the most important levers for innovation is something the company calls "dabble time." For half a day a week associates are free to explore their own projects. There are no limits; issues explored may be close to or distant from the company's goals.

Moreover, if one's dabble-time idea becomes compelling enough, it attracts other associates and, in a natural way, one becomes the leader of a newborn team, as long as others find it worth the time investment. If the new idea thrives and survives a rigorous process of probes, trials, market analysis, etc., it can then become one of the Gore production lines. Following are two examples of bottom-up initiatives that grew out of associates' personal passions and were transformed into winning market hits.

Gore Bike Wear™

In the 1980s, Gore had a few associates who were passionate road cyclists and wanted to pursue their hobby in all kinds of weather, but there were no suitable jackets on the market. They were looking for something waterproof and breathable, lightweight and with a small pack size, and short at the front and long at the back so it fit well in the cycling position. After a long process of probes, trials, verification, and marker analysis, Gore set up a new business unit in 1985. Thanks to the sporting enthusiasm and persistence of a few employees, the "Giro" jacket was born.

Consumer response was overwhelming. Word of the new product spread like wildfire in cycling circles, and the jackets sold like hot cakes. Today Gore Bike Wear™ sells well in many European countries and in the United States. The brand regularly receives awards from prestigious road and mountain biking magazines, and Gore Bike Wear™ has been ranked number one in the cycling clothing market.

Guitar Strings

Although the Gore engineer Dave Myers was principally engaged in developing cardiac implants and Gore had no business related to the music industry, he decided to spend his dabble time pursuing a speculative project involving guitar strings.

Myers was trying to make the gears on his mountain bike shift more smoothly. He coated the gear cables with a thin layer of plastic, and these became Gore's Ride-On line of bike cables. His next idea was to improve the cables used for controlling the movements of oversized animated puppets at places such as Disney World. He needed small-diameter cables, so he tried coating guitar strings with a similar plastic. The aha moment occurred in 1993, when Myers had the notion that this process could also improve guitar strings, making them less fragile.

Myers wasn't a guitarist himself, so he needed to attract others to the project. He involved another engineer, who was also a musician, and understood that the natural oils on musicians' fingers carry particles of dust and skin and so contaminate the strings. The accumulation of those tiny contaminates negatively influences the sound of the vibrating string. The solution was to use a grit-repelling coating similar to the one Myers used for bike cables on guitar strings.

After this discovery Myers easily received R&D's support and soon had a small team of volunteers working on his project. During three years of experimentation everything was done through bottom-up initiatives, without seeking any formal endorsement. Eventually, the team developed a string that held its tone three times longer than the industry standard. Currently, guitars equipped with these strings outsell their closest U.S. competitor by a two-to-one ratio.

Trust and Fun

The absence of formally chartered supervisors reflects one of Gore's core principles: In a high-trust, low-fear organization, employees don't require much control. Instead, they may need to be mentored and supported, often through a team's peer-to-peer relationships. In an interview[5] Gore highlighted the fact that "our organization is very trust-based, with a lower turnover rate compared to other companies in our market."

A survey of employees confirmed their pride in the company's products, their mutual respect and trust, and their recognition of consistent fairness and partnership as an integral part of their work. At Gore small operating units and self-managing teams support innovation and two common goals: to make money and have fun doing so. Studying the Gore process, it would seem that having fun is at least as valuable as making money.

---

[5] With Nicole Kochems and Michael Haag, March 18, 2016.

Figure 18. Morning Star tomato processing.

Tomato Game: Self-Management at Morning Star

Chris Rufer from the United States

The Morning Star Company was founded in 1970,[6] by Chris Rufer, a one-truck owner and operator[7] who transported tomatoes to factories. Rufer is still the company's president, and today, Morning Star is the largest tomato processor in the world, handling nearly 40 percent of the tomatoes processed each year in the United States, with more than four hundred year-round employees producing more than $700 million in annual revenue (see Figures 18 and 19).

This extraordinarily successful company also embraces EL principles of self-management. All employees, regardless of education or position, are called colleagues. They have no bosses and no top-down control and will commonly say that they can't wait for the weekend to be over so they can get back to the game of work as self-managers.

---

[6] Morning Star Web site: www.morningstarco.com; retrieved February 24, 2017; Hamel (2011), Wartzman (2012); interview with Doug Kirkpatrick (2015). Doug Kirkpatrick is a consultant partner with the Morning Star Self-Management Institute and is author of the book *Beyond Empowerment: The Age of the Self-Managed Organization*; interview April 27, 2016.
[7] Also at that time an MBA student at UCLA.

Figure 19. Morning Star tomato transporting.

Colleagues find this "game of work," called the Tomato Game, greatly satisfying. Photos on the company Web site depict colleagues as self-managing professionals, initiating communication and coordinating their activities with others, with no directives from above. Morning Star wants colleagues to find joy and excitement in drawing from their potential, and, above all, to take personal responsibility and hold themselves accountable for achieving the company's "Big Mission" as well as their own personal missions.[8]

Evidence that employees appreciate this management method can be found in the return rate of the seasonal cohort, which has been as high as 91 percent. This means that nearly everyone who works for three and a half months and then goes off to other regions in search of other work returns to play the Tomato Game.

Doug Kirkpatrick, of Morning Star Self-Management Institute, says that the company's leadership style took shape with the implementation of two simple rules. (Simple rules are one of the pivots of complex systems. See Chapter 5.) In 1990, a small team of colleagues working out of a little farmhouse in California was overseeing construction of the first Morning

---

[8] Each colleague sets his or her personal mission as part of the commitment, as discussed later in this chapter.

Star factory. The $27 million project was launched in December 1989. By the following March it seemed that it would be impossible to complete the factory by the July deadline.

Equipment was arriving on ocean freighters from Italy, and hundreds of contractors were fabricating, welding, erecting, and constructing twenty-four hours a day, seven days a week. The core team had plenty to do as well, coordinating engineering, architecture, fabrication, etc. But time was running out.

The solution, in part, was self-management. In March 1990, Chris Rufer called for a meeting. The team met in one of the construction trailers on the job site, and Rufer passed out a document called The Morning Star Colleague Principles, essentially boiling down the governance of the enterprise to two core principles: People shouldn't use force or coercion against others, and people should honor the commitments they make to others.

Those two simple rules made all the difference. The twenty-four-member team completed the factory, and production began on July 16, 1990. Organizational self-management enabled the team to weave their talents together as individuals, fluidly and with agility and flexibility. Rufer's two principles fostered more happiness, harmony, and prosperity, and as a result, the team had greater success.

Could such a feat be achieved using top-down command and control? Perhaps yes, but it's unlikely that it would occur with the same efficiency, speed, flexibility, and learning, because the people who built the factory learned how to operate it at the same time. Rufer's rules also initiated a specific culture of loyalty, commitment, passion, and innovation. Today, with those guiding principles still in place, Morning Star is the world's largest producer of tomatoes. Here is Morning Star in a nutshell:

- The company has no human bosses; the boss is the mission of the enterprise
- Employees negotiate responsibilities with their peers
- Anyone can purchase what he or she believes is necessary
- Each individual is responsible for acquiring the resources needed to do his or her work
- There are no titles and no promotions
- Compensation decisions are peer-based

Is this realistic? And how does this system operate? Let's have a closer look at Morning Star's core policies:

Personal Mission Statements

Every Morning Star colleague is responsible for defining a personal commercial mission statement that outlines how she or he will contribute to the company's goals. In other words, individuals not only plan their performance agreement: they also set a personal overarching mission. This means that employees aren't reduced to a simple list of goals and checkboxes, but rather, they see their role as one that serves the company's mission but also has meaning for them personally.

Colleagues become responsible for accomplishing their mission and for acquiring everything they need, e.g., training, resources, cooperation, to get the job done. Hence, they're driven by their mission and their commitments, not by controlling managers.

Colleague Letter of Understanding (CLOU)

To operationalize the Personal Mission Statement, employees negotiate a Colleague Letter of Understanding (CLOU). This isn't done vertically, with managers or superiors (who don't exist). It's done in partnership with those associates who are most affected by the employee's work.

Each year the CLOU is modified and adjusted to accommodate growing competencies, new interests, or the changing environment. However, once set, CLOU becomes nearly sacred. Remember the two honored Morning Star Colleague Principles? The second one says that people should honor the commitments they make to others; this is foundational to the organization. In this system accountability isn't tracked through performance reviews with managers. Instead, all employees in the company receive feedback from their CLOU colleagues. Ways to accomplish the CLOU commitments are all in employees' hands, as is equipment purchase.

You Know Best What to Purchase, So Do It

Morning Star colleagues are also empowered to the extent that they don't need anyone's approval to purchase equipment or materials. In some cases, when others need similar equipment, they team up and discuss how to merge and make the overall purchase cost-effective. However, the decision belongs to the individual. Everyone can spend the privately held company's money without explicit rule-based budgetary constraints. The real restraints in this self-management system based on trust are common sense, business-unit strategy, and policy.

Colleagues Hire Colleagues

Within this model, colleagues also trust one another to know when they are overloaded or whether a new role needs to be filled. Self-management guides staffing decisions, and colleagues are responsible for initiating the hiring process.

Self-Advancement and Innovations

Roles are open and flexible. There are no centrally defined boxes, layers of management, or positions. Instead, colleagues develop their skills and gain experience naturally. They simply take on greater responsibility to the degree they are willing and able. This means that advancement doesn't derive from above. It's within everyone's reach, reflecting a real change-and-needs process. This, in turn, makes people feel more responsible and engaged, willing to explore and innovate.

Identification and Internalization

The self-management model encourages employees to develop their skills and take on more responsibility. Hamel (2007) quotes Morning Star President Rufer, who believes that if people are free, they will be drawn to what they really like, as opposed to being pushed toward what they have been told to like. In that way people are free to discharge their creativity and realize their individual potential as they work together.

This system, including narratives and symbols (e.g., the company's Founding Principles), makes people internalize and strongly identify with the mission and goals, seeing the mission as their own and the goals as woven among *their* colleagues.

Self-Management Institute

To advance the knowledge of self-management, Morning Star launched a Self-Management Institute.[9] The organization's mission is to cultivate a superior organizational structure and happier, more productive colleagues by creating and refining principles, systems, and practices of attracting, developing, and organizing people. The institute analyzes the nuts and

---

[9] See: www.self-managementinstitute.org; retrieved February 24, 2017.

bolts of self-management on its Web site, recommends several resources, and shares case studies. Its focus is solely internal, driving the development of organizational self-management within Morning Star.

The Company as Village: Semco Partners

Ricardo Semler from Brazil

In the 1980s, Ricardo Semler took over an almost-bankrupt firm from his father, Antonio.[10] The first thing he did was to fire nearly all the managers, thereby delegating decision making to the employees. He also expanded the company's market by moving into the service sector, including environmental consultancy, facilities management, real estate brokerage, and inventory support. By 2015, the company had annual revenue of more than $240 million per year and employed more than three thousand workers.

Cultural Metamorphosis and Creativity

Semler's strategy was essentially to hand over total control of the company to his workforce. He implemented principles of democracy, transparent communication, constructive dissent, creativity, and employee advancement in what Richard Daft (2015) calls a "cultural metamorphosis" that reversed a top-down, autocratic setup. Semco evolved around the understanding that employees need to make their own decisions in the course of accomplishing their tasks.

Given the company's success, it would seem that the employees' identification with the company's culture made all the difference. Semler holds that people who are motivated by self-interest find solutions that no one else could envision; they simply see the world in a unique way – one that others (those "hired," who do not necessarily identify with the firm's goals) often overlook.

Semler also posits that the main objective of equipping Semco's employees with autonomy is to spur their creativity. His groundbreaking insight was that being self-driven increases the propensity for creativity. This includes limiting processes and procedures that encumber creativity. For example, in order to remove all possible obstacles to innovation, one of

---

[10] Semco Partners Web site: www.semco.com.br/en/; retrieved February 24, 2017; Semler, R. (1994, 1995, 2004), Maresco & York, (2005), Fisher (2005), Hamel, (2007); Daft (2015); interview with Ian Borges, July 8, 2016.

Figure 20. Semco teams socializing.

the company norms is that employees have to restrict all circulars, reports, letters, and minutes to a single piece of paper.

The Purpose of Work Is to Feel Good about Life

Ricardo Semler believes that the purpose of work is not only to make money. Rather, it is to make workers feel good about life. He thinks that companies ought to put employees' freedom and satisfaction ahead of corporate goals and, in that spirit, introduced a working environment with no job titles, no written policies, no HR department, not even a headquarters. In that way Semler turned an aging and nearly bankrupt family business into one of Brazil's most stunning success stories. He eliminated nine layers of management and introduced unprecedented democracy in the workplace. Today, employees vote for their managers, evaluate them, and publicly post their evaluations. Meetings are voluntary, and two seats on the board are open to the first employees who show up. The new delineation was "the company as village," (see Figures 20 and 21).

Figure 21. Semco's garden for the workers.

During the 1990 economic crisis the Brazilian economy went into a severe downturn, forcing many companies to declare bankruptcy. Workers at Semco demonstrated shared responsibility and agreed to wage cuts. They were also given the right to approve every expenditure. Semler created self-managed teams of six to eight workers who were in charge of all aspects of production. They set their own budgets and goals and agreed to tie compensation to budget and productivity. As a result, costs went down and profits went up. While many workers liked this model, middle managers were less enthusiastic. Feeling that they had lost their power and rank, one-third of them quit within a year.

Learning from the Economic Crisis

Performing multiple roles during the crisis gave workers greater knowledge of company operations, and boosted their identification with company aims. This resulted in more bottom-up insights and suggestions on how to improve the business. One of the employees commented:

Another significant experience was the discussion process with the Factory Commission (which I was part of) during an economic crisis in Brazil. The final decision was to not reduce personnel – which was the first option presented to the Commission – and instead to reduce salaries to reach the same reduction in costs. Salaries were (temporarily) progressively reduced, with the lowest salaries contributing less to savings than higher salaries. Savings achieved were returned to employees after the crisis was averted.

A decade after the crisis ended, in 2003, Semco ended up with annual revenue of $212 million, up from $4 million in 1982 and $35 million in 1994, with a compounded annual growth rate of up to 40 percent a year. Employee count went from ninety in 1982 to three thousand in 2003.

Lying down in Hammocks

Over the years, the idea of autonomous teams was adopted throughout the company. Teams began hiring and firing both workers and supervisors through a voting process, and policy manuals were replaced by a policy of common sense. In fact, the only actual manual runs about twenty pages long and is filled with cartoons.

Semler certainly believes in responsibility but not in pyramidal hierarchy. He also doesn't think that a company's success can be measured in numbers, since the numbers ignore what the end user really thinks of the product and what the people who produce it really think of the company. Moreover, he doesn't believe that control is either useful or desirable. For example, Semco Partners doesn't regulate business-related travel, and the company provides hammocks in its garden that actually encourage relaxation.[11]

Semler simply believes that those who are trusted are more coresponsible. Social influence results through identification and internalization, turning "employees" into reliable partners. Along these lines he suggests (in his recent book) that future managers should enable employees to blend work life and personal life with enthusiasm and creative energy. He also notes that smart bosses realize an employee might be most productive if he or she works on Sunday afternoon, plays golf on Monday morning, goes to a movie on Tuesday afternoon, and watches his or her child play soccer on Thursday (Semler, 2004).

---

[11] See: www.godlikeproductions.com/forum1/message2174175/pg1; retrieved February 24, 2017.

Semco-Style Movement

Convinced that "too many organizations trap their employees in rigid structures and controls,"[12] Semler founded Semco Style Institute[13] to share the theory and practice of his leadership style. The institute offers a master program in building organizations that show agility, stimulate performance, and foster entrepreneurship. It also facilitates a leadership program and an experience-exchange program with other similar projects.

In short, the Semco Style Institute organizes around humans instead of around structures and procedures. It puts people above organizational modes, and sees freedom and self- interest as the basis for collective alignment. Its five pivotal principles are to stimulate trust, self-management, extreme stakeholder alignment, and creative innovation, and to reduce controls.

Additionally, the organization maintains an online gateway called LeadWise[14] for leaders who want to transform their organizations to People-Centric Management.

Summary: From the Conceptual Perspective

Social Influence

At these three companies the core mechanisms of social influence seem to be *identification* and *internalization*. Employees (here associates, colleagues, or partners), regardless of their number (e.g., ten thousand in the case of Gore-Tex) take coresponsibility and are invited to influence the firm's small- and large-scale policies and innovate products or methods. All of this leads to *identification* and *internalization* of the firm's culture and goals, which create a higher level of motivation and loyalty (e.g., the Morning Star employees waiting for the weekend finally to end so that they can resume the Tomato Game on Monday), leading to innovation and higher performance.

Preconditions for Chaos-to-Order Dynamics

The preconditions for endogenous dynamics are all there. While these leaders might not use terms such as *complexity way of thinking*, employees

---

[12] https://semcostyle.org/events/semco-style-master-program-group-5; retrieved February 24, 2017.
[13] http://semcostyle.org/; February 24, 2017.
[14] www.leadwise.email/awareness/checkout/; retrieved February 24, 2017.

who participate in decision making on all levels of management, across all divisions, see the complex environment of multiple interrelations and interdependencies. The free and random (chaotic) interactions pave the way for novelties to emerge.

There also exists a *connectivity spirit*, which is augmented through multi-level working connections (horizontal and diagonal), as well as through more personal platforms where employees chat and cooperate in their private lives.

These three firms function on *empathetic* values, best verbalized by Ricardo Semler, who says that the ultimate goal isn't only making money, but making people happy about their lives, and that those who are trusted are more coresponsible. Morning Star is based on two foundational principles, one of which eliminates force or coercion between people. And Gore-Tex creates space for employees to realize their own passions.

In all three companies *creativity* is a central category. The bottom-up empowering environment is seen as a major lever for people's creativity and, as a result, for the company's innovativeness.

From the Complexity Perspective

From the perspective of complexity theory, Gore-Tex, Morning Star, and Semco's management structures enable free horizontal communication, which may be viewed as the *collection of interacting objects*, with certain *phenomena emerging* from these interactions, i.e., well-oiled cooperation, novel products, and market innovations. As decisions and control are delegated to the peer-to-peer level, this all happens in the *absence of any sort of "invisible hand" or central controller*. Moreover, there are *simple rules* of interactions among associates, leading to impressive achievements. *Chaos* is accepted and may be a gateway to a *new order*. The multiple, *horizontal interactions*, accompanied by a blend of *upward and downward causations* creating a variety of *feedback loops*, may yield new results in an often *unpredictable* way.

The complexity approach (even if not verbalized as such) also enables sudden *jumps*, e.g., market success with new products such as Gore Bike Wear™.

Chapter Coda

- Three Empowering Leadership case studies were presented:
- W. L. Gore & Associates, Inc.

- Morning Star
- Semco Partners
- In the Summary the companies' management system was delineated through three conceptual perspectives:
- Social influence mechanisms
- Preconditions for the chaos-to-order dynamics
- Complexity Theory

CHAPTER 12

Empowering Leadership in the Social Arena

The social arena is an overwhelmingly broad field – one without limits where all possible problems may become issues to be solved. Areas of social engagement include aging, disabilities, children with special needs, discrimination against minorities, education, unemployment, women's equality, renewable energy, environment, health, homelessness, conflict resolution, poverty, rural community development, sanitation, street children, domestic violence, chemical dependency, and trafficking.

As with the business sector, the social field features a whole tapestry of structures and management systems. Some social organizations may have well-defined goals and procedures matched by concrete structure. (Corporate foundations, for example, usually set strict, pragmatic goals.) Others take the form of umbrella organizations, supporting a variety of entities with the funds they raise. In this book we'll focus on a segment of social-sector organizations driven by the passion and commitment of the founders – individuals who have a big vision and won't sleep until they make it a reality, namely, social entrepreneurs (SE). We introduced the SE phenomenon in Chapter 4, and we'll elaborate on it here.

Most Social Entrepreneurs follow the complexity principles (often intuitively), as they usually start with nothing but a dream of a big system change. To advance, they need to use small impulses to effect immense results. Moreover, they must identify alternative attractors, serving as fulcrums, especially in situations where intractable problems are sustained by inveterate homeostasis.

A good illustration of this is in the area of peacemaking, where the essential challenge is to transform an apparently intractable sociopsychological conflict into a peace-enforcing environment (Lederach, 2003; Miall, 2004).

Intractable conflicts in societies lead to the establishment of a specific sociopsychological infrastructure (homeostasis), which includes a collective memory, an ethos of conflict, and collective emotional orientations

(Bar-Tal, 2007). Societal beliefs, e.g., shared narratives highlighting how "the other" was and still is bad, are the basic components of collective memories and may lead to an ethos of conflict. People adjust their lives to the antagonism, often finding some gratification associated with the conflict.

Instead of directly addressing conflict, social entrepreneurs usually find ways to circumvent it and find alternative attractors "somewhere else" (Praszkier *et al.*, 2010). These initiatives may appear to be irrelevant or unrelated to the central issue. But they can lead to the emergence of new, constructive attractors that, if successful, deepen and create a new, emergent environment. This new environment benefits from peace and, in that way, paves the way for and reinforces it (Praszkier & Nowak, 2012b). Following are two examples of social entrepreneurs who successfully circumvented potential conflicts.

Sustaining Peace through Building Alternative Attractors

Krzysztof (Chris) Czyżewski from Poland

Krzysztof (Chris) Czyżewski, a Polish social entrepreneur,[1] demonstrated that the attempt to overcome deeply ingrained cross-border and cross-religious prejudices can be far more effective when addressed through a variety of small, community-based initiatives rather than by tackling the issues head on. On the Poland–Lithuania–Belarus border, a previously economically disadvantaged area, Czyżewski works through his Borderline Foundation to encourage children to publish a local chronicle publicizing their efforts to collect and exhibit old postcards and photos and trace the multiethnic history of the area. The historic Catholic, Jewish, Orthodox, and Protestant roots in the region are thereby rescued from obscurity and disseminated throughout the community. Other initiatives involve teaching multitraditional crafts and cross-cultural music lessons. Also, local youth, who in the past were living lives dominated by a spirit of hopelessness and depression, are now involved in reviving the indigenous Jewish folk music, even founding a Klezmer Orchestra, which performs at home and abroad (Czyżewski, 2008). By transforming young people's

---

[1] See Ashoka: www.ashoka.org/node/2917; founder of the Borderland Foundation, see: http://pogranicze.sejny.pl/?lang=en; retrieved February 24, 2017. Sources of this section include interviews, site visits (in the case of the Borderline Foundation), and publications.

Figure 22. Borderline Foundation: discussing ethnosociology of the city.

perceptions and roles within communities scarred by historical divides, Czyżewski is creating a new vision for the future. His brand of entrepreneurship shows how many small initiatives can accumulate to foster a shift in the collective mind-set of a community, which eventually engenders a new social and economic order.[2] This creates an emergent peace-sustaining and mutually beneficial environment (see Figures 22 and 23).

Dr. Yehudah Paz from Israel

The second example is from Israel. The social entrepreneur Dr. Yehudah Paz[3] was building islands of peace in the Middle East region – a place where conflict and distrust underlie cross-ethnic relationships. His core conviction was that mere conflict resolution is not enough, given that peace leaves a void, which is very often difficult to bear for people accustomed

---

[2] Krzysztof disseminated the Borderline Foundation's approach to many regions of conflict in Central and Eastern Europe, the Caucasus, and Central Asia.
[3] See: www.ashoka.org/en/fellow/yehudah-paz; Dr. Paz passed away in 2013.

Figure 23. Planning the ideal city.

to war, especially if they don't see any prospects for the future. On the basis of this philosophy, he involved partners, mainly women drawn from clashing groups, in profitable Arab-Israeli joint ventures. Through cooperation in these ventures, Israelis and Arabs experience the great benefits engendered by joining forces. Dr. Paz's ideas for these joint ventures result in peace imbued with new prospects based on trust and success. From this activity not only did new enterprises blossom, but a secondary effect has been the empowerment of women, who found themselves in the forefront of building a new economy for their families and their community. The joint Israeli-Arab approach is reflected in the structure of Paz's organization,[4] where the most active leaders are Arab and Israeli women, e.g., the codirectors Amal Elsana Alh'jooj and Vivian Silver, who not only seed the new concepts but also serve as a model for change and cross-ethnic cooperation. By building bubbles of trust and cooperation, Dr. Paz prevented the potential outbreak of dormant conflicts between the two communities.

---

[4] See: http://nisped.org.il/; retrieved February 24, 2017.

Following are four case studies from the areas of health, environment, homelessness, and emigrants, operating in diverse regions (Netherlands, the United States, Poland, and Syria), that highlight the effectiveness of Empowering Leadership.

Self-Governing Nurses: A Better and Cost-Effective Home Care

Jos de Blok from Holland

After resigning from a good job with a good salary, Jos de Blok made a leap of faith and, in 2007, launched the nonprofit Buurtzorg, which in Dutch means "Neighborhood Care."[5] The initial team included four nurses. By 2013 it had grown to sixty-five hundred nurses organized into 630 independent teams, and by 2016, more than nine thousand nurses in 850 teams were part of the organization.[6] The Buurtzorg system spread from the Netherlands to Sweden, Japan, and, in 2015–2016, to the United States. It currently cares for sixty thousand patients a year.

Buurtzorg provides community care for the chronically ill and functionally disabled, elderly people with multiple pathologies, individuals in a terminal phase, persons with symptoms of dementia, clients who are released from the hospital and are not yet fully recovered, and many other persons in need. The nonprofit provides a full range of medical and support services to their clients. Some services require nursing expertise, but many others, such as help with daily living activities such as dressing, bathing, or toileting, can be provided by less-trained and less-expensive personnel or volunteers – all contracted, trained, and monitored by the nurses.

One of the group's core ideas is that of a community-based care system. Nurses are organized in small, twelve-person teams operating in a community of about ten thousand inhabitants. They get to know the specific characteristics of their community and establish alliances with doctors, hospitals, and other medical or social services. And here we arrive at the really revolutionary innovation: The teams are totally autonomous, with no overhead or top-down management. They're responsible for all integrated tasks, previously dispersed among several departments. They decide what range of services will be applied to particular clients and how much

---

[5] www.buurtzorgusa.org/about-us; retrieved February 24, 2017; de Blok & Kimball, 2013, Laloux, 2014, Gray et al, 2015, Betz, 2016; interview with Jos de Blok, June 3, 2016.
[6] There are other units based on the same principles; the biggest is Buurtdiensten/Familiehulp, which has four thousand employees, for a total of thirteen thousand in 2016.

Figure 24. Enjoying togetherness at Buurtzorg.

time will be invested. They also make decisions related to hiring, logistics, planning, renting the office space, and even redesigning it if necessary. Buurtzorg teams cooperate with the hospitals and doctors in the community and decide how to carry on with public education. Working autonomously with no vertical control or management, the teams develop their own ideas. For example, some shoot YouTube films for public education and prevention, while others publish flyers and deliver speeches, depending on the specifics of the community.

Buurtzorg nurses deliver not only technical services (e.g., injections), but also long-term care and medical support, establishing psychological bonds and trustful relationships. The goal is to increase the patients' potential and make them self-reliant to the extent possible.

While nurses on the team take on diverse roles according to their experience and preferences, the team has no formal leader, and decisions are made during round table discussions. At the end of the day, if there are no objections, a decision is made. To support the teams and prevent them from falling apart for any reason, Buurtzorg coaches provide preliminary training in a group format for new teams and, later, provide nonjudgmental support whenever it's needed (see Figures 24 and 25).

Figure 25. Buurtzorg nurses.

The critical challenge here is how to maintain strict medical standards within such a flexible system. In 2005, Jos de Blok and his friends had the vision that the Internet could support a horizontal means of communication, making information and knowledge available by using a special platform. With one integral system they could use the data and information from the nurses for different purposes. It would reduce bureaucracy by making it easier for nurses to log their time with patients and manage billing, payroll, and administration. And it would create a community where everyone could share experiences, ask questions, and innovate. The eCare platform combines these functions. So, for example, when someone uses the system for administrative purposes, he or she can also see the communication platform. Everyone is provided with a tablet, so each has the opportunity, at any time of the day, to login as he or she wishes. While online, they're invited to see the experiences of their colleagues through posted articles, messages, or questions. For example, if a nurse logs in to register a new patient, she might also see a post from a colleague with a very sick patient asking for treatment advice and responses to the inquiry from nurses all over the country. eCare also supports a network of experts. If a nurse becomes an expert on Parkinson's disease, for example, she can consult colleagues who have clients with this illness.

Blok says that eCare, above all, serves as a specific nurses' "Facebook." Nurses can log a problem, find solutions that others have tried before, and provide feedback. This platform works across all aspects of care delivery, also linking doctors and pharmacists outside the network to ensure proper sharing and management of patient information.

Much of the organization's activity results from bottom-up initiatives. Groups of nurses sharing a common interest on palliative terminal care, for example, may put together an online group, which, after discussion, creates a special eCare module with videos, brochures, and guidelines.

A good example of an eCare bottom-up initiative is the idea of a "walkers' race" for the elderly. A group of nurses initiated a walk for aging patients in one of Amsterdam's parks. Then many other nurses tried this idea at their locations, and eventually the concept caught on in the public media. Discussing their experiences activating the elderly, the nurses reached the conclusion that when one focuses on people's abilities rather than on their disabilities, one may find different ways to create more positive solutions. This insight, in turn, triggered many new initiatives.

In short, Buurtzorg proved that horizontal communication and bottom-up processes augment creativity. As Blok put it,

> When these nurses feel the ownership and the responsibility for their own daily processes, they will find all the solutions. If you compare this horizontal approach with a traditional way of planning, controlling and making top-down policy, then you see that in the latter people respond to what comes from above. It is important that they feel empowered, especially because the nurses operate in specific environments, dealing with different kinds of issues and problems; every team has different ideas fit to their environment.[7]

At Buurtzorg nurses strive to find consensus on identified solutions. Besides medical problems they focus on how they collaborate as a team and on the specifics of their environment. Usually they take advantage of all kinds of structures in their neighborhood and use them as informal networks to solve patients' problems. For example, patients who have been isolated are organized into group activities, such as walking groups. It's important to note that the nurses aren't paid for these kinds of community based social activities, but they initiate them because they create better conditions for the patients.

---

[7] From the interview with Jos de Blok.

The use of self-regulating teams with an integrated care system (previously split among departments) definitely provides flexibility in work arrangements to meet both nurses' and patients' needs. But are the clients satisfied with this approach? And aren't the nurses overwhelmed by this open, unstructured, multitasking approach? And, last but not least, doesn't this system cost too much?

In a 2015 study, Buurtzorg patient ratings on measures pertaining to physical care, staff quality, information, and participation were in the top 10 of 370 home health agencies.[8] This study also showed that by changing the model of care, Buurtzorg has accomplished a 50 percent reduction in hours of care and improved quality of care and has raised work satisfaction for their employees.

Patients' satisfaction was measured at 9.1 out of 10 in a study conducted from 2008 to 2010 (Monsen & de Blok, 2013). And in 2009, Buurtzorg had the highest satisfaction rates among patients anywhere in the country (Gray *et al.*, 2015).

The nurses also seem to be satisfied, as Buurtzorg Nederland was named the best employer in Holland in 2010, 2011, and 2012 by a Dutch company[9] that collects, analyzes, and uses feedback from employees and customers (Gray *et al.*, *ibid*).

And what about costs? NIVEL, the Netherlands Institute for Health Services Research, found (in 2009) that Buurtzorg had the highest satisfaction rates among patients anywhere in the country (de Veer *et al.*, 2009). A 2009 Ernst and Young study found that Buurtzorg was able to meet patients' needs while using 40 percent of the authorized patient care hours, compared with an average among other home care organizations of about 70 percent. The study also found that Buurtzorg's patients required care for less time, regained autonomy quicker, had fewer emergency hospital admissions, and had shorter lengths of stay after admission. In addition, the company had lower overhead costs than other home care providers (8 percent of total costs, compared with 25 percent) and less than half the average incidence of sick leave and employee turnover (Monsen & de Blok, 2013). Ernst & Young computed that if all home care organizations worked the way Buurtzorg does, it would create potential Dutch national savings of € 2 billion Euro per year.

---

[8] KPMG (2015). *The Added Value of Buurtzorg Relative to Other Providers of Home Care: A Quantitative Analysis of Home Care in the Netherlands in 2013* [in Dutch].

[9] "Effectory."

Community-Based Environmental Monitoring

Shannon Dosemagen from the United States

How can citizens defend their environmental rights after a major natural or man-made disaster, especially when they find themselves completely isolated and the costs of monitoring equipment are far out of reach?[10]

This was the question posed in the aftermath of Hurricane Katrina (August 29, 2005), which exposed the ineptitude of the state and federal government in New Orleans, where at least fourteen hundred people died because of levee failure. People were still without help months and years after the catastrophic event, not even able to estimate the extent of the damage. The question of how to empower citizens in monitoring environmental threats became essential – even more so five years later, in the same Gulf of Mexico, during the Deepwater Horizon oil spill (April 20, 2010). This BP oil disaster was considered the largest accidental marine oil spill in the history of the petroleum industry. Because of the months-long spill, extensive damage to marine and wildlife habitats and fishing and tourism industries was reported. It seemed critical that people be able to determine for themselves the size of an oil slick or the direction it was heading, especially vis-à-vis an evident information blackout for residents of the coastal region, as well as the rest of the world.

Shannon Dosemagen,[11] always passionate about environmental issues, had a dream to give power to the communities most affected by environmental degradation. There were, however, two major bottlenecks. First, to document in a methodical, reliable, and scientifically justified way, one needs commercial equipment that costs thousands of dollars. Second, this is not work for lone rangers; it takes a unified community effort to cover a large-scale disaster. Dosemagen realized that the pivot for launching "community-based science" is a collaborative network of practitioners, each of them equipped with do-it-yourself (DIY) monitoring devices.

So, in 2010, after the BP oil disaster, Dosemagen helped a group of concerned residents make "community satellites" from balloons, kites, and digital cameras and distributed them over the spill area to collect real-time data about its impact. They loaded more than 100,000 aerial images into maps of the coastline documenting the oil spread. These high-resolution

---

[10] Public Lab Web site: https://publiclab.org/; Blodgett (2016), Gibney (2016), interview with Shannon Dosemagen on June 16, 2016.
[11] See: www.ashoka.org/fellow/shannon-dosemagen.

Figure 26. Setting up a monitoring balloon.

maps were featured by BBC and the *New York Times*, among other media, allowing residents to show what was actually going on in the Gulf. This experience led Dosemagen to found the Public Laboratory for Open Technology and Science, also known as Public Lab, which supports community environmental movements.

Public Lab's goal is to increase the ability of underserved communities to identify, redress, remediate, and create awareness and accountability around environmental concerns. They achieved this by providing online and offline training, education, and support, and by focusing on locally relevant outcomes that emphasize human capacity (see Figure 26).

Public Lab is focused on community and movement building, not on creating isolated technology-centered projects. Hence, it disseminates and supports communities of technologists, educators, activists, scientists, urban planners, and engaged citizens to gather critical information about the adverse impact of events on the environment and use it collectively to build aggregated professional documentation – just as they used small helium balloons and kites to collect hundreds of thousands of images of the spill that wouldn't have been available otherwise.

The Public Lab community interacts at all stages, including problem identification, development, data collection and analysis, and advocacy. Groups break projects into smaller pieces, work on them intensively, and return to share information with the broader community, asking for input and feedback. Public Lab bases its efforts on a traditional model of community organizing referred to as "barn raising." Eighteenth- and nineteenth-century-style barn raisings in the United States occurred when a community joined together to help literally raise a barn or house structure. Traditionally, a barn raising was the time for people to support one another and socialize after the barn was raised. Public Lab borrowed the term to encapsulate their goals.

In the context of this group, barn raisings are about conversations among people interested in helping to organize mapping efforts. Public Lab directly supports community groups interested in collecting information. On Tuesday afternoons they hold weekly "barn raising" training sessions in city parks, where people can receive hands-on training in mapping, including actual mapping trips. The group facilitated barn raisings in Plymouth, Massachusetts, in 2014; in Chicago in 2015; and in Los Angeles County in 2016.

To grow the community Public Lab also launched an Internet platform and encourages people to establish various mailing lists, organized both geographically as well as around different topics. In 2016 there were thirty-three different mailing lists.

Open technology is also an important organizational tenet. Dosemagen says that the development of open, replicable, low-cost tools for people to do their own monitoring helps set the stage for a future when pollution-sensing devices for checking your own air or water quality will be as common as household smoke detectors. A Public Lab balloon-mapping kit costs less than $100 and captures images with 2-cm pixel resolution, ten-times more detailed than Google Earth images. It took three of these kits to document more than one hundred miles of coastline after the BP spill, as opposed to a so-called low-cost drone with GPS and camera at $1,200. Similarly, Public Lab spectrometer kits start at $10, and the Infragram kits cost from $10 to $135, compared with commercial off-the-shelf infrared photography options, which cost anywhere from $300 to more than $1,000.

The comment on the 2014 Innovation Award Dosemagen received read, "A broken CD, an old VHS player and an inexpensive webcam. These three items usually end up as trash, but the innovators at Public Lab have turned them into a low-cost, do-it-yourself alternative to the traditional

spectrometer – a tool used to detect neurotoxins and which ordinarily costs thousands of dollars."[12]
Dosemagen thinks that

> any time we put more minds together with different experiences in different backgrounds the more innovative a project is going to be. Open Space Technology style events are where people come together and they can ideate, think and build together. And the topics that end up getting covered are incredibly broad, ranging from the ethics of data collection to hacking on different water monitoring tools. Out of those sessions come new collaborations, come new partnerships, come new ideas for tools.[13]

> In 2016 Public Lab operated in more than fifty local organizations and organized thousands of individuals around the United States and beyond. It actively participates in the global movement, and Dosemagen is one of the coorganizers of the first international conference dedicated to the field of open hardware, at CERN, Europe's particle-physics laboratory near Geneva, Switzerland, 2016.

Those Most Marginalized Help Others: The Barge (Barka) Foundation

Tomasz Sadowski from Poland

Tomasz Sadowski's[14] big dream is to empower and move into the mainstream marginalized people, in particular those whom the authorities and social workers consider to be the most difficult cases.[15] Often labeled "hopeless" and "unreformable," these are people who have often been doubly rejected, first by the society and then by the aid system. Around 1989, Sadowski realized that the only way to address the root causes of distress was to empower marginalized people to build their own homes and create their own job opportunities. That is how the Barka Foundation was born, by settling groups of homeless people in previously abandoned farms in rural Poland.

---

[12] See: http://svn.org/meet-our-members/svn-innovation-award-winners–3/2014-innovation-award-winners.
[13] Interview June 16, 2016.
[14] See Ashoka: www.ashoka.org/fellow/tomasz-sadowski.
[15] Site-visits (I interviewed Tomasz Sadowski twice in 1995, also in 2015; I visited the Barge facilities several times and interviewed its participants in 1995–1997), interviews with Tomasz Sadowski and his colleagues, Barka website (http://barka.org.pl/taxonomy/term/28), Sadowska (2009).

The many Barka farms in Poland are managed solely by the previously homeless. Some of them are ex-prisoners, alcoholics, ex-bums, ex-prostitutes; some are aging and lost their homes. I will never forget being invited to lunch by one of the Barka farming communities. The meal was prepared from products they had grown and prepared themselves, and all acted with great hospitality, clearly proud to be hosts.

The farming communities (around twenty-five people each) meet over dinners to discuss current issues. Some are related to day-to-day agriculture and management problems, some to people's behavior. (I remember, for example, a discussion related to one of them who had had a few beers and thus violated the agreement for staying clean.) They also discuss future dreams and plans. I remember someone saying that now that they feel privileged, it might be righteous to start helping others in need. In fact, that was probably the moment when the idea of becoming a community of helpers and trainers was conceived.

The Barka farms are profitable, and Barka residents spend their income in their villages, contributing to the underdeveloped rural communities. This, in turn, creates jobs for village residents and leads to an atmosphere of cooperation and respect between village dwellers and the former homeless people.

The Barka farmers, being proud of their achievements, developed a much higher level of self-esteem and self-confidence. It's an unforgettable impression seeing previously rejected and disdained individuals speaking confidently about their jobs, personal plans, and vision for the community.

Strategic decisions are made by an assembly of all Barka communities. A key decision was made in 1995/96 to launch an international training center called Schools of Social Animation at Chudpoczyce, another bankrupt, post-*kolkholz* farm restored by the Barka community. This was, at that time, a breakthrough leverage point. Instead of being cared for, marginalized people now train professionals how to help others. In the first year they trained fifty activists from Belarus, Belgium, the Czech Republic, Estonia, France, Germany, Serbia, and Slovenia. Barka inhabitants also visited European job-training centers to learn new skills. The Chudopczyce group is also preparing to include ecotourism in its programs, managed by the formerly homeless residents.

In addition to local successes, Barka expands social awareness of homelessness throughout Poland through various TV programs and articles in national magazines and newspapers. It also informs legislative authorities regarding homelessness and lent substantial support to a new bill on combating poverty.

The next turning point was the decision to provide help to marginalized people outside Poland. Following identified needs Barka members set up chapters in several European countries facing growing problems with immigrants. Today there is a strong Barka presence in Great Britain,[16] Ireland,[17] and the Netherlands,Holland[18] empowering Polish and other emigrants. Needless to say, those EU programs are run by ex-homeless and ex-marginalized Barka participants and managed by their teams and through bottom-up initiatives.

Self-Reliant Emigrants

Ahmed Edilbi from Syria

In 2015–2016, Syrian refugees were facing an unbelievable displacement tragedy: panicked escape as war victims in the midst of disaster, loss of roots, loss of family members and belongings, and threats from middlemen and various natural and man-made disasters.[19] We can't even comprehend the degree of their suffering. Syria's population has diminished from a prewar level of around 22 million to 16.6 million.[20] This has created a huge problem. On the one hand, refugee-hosting countries face the enormous challenge of coping with the skyrocketing number of Syrian refugees. And on the other, emigrants in hosting countries feel that they are an unwanted burden and often face hostility and harassment. This influences their self-esteem, self-reliance, and self-confidence and can perpetuate a cycle of dependence, hopelessness, and frustration.

Scattered throughout Europe and the Middle East, emigrants become dependent on the hosting countries, where they're usually treated as an unwanted hardship and in that way, lose their human dignity and self-reliance. In response, the hosting countries turn to top-down solutions, offering aid and making the recipients more dependent on external support.

It's a disheartening scenario, but one Syrian emigrant, Ahmed Edilbi, innovated a solution to overcome it.

---

[16] Barka in the United Kingdom, see: www.barkauk.org/; retrieved February 24, 2017.
[17] Barka in Ireland, see: http://barkaie.org/; retrieved February 24, 2017.
[18] Barka in the Netherlands, see: www.barkanl.org/?page_id=173; retrieved February 24, 2017.
[19] Sources: Interview with Ahmed Edilbi and the Dubarah website. Interview in Cairo, December 11, 2013.
[20] *Economist*, Syria's drained population, September 30, 2015; www.economist.com/blogs/graphicdetail/2015/09/daily-chart-18; retrieved February 24, 2017.

Edilbi earned a degree in mass communications at the University of Damascus and worked successfully introducing information and communications technology (ICT) for business. When the Syrian conflict broke out, Ahmed was married with three children. In the blink of an eye he lost all his belongings, beginning with his home and car. Ahmed had to leave Syria for Dubai. He was separated from his wife, children, and members of his extended family, who moved to Lebanon, and a brother who went to Turkey.

Being a Syrian refugee, Edilbi[21] wondered how he could avoid the existing dynamic. He was especially interested in how to change the status quo of "relying on help" to a "self-helping paradigm." This, he said, could totally change the position of refugees in hosting countries, alleviating the burden and shifting predominantly anti-immigrant attitudes. Even more importantly, it could empower the refugees, restoring their dignity and self-reliance. He dreamed of changing their position from the one of "beneficiaries" to that of full citizenship – contributors to the mainstream society.[22]

Edilbi's solution was to weave a bottom-up network of mutual support and self-empowerment. To do so he launched the Dubarah platform, which links Syrian emigrants from all over Europe and the Middle East, providing a space for mutual exchange and peer-to-peer sharing with a variety of opportunities for employment, accommodation, health care, education, and business. The user-friendly platform enables Syrian emigrants to find their own solutions, to build mutual support networks, and to become independent and fully participating citizens in their hosting countries.

Ahmed's bottom-up solution is much less expensive than the top-down traditional way. It's based on endogenous processes, keeping people in charge, building social capital, and providing a tapestry of value-added benefits. During the first year of the program, 1,800 Syrian diaspora members around the world participated in producing content for the Dubarah guidebooks, which were then distributed to 300,000 Syrian refugees in thirty-six countries. Within a few months of opening, just the employment section of the portal posted eight thousand opportunities, four thousand of which were quickly filled by Syrian refugees. This was accompanied by career counseling, job advice, and coaching to increase the capacity of the participants.

---

[21] Ashoka Fellow, see: www.ashoka.org/fellow/ahmad-edilbi.
[22] From author's interview with Ahmed Edilbi.

Keeping in mind the disastrous situation the refugees faced, Edilbi has created "Emergency Relief" teams to provide immediate aid if, for example, a refugee has lost his home or job.

Dubarah participants have averted total dependency on the hosting countries and instead found a new way of solving their pressing life problems. This, in turn, has gained them the satisfaction of identifying their own solutions. They've enjoyed finding new jobs, educational opportunities, accommodation, and health through peer-to-peer support, and they've become more self-reliant, fully active, contributing citizens of the hosting countries. Satisfaction derived from their own inventiveness and ingenuity, reinforced by concrete solutions to their problems, has also helped create and reinforce harmonious relationships with the hosting population. Edilbi says that his dream goes beyond providing help for emigrants. He envisions "building Syria again. We need for that good people. We are creating community solidarity and empathy," he says.[23] And indeed, he carries on, directly and between lines, the message of human dignity, mutual care, and empathy.

Example from My Own Experience

At this point I would like to share an example of social EL from my own professional experience. When I became a Polish representative for Ashoka[24] (the global association finding, selecting, and empowering leading social entrepreneurs),[25] I not only wanted to find many candidates for its fellowship (especially in remote disadvantaged areas), but wanted to turn those outstanding individuals into a well-connected community delivering, through mutual trust and cooperation (i.e., social capital), a second layer of value-added achievements.

This dream was realized successfully, and I'm frequently asked how I did it. The answer could be very simple or quite complicated. The simple version is that I gave them an unstructured space to discuss, interact, brainstorm, play with "crazy" ideas, and create horizontal connections freely. In other words, even though I didn't know the terminology at the time, I created chaos, which turned into a higher-level order. After each Ashoka official meeting there was an off-the-record round table gathering. These

---

[23] Interview with Ahmed Edilbi.
[24] November 1994.
[25] Operating since 1980 in over 80 countries, see: www.ashoka.org.

brainstorming powwows were also called randomly in order to strategize around some issue or, as they called it, "charge their batteries."

At that time the prevailing paradigm for meetings was a well-organized structure with top-down control, possibly with acknowledged experts or known public figures present. It wasn't easy to convince people that much better results could be achieved by facilitating an endogenous process – one based on the group's own potential, with no external experts or celebrities, that gave people space for free (chaotic) interactions. Similarly, it was hard for them to believe that chaos could beef up the feeling of belonging, bolster identification with the fellowship, and, on top of that, through mutual collaboration, augment the propensity for generating value-added ideas. But after a few successful gatherings, the group saw the value and restructured meetings going forward.

The more complicated answer is an account of how a new value-added idea was generated through this sort of chaotic interaction. The story is about the Ashoka School of Young Social Entrepreneurs.

In May 2000, we had a debriefing meeting with the Polish Ashoka Fellows, summarizing the Central European All-Fellows assembly in the Czech Republic.[26] As usual, I gave the Fellows time and space for free discussion. At some point someone said that he or she had already gotten a lot from Ashoka, so maybe it was time to start giving back to society. During a heated discussion the group considered pros (mostly values-driven) and cons (related to strained resources within their own projects). They also came up with several options for whom to target and made a decision to address young people. The next question was what segment should it be: secondary, high school, or university students? And, if university students, which specialties? Someone made the suggestion to target business students. Reaction was strong. Some objected, saying that business students are usually narrowly profit-driven and would have no understanding of social issues. Someone else countered that business students usually falsely think that to pursue their business career they need to compromise their well-hidden dreams, whereas Ashoka Fellows could demonstrate that whatever their dreams are (e.g., helping children from endangered families because their own father was alcoholic and abusive or helping the disabled because they had a disabled sister), they can pursue a business career without postponing those dreams. Another Fellow argued that business students think that making a real difference can be done only in business,

---

[26] This happened on a bus, on our way back, which was one of the reasons why this program was called Bus.

following the iconic examples of Lee Iacocca or Bill Gates, and that they would be thrilled to discover that one can also do something really big in the social sector (e.g., Mohammad Yunus). Finally the decision was made to launch the Ashoka School for Young Social Entrepreneurs (ASYSE) targeting business students.

The next step was to determine how to do it. Obviously, the Fellows decided to capitalize on the capacity of Ashoka Fellowship. They decided to provide hands-on experience with real social entrepreneurs, both conceptually as well as practically. Hence, the students would receive a booster shot of sorts from Ashoka Fellows, learning about their ideas, visions, and creative approach. They would participate as interns in their projects and track the bumpy ups and downs that would lead them forward. Someone suggested that that wasn't enough and that they should work on their own social projects simultaneously.

Ultimately, the ASYSE was launched in Poland and spread to Nepal and Indonesia. Students participated in a series of hands-on experiences with active social entrepreneurs, including seminars, workshops, internships, and mentoring. They also created a peer-to-peer community (horizontal connections), providing mutual support and feedback on planning their own projects. Moreover students could tap social entrepreneurs for mentorship. At the end of each cycle, participants have had the opportunity to start a social project on their own. After five months they gather again for a follow-up meeting to report, debrief, and discuss their achievements. On top of that they plan goals for their own alumni platform (again, through a free, "chaotic," bottom-up process). This alumni network and the projects pursued by the students came about organically, as sort of a second-layer offshoot of the initial idea.

ASYSE has influenced many students' lives. Following are some quotes from students who participated in the program (Praszkier & Nowak, 2012):

> Enormous experience, which will influence my entire life. I want to send my brother for an internship with the social entrepreneur I visited. – Gretchen, MBA student, United States
> ASYSE showed how to change the reality, having nothing but a vision, strong will, commitment and faith, plus innovative and entrepreneurial ideas; that there exists such a thing as goodness, which helps in realizing the dreams. After ASYSE I learned how to fill the gap between the dream and just doing it. – Gabi, MBA student, Poland
> A lifetime experience. It will not only help me in my professional life but also my personal life. One of the most important things that I learnt from my Ashoka Fellow mentor is to follow the heart. The tools can be always

Figure 27. ASYSE in Nepal, 2007.

obtained; support from exceptional individuals is rare. – An anonymous ASYSE student from Nepal (see Figures 27–29)

The multiple student projects usually addressed pressing social problems. For example, Marta, one of the Polish alumni, carried on a project in the most disadvantaged part of Warsaw for children from endangered families (see Figure 30).

Summary: From the Conceptual Perspective

Social Influence

Similar to the business cases, the core social influence mechanisms at work in these examples of social EL are *identification* and *internalization*.

As the homeless and the nurses take coresponsibility into their own hands, they influence their social undertaking and innovate new methods or techniques. As the emigrants and the potentially conflicted communities become self-driven and committed in pursuing their mission, undoubtedly their commitment is based on *internalization* and identification.

Figure 28. ASYSE students in Indonesia, 2007.

Figure 29. Discussing and planning own ideas; ASYSE in Poland, 2005.

These social influence mechanisms create a higher level of motivation and loyalty, leading to self-development and creativity. Moreover, they perpetuate "something out of nothing" paths of development.

Preconditions for Chaos-to-Order Dynamics

Both in the interviews as well as during site visits with these remarkable social entrepreneurs, I could sense an instinctual ability to delegate responsibility and create a space for free interaction, which, from our point of view, may be encapsulated as the *complexity way of thinking* – one of the preconditions for chaos-to-order dynamics.

Figure 30. One of the Polish ASYSE alumni projects aimed at children
from endangered families, 2007.

The *connectivity spirit* is also evident. Take the Public Lab, for example, with multiple mailing lists and a robust communication platform. Not to mention the Dubarah platform, which connects emigrants scattered throughout the world.

Peacemaking, caring for marginalized people and emigrants, building up a novel community-care system, protecting the environment – all of these efforts are based on *empathetic values* shared by people driven to give the disadvantaged a voice and the power to make decisions.

And finally, these cases also show how the EL method enhanced *creativity* as a result of direct horizontal communication and teamwork.

Complexity Theory

Applying complexity theory to these cases we can track down nearly all twelve of the complexity dimensions. In each of these cases there are freely interacting individuals (the homeless people set a course, the emigrants interact through the Dubarah platform, citizens join together and collaborate on disaster mapping, etc.). In each case there is an emergence of a new phenomenon: e.g., out of the citizens' bottom-up environmental engagement there emerge professional reports influencing national and international policies. In each a blend of upward and downward causations is evident: The nurses decide on the pragmatics, and their ideas spread throughout the entire system, serving as a resource for other nurses.

Similarly, the reader may identify multiple feedback loops (e.g., marginalized people decide on the legal regulations for combating poverty, thus influencing the lives of those marginalized). And in each case we can see chaos turned into order (e.g., the chaos of lurking potential conflicts is turned into an order of cultural or business cooperation). And what about small impulses creating big changes? The example of the Dubarah platform where emigrants interact, develop self-reliance, and, hence, experience better integration with mainstream societies certainly qualifies. Additionally, the fractals syndrome is evident in the groups of nurses who self-replicate and hire new nurses on their own initiative, creating a fractal model of development.

Chapter Coda

- Peacemaking and peace-preventing cases from Poland and the Middle East
- Cases of self-governing nurses building up a novel system for social care (Netherlands), community environmental monitoring given to the people (United States), homelessness and marginalization combated by ex-homeless people (Poland), and emigrants empowered through mutual help and horizontal communication (Syria)
- An example from my own experience: the second layer impact through chaotic interactions on the lower level
- The conceptual recap related to the mechanisms of social influence, preconditions for constructive endogenous dynamics, and the premise of complexity theory

SECTION 5

Being an Empowerer

We have defined a new kind of Empowering Leadership and introduced the concept of an Empowerer as someone who is maximizing the contributions of others through recognition of their right to guide their own destiny. To do so Empowering Leaders create an enabling environment that encourages and supports bottom-up decision-making processes, provides opportunities for others to make and act upon their own decisions, and gives space for others to enjoy and celebrate their success.

We have also reviewed several case studies of the Empowering Leadership at work. A key question, however, is whether or not the EL style is effective only in the work environment, or whether it's also applicable outside the office. And if some use an EL approach in their personal lives, is it a style specific to the person – a way of life and a habitual way of relating to others?

The word "leader" in the case of family life would seem to be a misnomer. You probably wouldn't want to declare that you're an Empowering Leader of your spouse, adolescent daughter, or aging father. I certainly wouldn't want to imagine myself in such a situation with my teenage daughter.

On the other hand, there is a specific way of giving space, and it's not because you want to read the newspaper or watch the news or you don't care what others do (laissez-faire style; see Chapter 1). On the contrary, it's because you care deeply about your family and want to create an enabling environment where they can thrive. Isn't this approach worth a neologism, such as "Empowerer"(introduced in Chapter 9)? And what does it mean to be one?

In this section we will delve into some mechanisms that foster empowering relationships (Chapter 13) and review some real-life situations when this approach may be especially significant (Chapter 15). We'll also revisit a specific competence, which is basic and worth educing, be it in business or in everyday life. Augmenting others' creativity, will be discussed in Chapter 14.

Some Characteristics of an Empowerer

We're taking off on a trip far beyond work and the professional environment. The purpose of our journey is to become an empowerer, regardless of the context – to be an Empowerer in life.

But what makes an Empowerer? What are the cardinal mechanisms that enable empowering behavior? Challenging questions, as we open up this new avenue of investigation.

All that's been said about the characteristics of an Empowering Leader remains substantial, especially *complexity thinking*, or in this case understanding the complex processes and feedback loops involved in human relations such as love, caring, growth, maturity, dependence and independence, connectivity spirit – seeing the importance of relationships and networks – and probably most important, empathy. Creativity is another important piece; the practical side of it we'll explore further in Chapter 14.

Drawing from literature and interviews, as well as from my practical experience in fostering inventiveness, I would posit that the central skills of an Empowerer are:

- Being a social capital transmitter
- Mastering the bridging properties of social networks
- Facilitating the process of emergence
- Enabling others to act while keeping one's own ego on a short leash
- Believing that the world is changeable, and that change may result from bottom-up initiatives, not necessarily be imposed from the top down
- Having a propensity for building a creativity-augmenting milieu

Social Capital Transmitter

Social capital was briefly mentioned in Chapter 6. Here we elaborate on this phenomenon.

An Empower builds cohesiveness around and glues together people and groups. The question of what adheres people to one another has intrigued sociologists and psychologists since the first half of the nineteenth century, when the French writer Alexis de Tocqueville, in his book *Democracy in America* (de Tocqueville, 2003), expressed his fascination with the vibrant associational life that bolstered American democracy and economic strength. For de Tocqueville, personal interaction in voluntary associations provided the *social glue* that helped to bond individual Americans together (Field, 2008). This "social glue" was probably on Emile Durkheim's mind when he coined the term *organic solidarity* (Durkheim, 1984) and may be related to Francis Fukuyama's concept of *spontaneous sociability* (1996).

This social glue is also called *social capital* (see Chapters 7 and 9). Seen as a blend of networks, trust, and cooperation, it perpetuates development, empowers people, raises their self-esteem, and makes people happier and more optimistic (Putnam, 1996, 2000). To bond people together one needs not only to create connections among one's own group members (the *bonding* type of social capital) but also develop linkages with other social groups (*bridging* type of social capital; Putnam, 2000). Strong ties inside close-knit circles seem more natural. We usually trust and socialize with those best known (e.g., families, friends, neighbors, or professional colleagues). Less obvious are the relationships with other groups and with less-well-known or unknown people.

As said before, social capital is predominantly perceived as an important value, both for individuals and for groups or societies. It refers to connections among individuals (e.g., social networks) and the norms of reciprocity and trustworthiness that arise from those connections. In other words, social capital refers to any feature of social relation that contributes to the ability of groups and societies to work together and accomplish their goals (Putnam, 2000; Foley & Edwards, 1998). It may also be seen as the aggregate of actual or potential resources that are embedded in a durable network (Bourdieu, 1986; Coleman, 1990). In simpler terms, social capital appears when a person's family, friends, and associates constitute an important asset, one that can be called on in a crisis or enjoyed for its own sake (Woolcock & Narayan, 2000).

Social capital is not only a collection of relationships among people, but also the shared values and understandings that enable individuals and groups to trust each other and so work together. Mutual trust reinforces societal development and yields better societal outcomes, and these, in turn, raise the level of mutual trust, which, in its turn, positively influences further outcomes (Putnam, 1993; Fukuyama, 1996; Coleman, 2000; Bourdieu, 2003).

Social capital is sometimes also perceived as a consequence of individuals' mutual trust with others, arising through bonds, bridges, and links within various social networks. Social capital also has positive outcomes at the individual level (Tyler, 2003; Cook *et al.,* 2005). For example, it empowers the individual to take some risk and explore new opportunities (Coleman, 1988; Brehm & Rahn, 1997). It also influences career success (Burt, 1992; Podolny & Baron, 1997; Gabbay & Zuckerman, 1998).

Understanding the positive impact of social capital, the central question becomes, What factors support its development? And especially, what personality characteristics help an individual build up his or her social capital? In what situations does the propensity for building social capital become not only a bonding capability (inside close-knit personal circles), but also an opportunity for bridging (i.e., extended to external circles, groups, and individuals)?

These questions strongly relate to leadership in business, given that the business leader deals with sections, departments, working groups, divisions, etc. They also relate to being an Empowerer outside the office and how people build bonds and bridges among friends, family, and neighbors and foster social capital in the community.

In our research we maintained that there are three dimensions that foster an individual's propensity for building social capital.[1] They are:

- Having a high level of trust

Trust is seen as an essential dimension of social capital. Trust, as it exists among neighbors, peers, and group members, leads to a high level of solidarity. It's the key driver for undertaking cooperative actions (Fukuyama, 1996; Putnam, 1993, Bourdieu, 2003; Coleman, 2000; Tyler, 2003; Cook *et al.,* 2005). Some authors equate trust with social capital, as in "Trust or social capital determines the performance of society's institutions" (La Porta *et al.,* 1996, p. 3).

With regard to individual propensity for developing social capital, we posit that trusting others, as a personality characteristic, plays an essential role (Praszkier *et al.,* 2009; Praszkier & Nowak, 2012).

- Tending to cooperate with others

---

[1] In 2015 and 2016 we developed a questionnaire measuring the propensity for building social capital based on those three dimensions (Zabłocka *et al.,* 2016).

The second pivotal dimension of social capital is cooperation (Putnam, 1993; Knack & Keefer, 1997; Woolcock, 2004; da Silva, 2006; Bouma *et al.,* 2008).

It takes mutual commitment and cooperation from all parties involved to build social capital (Adler & Kwon, 2002). The more individuals are in regular contact with one another, the more likely they are to develop a "habit of cooperation" and act collectively (Wasko & Faraj, 2005). Cooperation, one of the central tenets of social capital, is seen as a value per se (Kenworthy, 1997; Maxwell, 2002; Praszkier & Nowak, 2012). We therefore suggest that willingness to cooperate is a personality trait essential to the propensity for developing social capital.

• Having a strong sense of support

Adding to trust and cooperation, we hold that the third variable indicating an ability to build and develop social capital is sense of support. Sense of support is strongly related to a feeling of security in social relations and asserts their permanence. In that vein, all kinds of perceived support are significant (emotional, informative, instrumental, or spiritual), as is the perceived accessibility of this support (Tardy, 1985). Various research (Sheridan & Radmacher, 1998; Knoll & Schwarzer, 2004) demonstrates that participation in social networks and social contacts delivers positive experience and strengthens the sense of security, as well as the feeling that life is predictable and stable (Sęk, 2001).

Social capital can be an individual asset (Portes, 1998), defined as features of social groups or networks that individuals can access and use to obtain further benefits (Yang, 2007). Someone with a strong sense of support, through diversity of connections, opens up avenues to various, previously inaccessible, resources. These assets empower the individual to take some risk and explore new opportunities (Coleman, 1988; Brehm & Rahn, 1997; Praszkier & Nowak, 2012).

The opposite – we call it the Lone Ranger syndrome – disregards the need for support from others. This individual is doomed to fail in the long run (Praszkier & Nowak, 2012), and is definitely less able to develop social capital.

Mastering Bridging Networks

In Chapter 6 we introduced the concept of "the power of weak ties." To recap, strong ties are relationships among people who work, live, or play together. They engender a tendency for group members to think alike, reducing the diversity of ideas (Porter, 2007). To glue the society one needs not only to create connections among homogeneous groups (the *bonding* type of social capital) but also to develop lineages across diverse social groups (*bridging* type of social capital; Putnam, 2000). As said before, strong ties inside well-known groups seem more natural. Less obvious is the "gluing" and bridging with other groups and with less well-known or unknown people.

Establishing weak ties requires cognitive flexibility and an ability to function in complex organizations. Weak ties not only provide access to heterogeneous resources but also enhance a person's opportunity for mobility (Granovetter, 1973, 1995; Lin, 2001; Praszkier, 2012). They also require a capacity to maintain a diffused level of empathy. Moreover, weak ties have a special role in an individual's propensity for mobility (Granovetter, 1983).

Csermely (2009) maintains that there are two types of personalities: "stronglinkers" and "weaklinkers." Stronglinkers tend to rely on family links and just a few good friends – in other words, reliable, lifelong contacts. They find it difficult to change their mind-sets, as they are generally rigid and usually fold new concepts into preset notions, and, finally, they are rather intolerant.

Weaklinkers, on the other hand, have friends from wide and diverse circles. They have a high tolerance for varied ideas, emotions, and attitudes and are comfortable interacting with a large number of people. They are flexible and highly adaptive to new information and unfamiliar environments. They are also rather tolerant.

Stronglinkers perform better and are more creative in a highly structured environment, whereas weaklinkers are creative in diffuse structures. The former tend to operate in starlike networks (in which all participants communicate with the centrally positioned node and not with each other), whereas the latter prefer a random network.

It seems important to add that weaklinkers may feel a bit lost with multiple feeble and low-value connections. Rather, in an analogy to social dynamics, the most adaptive and "healthy" state is characterized by the coexistence of strong and weak bonds, both playing a significant role in building the balance between cohesion and openness of groups, communities, or societies (Praszkier, 2012). Weak links stabilize all complex systems. They provide a "small-world" atmosphere, enable synchronization of bottom-up networks, provide communication channels, and ensure that the relaxation of the stressed networks goes smoothly and the network is integrated and behaves as a whole (Csermely, 2009). Strong links provide the backbone, help in maintaining and transmitting values and traditions, provide a sense of identity, and are reference points in case of disturbances.

Facilitating the Process of Emergence

It seems obvious that Empowerers are not hands-on facilitators. On the other hand, they are far from being laissez-faire kind of people, lying back and letting things go. On the contrary, an Empowerer is committed to and deeply involved in relationships and passionate about his or her dreams and visions. So if neither of the two extremes fits, what is the Empowerer's role?

It is to create the prerequisites that will enable others to thrive, learn, be happy, innovate, make their own choices, etc. While difficult to assess these prerequisites include:

• Creating a safe-to-explore environment

An infant is starting to explore and is likely to get into trouble by pulling a lamp onto his head or slamming her fingers in the drawer. You remove potentially dangerous "traps" so that the infant may safely wander, yet the environment remains full of colorful and attractive shapes for a young child to touch and take into his mouth, without harming himself. Moreover, your height prompts the child to pull herself up and experiment with standing.

Your teenaged kids start exploring the world of social and emotional relationships with backing from your supportive, listening, loving family.

Your spouse is facing a new job dilemma. He or she feels supported not because you are telling him or her what to do, but because you listen to the pros and cons of taking a new job, sharing thoughts and providing caring support that helps your mate make the right decision.

Creating a safe environment can also mean establishing firm boundaries. Imagine a soft chair. If filled with liquid without some solid structural support (e.g., a support for your back or arms), it wouldn't provide any comfort. The solid structures of a safe environment are your values and norms. Setting boundaries is an important part of any relationship;[2] "one of the most vital components to creating a happy, healthy and fulfilling relationship is to become a master at setting boundaries" (Twardowski, 2014). This means that safety is defined by open space as well as clear boundaries. From the complexity theory we know that the fewer rules

---

[2] See, for example: www.loveisrespect.org/healthy-relationships/setting-boundaries/ and http://psychcentral.com/lib/10-way-to-build-and-preserve-better-boundaries/; retrieved February 24, 2017.

there are the better. This suggests that for growth to occur there should be as few boundaries as possible; however, those that exist should be clear and strongly guarded.

• Dedication and determination

Remember the mission-based charisma that we delineated as a specific "radiating power" associated with the particular mission being pursued and passion for the pursuit of this mission? People around Empowerers sense, without being told, their absolute dedication and determination. This doesn't necessarily mean action, although sometimes it does. It's a message primarily conveyed through body language. Even when you play, relax, or have fun, there is this absolute dedication and determination associated with your meaningful relationships.

When your stance is unwavering, people around you feel safe to explore, experiment, initiate, and innovate and are simultaneously inspired by your "inner fire."

Enabling Others to Act While Keeping Your Own Ego on a Short Leash

Leadership is more than an affair of the head. It is also one of the heart (Kouzes & Posner, 1992). Through both head and heart, the best leaders enable the full potential in others to be achieved (Llopis, 2014).

Empowerers stress cooperative goals and build relationships of mutual trust. They make others feel important, strong, and influential. It's about creating a milieu of mutual help and team playing (Kouzes, J. M. & Posner, 2011; Armbruster, 2014). The two essential skills for "enabling others to act" are fostering collaboration and strengthening others (Kouzes & Posner, 1987, 1992, 1993; Krill *et al.*, 1997).

Empowerers are also humble. That's not an easy thing to be these days, when narcissistic business leaders are treated as rock stars. However, humility is an essential trait for creative leaders, even if it sounds a bit anachronistic. Humility and the ability to admit error may be two of the most important qualities a truly creative leader must have (Guthrie, 2012).

Creative leaders must also be in tune with human behavior. They must be deeply convinced that, in some areas and at some level, everyone is, or potentially could be, a leader; that leaders must know themselves, alert to their own failings, to serve the organization better; and that only by mastering complexity will they be able to release others' potential and, at the same time, maintain overall harmony (Guthrie, 2012).

It's not easy to keep a handle on one's ego. It means not only delegating responsibilities and partnership to others but also allowing them to celebrate their successes. In your private life it means that you can express happiness when your spouse's prediction or decision turns out to be correct, even if your ego prompts you to claim that it was you who made it first. You avoid telling your son, "Didn't I say so?" And you try to downplay your ego's claims that you're not sufficiently respected, that nobody listens to you, and that you deserve more acknowledgment. It doesn't mean you should give up and remain in the shadows. It's more about tone – your way of expressing your needs, your vibration, and whether you're fostering harmony or being driven by ego prompts. It means that you simply give benevolent space to others.

Belief in Changeability

An Empowerer gives space for people to explore, thrive, and change. It's trivial to say that change is inevitable: your children turn into teenagers, become independent, and leave home; your professional career goes through several hurdles; people around you change from Republican to Democrat and the reverse; fashions become out of vogue, etc.

Interestingly, Professor Carol Dweck's team documented that mere belief that people and the world are changeable can sustain our persistence and tenacity in pursuing our ideas (Dweck, 2000, 2006; Chiu *et al.*, 1997). In other words, belief in the malleability of people and the world makes you a committed person, which, as said before, creates a supportive message for others.

Of course, some people simply don't believe in this malleability. They think that conditions are set once and for all. And, as research has documented, they have a much higher tendency to stereotype others (Levy, Dweck, *et al.*, 1998), and they're more inclined to seek acceptance and, in that way, avoid the risk of rejection. Conversely, those who believe in the malleability of the world tend to learn by failure instead of focusing on avoiding rejection (Dweck, 2000).

People can sense whether you're an Empowerer. They feel that you trust them even if they change (e.g., from a sweet child to an explorative teenager), and they can read between the lines that you believe conditions *may change*, that you and others *may influence the world*, and that *exploring is worth a try*. Empowerers also convince the people around them that they won't avoid taking reasonable risk to pursue change.

The Empowerer – in Short

At its essence, being an Empowerer means creating a specifically safe milieu from which to explore the environment, developing trustful relationships (both bonding as well as bridging), and radiating dedication and commitment. It also means downplaying your ego and allowing others to take initiative and explore. The Empowerer should be deeply convinced that people and the world are changeable, a belief that is a gateway to taking on insurmountable challenges and learning through probes, trials, and failures.

It's quite a long list and a tall order, but these are not "tasks" to accomplish. Rather, this is a lifestyle that may become quite natural and habitual. If it does, in a feedback loop, it can be very rewarding and enjoyable.

In Chapter 1 we'll see how the Empowerer can help augment the creativity of individuals and groups.

Chapter Coda

- Some key characteristics of an Empowerer were delineated:
  - Being a social-capital transmitter
  - Mastering the bridging properties of social networks
  - Facilitating the process of emergence
  - Enabling others to act while keeping one's own ego on a short leash
  - Believing that the world is changeable, and that change may result from bottom-up initiatives, not necessarily be imposed from the top down

CHAPTER 14

How to Enhance Creativity

We conclude our exploration of creativity with some practical guidelines. In Chapter 7 we noted the feedback loop between creativity and joy: creativity delivers joy and joy enhances creativity. Here we'll elaborate on this phenomenon and look at other (cognitive and social) mechanisms and activities that augment creativity.

Music, Play, Humor, and Dance Accelerate Creativity

Like any skill or talent, creativity is something we can develop and improve. Music, dance, play, and humor are among the most effective ways to boost creativity and sustain the creative drive.

- Music

The brain is a music lover. Much research has shown that music can improve neuronal connections and brain plasticity, including the release of important neurotransmitters,

Music is a powerful tool for recovering memories and enhancing the capacity to learn. Listening to music or learning to play it boosts one's mental sharpness (Majd, 2012).

- Play

Playful activity leads to the growth of more interneuronal connections, particularly in the frontal lobe – the part of the brain responsible for uniquely human higher mental functions (Pellis & Pellis, 2009).

Pretend play also fosters the development of cognitive and affective processes related to divergent thinking in children. In a longitudinal study, the quality of fantasy and imagination in play predicted changes in divergent thinking over time. Play also facilitates insight (Russ, 2003, 2016).

Interestingly, experts on animal behavior posit that play also generates creativity and stimulates innovation. Through observation of animals they conclude that play helps the subjects find novel solutions. Play enables "breaking rules" in a protected environment and generates new ideas (creativity) and new ways of doing things (innovation). The same effects can be observed in human children (Bateson & Martin, 2013).

The influence of unstructured play on creativity in young children is documented by the following research: Two randomly selected groups of children (age range six to seven) were asked to perform a task involving playing with colors using their imagination. Before performing the task, children in the experimental group played freely with salt dough for twenty-five minutes. In the control group, the children followed a structured exercise in which they copied text from a blackboard. During the task that followed, the children who had played freely beforehand used more colors and were more creative (Howard-Jones *et al.*, 2002).

- Humor

Humor also has the power to get your creative juices flowing (McFadzean, 1998; Couger, 1995). "Getting into a humorous frame of mind not only loosens you up, it also enhances your creativity" says Von Oech (1983, p. 91).

In a group setting humor can stretch participants' thinking and help them change mind-set. It can also prompt them to combine ideas they hadn't associated before, and it can help them relax, encouraging them to take matters less seriously and thus reducing one of the primary obstacles to creativity: feeling foolish or fearful of making a mistake (Couger, 1995; Von Oech, 1983).

- Dance

Dancing stimulates creativity by calling on multiple brain activities simultaneously (Majd, 2012). Dancers maximize cognitive function through practice. And dancing improves brain function on a variety of levels. Studies show that different types of practice allow dancers to achieve peak performance by blending cerebral and cognitive thought processes with muscle memory and "proprioception" held in the cerebellum (Bergland, 2013).

Consistent with recent work on simpler, rhythmic motor-sensory behaviors, these data reveal the interacting network of brain areas active during spatially patterned, bipedal rhythmic movements that are integrated in dance. Dance, as a universal human activity, involves a complex combination of processes related to the patterning of bipedal motion and to metric entrainment to musical rhythms (Brown *et al.*, 2006). In all likelihood empathetic "feeling into" a partner's movements and achieving kinesthetic synchrony with another augment creativity. Moreover, research supports the idea that frequent dancing can reduce the risk of dementia by more than 70 percent (Majd, 2012).

Distance and Metaphors

So far we've considered the emotional side of creativity and the associated neuroscience triggered through activities involving joy, humor, music, and dance. But other cardinal aspects to consider are the cognitive dimensions of creativity.

The Power of Distance

Probably the most influential aspect of creative problem solving is the perceived psychological (spatial or temporal) distance: The closer to the problem we are, the less likely it is that we will find creative solutions. Directly confronting and struggling with a problem narrow one's perspective, whereas a glance from a distant perspective opens more options. David Kuria's (Chapter 7) attempts to solve the sanitary disaster in the Kiberia slums had two phases. During the first Kuria used direct communication to try to convince people to make changes (maintaining minimal psychological distance). When that failed, he withdrew from the situation for a while. This created an opportunity to look at the problem from a distant perspective, which produced an "aha" reaction. Instead of patronizing people, Kuria helped them identify with the issue simply by encouraging them to draw their ideal toilet.

Psychological distance affects the way we mentally represent things. Distant ones are represented in a relatively abstract way while those psychologically closer have more detail and seem more concrete.

As for temporal distance, in one exemplary study the participants were told to imagine their lives tomorrow (near future) or on a day one year from now (distant future), and then to imagine themselves completing a task on that particular day. Those who imagined a day in the distant future performed the task better than those who focused on the near future. In a series of experiments it was documented that the distant-future perspective facilitates abstract thinking (Förster *et al.*, 2004).

The role of the spatial distance in creative thinking is illustrated by a study from the University of Indiana at Bloomington. Researchers randomly divided subjects into three groups and told them that a friendly academic team needed some support in their research. The only difference between groups was that the introductory story for one group indicated that the friendly academic team was located at a far spatial distance ("in California, around two thousand miles away from here"). Another group was told that the academic friends were "just two miles away from here," and the third group (the control group) received no information regarding the team's location. Next, all groups heard the same thrilling story:

> A prisoner was attempting to escape from a tower. He found a rope in his cell that was half as long as needed to permit him to reach the ground safely. He divided the rope in half, tied the two parts together, and escaped. How could he have done this? (Jia *et al.*, 2009, p. 1129)

The participants were given one minute to find the solution.

Finding the solution in this case requires creative thinking, as you need to detach your mind from the conventional thinking that "dividing the rope" automatically means cutting it into two pieces. It doesn't. The solution isn't that he cut the rope in halves; instead, he divided it by unraveling the rope lengthwise and tied the resulting strands together.

The research question was, Which group was better at "discovering" the solution? The result was that the group told that the solution was for a distant academic team did markedly better than the group told that the solution was for a group located quite close by. Distance helped. Because the problems seemed farther away, they seemed easier to solve (Shapira & Liberman, 2009).

These and other studies suggest that merely the perception of temporal or spatial distance from a problem can generate more creative solutions.

The Magic of Metaphors

Here's a little test to try on your own: Close your eyes and imagine taking a walk with someone you love. Afterward, open your eyes and put your mind on a task or problem. Are you more creative (divergent thinking) or more analytical (convergent thinking)? Now close your eyes and imagine having casual sex without emotional connection. Then go back to the task or problem. What is your approach now? More creative or more analytic? If there is a difference, then we might be able to conclude that our imagination might influence our propensity for creativity, or that the impact on creativity of more abstract imaginings differs from the impact of more concrete ones.

This research was carried out at the University of Amsterdam. Participants imagined one of three situations: a long walk with their beloved one, casual sex with a person whom they were attracted to but not in love with, or a nice walk on their own (control group). Participants then attempted to solve two kinds of problems, some requiring creative insights and others calling for analytic thinking. The results were that participants imagining a walk with a loved person solved more creativity problems and fewer analytic problems than those in the control situation. Participants imagining casual sex, on the other hand, solved fewer creativity problems and more analytic problems compared with participants in the control group (Förster *et al.*, 2009; Liberman & Shapira, 2009).

Imagining love activates a long-term perspective that elicits global processing, which promotes creativity and impedes analytic thinking. In contrast, thoughts of casual sex activate a short-term perspective that elicits local processing, which encourages analytic thinking and hinders creative thinking (Förster *et al.*, 2009; Liberman & Shapira, 2009).

Instead of using verbatim delineation of reality to reveal this phenomenon, we can achieve a similar result by building metaphors. A metaphor, by definition, implies divergent thinking, as it is a comparison that shows how two things that are not alike in most ways are similar in another important way (Lakoff & Johnson, 2003). Interestingly, it was Aristotle who highlighted the pivotal role of metaphors in human communication.[1] And indeed, metaphors open up new perspectives and are motivational and inspiring (Kolar, 2012). Some even see metaphors as a "liberating force" providing new perspectives (Inkson, 2002). Moreover, they increase *distance*, and distance, as we know, is a powerful lever for creativity.

In business metaphors are frequently used to reveal the complexity of the organization (Morgan, 1980). And many suggest that each situation or problem should be "metaphorized," i.e., simulated for various settings (McFadzean, 1998). Some metaphors are quite simple and popular, e.g., "putting two and two together," "connecting the dots," or "thinking outside the box." More elaborate ones may be found in marketing: "This vacuum cleaner is so powerful that it can suck the light out of a black hole." When planning one may replace familiar sayings for more impact, swapping "increase sales" with "building larger muscles" or "attract more investors" with "harvest more corn."[2]

One of the most illustrative examples of a business metaphor can be found in the well-known writing of Eric Raymond: The Cathedral & the Bazaar. The "closed" Microsoft software is depicted as a cathedral

---

[1] See: Kirby (1997); Levin (1982).
[2] Cited from: www.mindtools.com/pages/article/newCT_93.htm; retrieved February 24, 2017.

built by a cloistered team of developers under the authority of a bishop, while the open-source software Linux is portrayed as an open bazaar (Raymond, 2001).

Some business consultants use the warfare metaphor, drawing strategic approaches and knowledge from the military field and applying them in business (Talbot, 2003). Others argue to stop using battle metaphors for business strategy (Cespedes, 2014) and replace them with the Blue Ocean metaphor, which suggests that effective strategy shouldn't aim to confront competitors, but instead, should make competitors irrelevant (Kim & Mauborgne, 2005). Success results from creating one's own "blue oceans" of uncontested market space, and one's own values and approach, regardless of what the competitors do. In the language of complexity theory, the blue ocean strategy means creating new attractors, instead of confronting the old ones (see Chapter 5).

One of the most common business metaphors is Edward de Bono's six hats of different colors (de Bono, 1995, 1996). Each color represents a different type of thinking used to solve a problem. To clarify the thinking process one has to don the hat representing the current mode of analysis: The White Hat covers facts, figures, information, asking questions, and defining information needs and gaps. The Red Hat relates to intuition, feelings, and emotions. The Black Hat is a logical critique representing judgment and cautions and is used to point out why a particular suggestion doesn't fit the facts, the available experience, the system in use, or the policy that is being followed. The Yellow Hat is also embedded in cognitive thinking, finding reasons why something will work and why it will offer benefits. The Green Hat is the hat of creativity, alternatives, proposals, provocations, and changes. And the Blue Hat represents surveying the entire process and controlling its proper flow.

Broken down like this, the process of innovating appears to be much more complex than a mere bubbling up of ideas. It involves a blend of instinct, emotions, and cognitive analysis. For our purposes here, I would complicate matters further and add a seventh, Brown Hat, which would represent simulating and analyzing future trends, especially in a complex environment (see Chapter 16).

Guided Imagery: Exploring the Unexplorable

An elaborate form of metaphor is a technique used to activate imagination called *guided imagery*. Guided imagery recalls images from long-term or short-term memory, or those created from fantasy, or a combination of both, in response to guidance or instruction (Kosslyn *et al.,* 2001; Pearson, 2007). It has the built-in capacity to deliver multiple layers of complex, encoded messages by way of simple symbols and metaphors (Naparstek, 1995). As such, it promotes divergent thinking, which enhances problem-solving ability (Sarnoff & Remer, 1982).

Guided imagery is sometimes used in therapy as a way to explore the subconscious in a talelike projection, taking clients from their current struggles to a distant time and location. The counselor provides a narrative structure for the imaginary journey[3] (e.g., Hall *et al.,* 2014). For example, the counselor might ask a client to close his eyes and imagine trekking in the mountains, arriving at a scary cave, exploring this cave, and – simultaneously – identifying the emotions he experiences. Trekking high may trigger memories of achieving something difficult in life, while exploring a dark cave may resemble anxiety-producing situations. The journey may be improvised and include significant details, such as putting on and taking off a backpack as a metaphor for a carried burden (Hall *et al.,* 2014). Guided imagery[4] explores perception and motor control (especially with brain damaged patients) and is one of the avenues for harmonizing "higher" cognitive functions (Kosslyn *et al.,* 2001).

In order to use any of these metaphors effectively in business, we must tap into our imagination. Through imagination "the impossible becomes possible; the unexpected happens; the unexplainable occurs" (Faucette, 2012). Especially when we teach others how to run businesses, the single most important contribution we can make is to cultivate the "entrepreneurial imagination" (Chia, 1996).

Similarly, imagination supports family creativity. For example, the popularity of the Soule Mama blog[5] demonstrated that there is great interest in fostering family creativity by enhancing imagination (see also the book by the author of this blog: *The Creative Family: How to Encourage Imagination and Nurture Family*; Soule, 2008).

Following are some of the guided imagery scripts I've used in my practice, in various settings.

The Empowerer's Role: How to Boost Creativity

With these tools, let's look at methods to enhance a group's creativity:

---

[3] Mostly in a group setting, though sometimes also within individual therapy.
[4] Sometimes also called mental imagery, neuroimaging, or visualization
[5] www.soulemama.com; retrieved February 24, 2017.

Enriched Environment

Like a farmer sowing seeds, an Empowerer who wants to "grow" creativity within a group should work to create an environment ripe with opportunities to enjoy music, laughter, fun, and dancing. He or she should also support a variety of ways to look at ideas and problems from a distance, through metaphors and other means, such as guided imagery. All of this contributes to a so-called Enriched Environment (EE). Multiple studies indicate that EE – a totally noninvasive effort – has powerful effects on brain plasticity. In its many forms it evidently supports child and adult brain development, under normal as well as physiological and pathological conditions (Rosenzweig & Benett, 1966; Van Praag *et al.*, 2000; Diamond, 2011; Sale *et al.*, 2014).

Rituals and Metaphors

Another way to augment creativity is through rituals. Fun rituals you can incorporate into your personal or family life, as well as your business, include brainstorming and brain-writing. Try brain-writing before brainstorming. Have everyone in the group write down his or her ideas on a topic. Then have the group read and discuss them. Interestingly, research has shown that brain-writing groups generate more original ideas than traditional brainstorming groups do (Thompson, 2013).

Rituals can also involve games related to metaphorizing. One to play with your family is to compare an encountered problem (e.g., a noisy neighbor) with a book. Have everyone complete the sentence: "If the problem with this guy were a book, then this book would…" One might say, "This book would have stiff and thick covers," or "This book would be heavy," or "This book would be written in unreadable fonts." This game may be played in various forms, for example, comparing someone to an animal ("What if this person were an animal?"), etc.

Let's imagine a group of overly territorial participants discussing competencies rather than future strategies. The game is to compare the group to a river. Members share such metaphors as "If this group were a river it would be blocked by a dam," or "It would flow slowly, often as if moving in circles," etc. Then someone suggests, "This river would encounter several obstacles, splitting each time into small separate streams." A discussion follows. Should the group break down into smaller groups or even individuals? This "lone ranger" vision seems inappropriate, as the task requires group work; however, many single-stream visions can mobilize the group to work out new modes of efficient collaboration.

If you've encountered a problem in your business, let's say with declining market demand for your products, you might start your team meeting with an icebreaker. Ask everyone to imagine the current market as a forest: "Close your eyes and try to identify the density of trees, the smells, the sounds. You reach a really wild part of the forest with thick bushes. How do you find your way back? Do you see clues or tracks? Hear sounds? Now imagine returning to a safer place in the forest. What does it look like?" The group's answers can be illuminating and serve as an inspiring warm-up before a serious discussion.

Haiku Poems

The more pressing the encountered problem is, the more important it will be to create some distance. That's a tall order, given our inclination to be preoccupied with problems or obstacles at hand. The natural tendency is to confront the problem head-on, jumping into it at the start of the meeting. However, this decreases the distance and increases the likelihood that group members will fixate on the problem, become overwhelmed, and have trouble thinking outside the box. In such situations some business counselors advise starting the meeting with a specific icebreaker, such as writing haiku poems[6] and then reading them out loud. In some cases participants will be asked to write poems that reflect the current business situation,[7] but often it's advisable to avoid the situation at hand and, for example, write about nature. After such a haiku round, the team will have gained some distance, which, we know, augments creativity.

Dancing the Problem

Another way to increase distance is dancing. In my practice I sometimes use dancing to reflect a difficult family or team situation. In one case the problem reported by a young, vigorous team was that the director often agreed with their new ideas initially, but after some time would back away or change course. A communication analysis revealed the following

---

[6] For some recommendations for writing haiku see: www.linkedin.com/pulse/can-you-write-your-business-haiku-dave-jarecki; February 24, 2017.
[7] See www.haikupoemsandpoets.com/poems/business_haiku_poems for some examples of business-related haikus; retrieved February 24, 2017.

recurrent sequence: The young team was usually represented by the deputy director, who would present the new ideas to the director. The director would react positively, but then he would share the new ideas with his secretary, who was conservative and skeptical and would advise against them. That would prompt the director to change his mind.

The verbatim analysis of the communication dynamics didn't move matters forward; it was cumbersome, and people became mired in the process. So I asked them whether, instead of talking, they might want to dance their problems. I proposed that they reflect, in a choreographic sequence, the consecutive steps: The deputy approaches the director, who likes the idea, then consults his secretary, and ultimately rejects the idea. Someone volunteered to "play" the director, and two others took the roles of the deputy and the secretary. My role was that of choreographer, transforming the action into simple *pas de trois*, in which the "deputy" made a body move toward the "director," reaching out with his arm; the "director" turned and bent toward the "deputy," and in the next *pas* turned to the "secretary," moving his hand toward her. This sequence repeated from the beginning, with someone simulating a drumbeat and the rest clapping rhythmically. The "dancers" gradually danced the sequence more and more fluently, becoming involved in the bodily representation of the real-life dynamics.

As a result the group became energized and approached the problem with humor and joy. The main actors easily gained insight on the patterns that had them trapped. At that moment I asked whether they would like to repeat the dance with some modifications. In the new dance, after consulting the secretary, the director moved back to the deputy, pulling slightly on the secretary's hand. The dancers, accompanied by joyful drums and clapping, made everybody laugh and easily overcome old patterns.

So, what happened? First, the participants could look at their problems from a distant perspective. Second, dancing and music enhanced creativity. Third, some difficult insights became naturally acceptable without verbal or intellectual analysis, which usually triggers resistance. If the flow is on the level of metaphorized simulation, conditions become much easier to understand and digest.

Two Thousand Years Ago, Two Thousand Miles Away

In some cases guided imagery techniques may also help enhance creativity. Some years ago I was working with a family with multiple problems. After a few sessions the tension increased and communication stalled. I proposed that the family members close their eyes and follow my guidance:

> Imagine that your family is part of an Indian tribe, two thousand years ago, two thousand miles away, in the Rockies. Families, each in their tipi, are preparing for a gathering in which they will have their turn to step out to the center of the circle and dance their family dance. You already hear the drum (pretending a drumbeat on my desk). You are preparing with your family for this dance. Who is doing what? Who is painting whose face? Who helps others to dress up? What are you doing? Take your time to imagine. Slowly you walk out to the center. Imagine who walks first, who joins whom, where you are. Your family sits down, observing others dancing. You hear the drum. Now it is your family's turn. You all step forward and start to dance. How is this dance shaped? Who is where? Who leads? Who is closer to whom? Who dances at a distance? Take time to imagine. Now slowly come back to reality and open your eyes.

The discussion that followed was lively. All wanted to share what they had imagined. The scenes they imagined were metaphors of their real-life relationships. In one the father was leading, and the daughter was dancing close to the father. The older daughter envisioned her younger sister dancing in isolation, and reflected that she never realized that she was sort of acting out. The mother saw the son as a bit helpless and was willing to support him in the dance by holding his hand. The son reflected that this is what really happens: Mom never accepted him as being self-supportive. The family engaged in a lively but friendly discussion, based on their choreographic images. In an easy atmosphere, without any pressure, their hidden patterns, thoughts, and feelings were revealed – being projected thousands of years backward and thousands of miles away. The metaphor and the distance, in addition to humor, joy, and envisioned dance, opened the way to insights that, otherwise, were too painful to verbalize and accommodate.

Physical Activities That Stimulate Brain Plasticity

Finally, for my own development and for the people I work with, I occasionally use the Feldenkrais approach,[8] which can trigger new neuronal connections and allows people to rediscover their innate capacity for graceful, efficient movement that can enhance functioning in many aspects of life.[9]

---

[8] Also recommended is Alexander technique, see: www.alexandertechnique.com/at.htm; retrieved February 24, 2017.
[9] See: International Feldenkrais Federation at http://feldenkrais-method.org/archive/feldenkrais-method/ also www.uta-ruge.de/what_is_feldenkrais_en.html; retrieved February 24, 2017.

The idea is to replace old, habitual movement patterns stored in the memory with new sets of movements. This is done gently, instead of through intensive and potentially damaging stretching and bending. Practitioners are advised to stop if they feel pain and continue the sequence in their imagination. Simply imagining certain movements is enough for the brain to initiate new neuronal connections. The new sequences, whether performed or imagined, stimulate new connections, similar to those formed in a child's brain to accommodate new movements. The limits, according to Feldenkrais, are mostly controlled by your brain. Hence the transformation should take place in your brain, providing new patterns of movement.

Feldenkrais approach has also proved efficient in therapy to treat eating disorders and other problems, by repairing impaired connections between the cortex and the body (Laumer *et al.*, 1997).

My practice-based conjecture is that intertwining the Feldenkrais techniques with metaphorizing and guided imagery can stimulate plasticity on various levels and lead to a generalized "creative state of mind" and enhanced "creative drive." Ideally the Empowerer would use a combination of these techniques to create a diverse Enriched Environment. Understanding the basic components opens the field for an Empowerer to explore and find his or her own ways and methods.

Chapter Coda

- How music, humor, play, and dance augment creativity
- The critical role of temporal and spatial distance
- The magic of metaphors and guided imagery
- How the Empowerer can help to enhance creativity
- The role of Enriched Environment
- Rituals and examples of metaphors and guided imagery
- Dancing your problem
- Physical activities and the Feldenkrais approach

CHAPTER 15

Empowering as a Lifestyle

Aging is an issue of mind over matter. If you don't mind, it doesn't matter.

Mark Twain

This chapter focuses on Empowerers and their relationships with people who are in some way dependent on them. Life is full of opportunities to help others grow by adopting an empowering attitude. The two instances we have chosen – child rearing and aging – are probably the most obvious.

Empowering Child Rearing

One of the most effective ways to empower a child is to create a playful environment. Playful activities establish more connections among neurons, particularly in the frontal lobe – the part of the brain responsible for uniquely human higher mental functions (Pellis & Pellis, 2009). Paradoxically, at some ages, play results in greater learning than teaching does. Studies that compared children who started formal literacy lessons at age five with those who started at age seven document that early formal learning doesn't improve reading development and may even be regressive. In a follow-up study it turned out that, by the time the children were eleven, there was no difference in reading ability level between these two groups. However, those who started learning at age five developed less positive attitudes to reading and showed poorer text comprehension than children who started later (Whitebread & Bingham, 2013).

More generally, creating an enriched environment for children contributes to enhanced brain plasticity (Rosenzweig *et al.,* 1966; Van Praag *et al.,* 2000; Sale *et al.,* 2014). And of course, the benefits of creating open space for creative play with some well-defined boundaries are well established (e.g., Gray, 2013).[1] An Empowerer provides an environment for the child that encourages safe exploration of ideas. Games to play include brainstorming activities, in which there's no such thing as a bad idea, and children may enjoy coming up with more or less "crazy" concepts. An Empowerer's role in this situation is to refrain from judgment or criticism while the child shares new ideas. On the contrary, Empowerers teach children to think in terms of "no limits" (Goss, 2011; Frost, 2014).

Another game that creates an explorative environment is Synectics, in which the players find links between distant and seemingly unrelated ideas. (This is divergent thinking, which is at the core of creativity.) You might make a strange idea familiar through the use of metaphors and analogies (Gordon, 1961), e.g., imagine, tell stories, and draw the idea that umbrellas don't need to be held, but instead, fly over your head and follow you wherever you go. What if they also want to follow you to the classroom and hang over children's heads? How would they behave at a basketball game? Would they bump against each other? Synectics creates a positive emotional climate that allows children to use analogies and metaphors to construct creative explanations and narratives through collaborative discussion (Faulkner, 2011).

The Paradox of the Empowerer

A stimulating, supportive, and positively challenging environment can do much to enhance and maintain creativity (Amabile, 1996). Empowerment is more about creating a specific kind of milieu than facilitating concrete activities, setting expectations, or distributing rewards. And, in fact, expectations and rewards can counter creativity (Amabile, 1996). It's true that, in some cases, rewards can empower, as acknowledgment for an original performance, for example. However, rewards for conventional performance can decrease intrinsic motivation and creativity (Eisenberger & Shanock, 2003).

To be an Empowerer, one must radiate support for exploration, fun, and joy, while establishing well-defined values and limits that help keep the empowered safe. Limits should be communicated as rarely as possible, only if necessary, and then with emphasis. Children should feel that the

[1] Web sites on this topic worth exploring include http://health.howstuffworks.com/pregnancy-and-parenting/teenage-health/how-to-know-when-to-give-your-child-space.htm and http://talkingtotoddlers.com/parenting-articles-tips-and-advice/successful-parenting; retrieved February 26, 2017.

Empowerer is at ease in the situation but reliable, with the strength and structure to serve as a support.

Critical to empowering children is forging their intrinsic motivation (Amabile, 1996). This is probably the central paradoxical challenge for the Empowerer: to stimulate endogenous processes with exogenous interventions.

In our previous book *Social Entrepreneurship: Theory and Practice* (Praszkier & Nowak, 2012), we argued that social entrepreneurs master this paradox by building an enabling environment where endogenous dynamics can unfold, instead of applying hands-on management, or teaching, preaching, or inviting experts, etc. (preconditions for complex processes). The same tactics can be used with children. But how?

Luckily there are some hints for nurturing intrinsic motivation:

- Provide a feeling of meaningfulness. Even when children are playing with sand or paints, you can add a background story (e.g., that a princess can be liberated if someone builds a nice sand castle or paints a beautiful tree). Use metaphors or fairy-tales to spark their imaginations. For example, ask them to figure out how to save their brothers and sisters lost in a forest that is home to a wicked witch.
- Make sure they always have a choice. Map out several ways to go, depict a choice of what is to be built or painted, give options for ways to choose how to defend themselves from a bad troll, etc.
- Give them a feeling of competence. They should be the masters of their actions, both in simple play as well as in more complicated adventures of the imagination.
- Allow them to experience and enjoy their progress. Celebrate each stage of building a sand castle, or sing a song together after the tree is finally painted. Use metaphors and narratives to mark the achievement of milestones along the way.

These four suggestions are presented in a book titled *Intrinsic Motivation at Work* (Thomas, 2009), which describes their use in a business environment. But they can be just as easily applied within family and social structures.

Guided imagery games can also spur endogenous change, through diverse and breathtaking feats of the imagination. These techniques are especially recommended for sick or disabled children, as there are no physical limits to the expansion of imagination.

Teresa Ogrodzińska from Poland

One example of an effective parent–child activity is the Playgroup model, initiated and implemented across Poland and beyond by Teresa

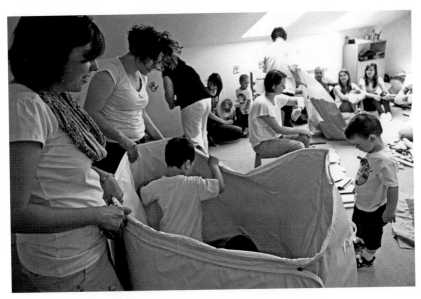

Figure 31. Parents playing with children 1.

Ogrodzińska.[2] In a Playgroup parents and their children play in small groups, with guidance and inspiration from play animators. Both the parents and the children benefit from these coordinated activities. The parents report that they not only learn how to interact with kids in general, but also discover things about their own children. And research conducted right after the program and in follow-up sessions two and four months later documented that children participating in this program gained significant social competencies[3] (Roehborn, 2012; see Figures 31–33).

Aging in Harmony

In 2008, I received a call from young business leaders asking me to create and facilitate a program to help them cope with their elderly parents. It soon became apparent that despite the fact that they were all young, healthy, athletic, and successful and developing their professional careers, issues the older generation faced were also present in their own lives. They reported multiple problems, e.g., how to energize or activate their aging

[2] See: www.ashoka.org/en/fellow/teresa-ogrodzi%C5%84ska#intro.
[3] Understood as empathy, tolerance, and scrupulousness (after Sarason, 1981).

Figure 32. Parents playing with children 2.

parents. It became obvious that building a path to a harmonious future starts early, and one's lifestyle in youth can foster healthy and happy aging. I called this program Aging in Harmony. Participants learned not only how to help their parents be healthier and happier in their later years, but also how to care, in advance, for their own future well-being. They did so using an Empowering approach.

The challenge of how to enjoy one's preparation for harmonious aging as well as one's twilight years seems universal. Those who meet the challenge may find the second half of life to be as gripping and enjoyable as the first. Aging doesn't have to include absentmindedness or loss of memory. Numerous studies have shown that a decline in mental function has nothing to do with aging, in and of itself. It's the lifestyle you choose that largely determines how your brain ages (Majd, 2012). Aging is a complex process, involving both physiological and psychological dimensions. And our attitude toward aging is the leading driver of the way we age (Carstensen et al., 2006; Hess, 2006). Paradoxically, declining activeness may not be a consequence of aging, so much as aging may be a consequence of limiting activity (as Mark Twain's quote at the start of this chapter suggests).

Eric Ericson, known for developing the stages of lifelong psychosocial development, focuses in his book *Vital Involvement in Old Age* (Erickson *et al.*, 1986) on the optimal model for harmonious aging. He asserts that there should be something worthwhile and desirable to do, the ability and resources to accomplish it, and, probably most importantly, a sufficient will or positive attitude.

Moving from a theoretical model to what older people actually think showed, in one study, that, for them, health meant doing something meaningful, while maintaining a balance between abilities and challenges. They also mentioned as important both appropriate external resources and a positive personal attitude (Bryant *et al.*, 2001). This was affirmed through an analysis of community-based programs that engage the older (sixty-five-plus) generation in cultural activities. The results reveal strikingly positive change[4] including health stabilization and improvement, despite the fact that most participants had surpassed average life expectancy. This demonstrates that these community-based cultural programs for older adults appear to reduce risk factors, by improving participants' general and mental health and deepening social engagement (Cohen, 2006).

Nijole Arbaciauskiene from Lithuania

An illustrative example of an Empowering approach to aging is the story of a Lithuanian engineer, Nijole Arbaciauskiene,[5] who worked for forty years in a research institute. A year before retiring she decided to make the next period of her life valuable both for herself and for society. To prepare she founded the Seniors Initiatives Centre[6] to improve quality of life for older people through creativity, tolerance, and positive motivation. The center helps seniors adapt to changes in modern society and encourages their self-expression and participation in social life by engaging them in volunteerism and matching their lifelong experience and knowledge with the needs of the community. The center also encourages international interaction among all age groups. To facilitate involvement it helps participants learn other languages and become technologically proficient. Needless to say, the center also promotes physical activities for the seniors (see Figure 33).

---

[4] The intervention group (i.e., those involved in intensive participatory art programs) compared to a control group (not involved in intensive cultural programs).

[5] See: www.ashoka.org/en/fellow/nijole-arbaciauskiene#intro; I interviewed her in January 2000.

[6] See: www.senjoru-centras.lt/en/; retrieved February 24, 2017.

Figure 33. Senior citizens playing and dancing.

These programs, at their essence, improve seniors' health and well-being by maintaining and enhancing brain plasticity. In Chapter 7 we mentioned three kinds of brain plasticity: *synaptic plasticity* (the propensity for creating new neuronal connections), *neurogenesis plasticity* (stem cells reproducing functioning brain cells), and *functional compensatory plasticity* (where parts of the brain take over for other parts that aren't functioning well). Interestingly, new research has shown that all three paths function regardless of age. The normal aging process leaves most mental functions intact, and may even provide the brain with unique advantages that form the basis of wisdom. Dopamine plays the critical role by influencing the formation of new neurons deep in the center of the adult brain. Once formed these neurons move to areas of the brain associated with higher brain function (Shelton, 2013).

An enriched environment that empowers intrinsic improvements to neuronal health through brain exercise could include:[7]

[7] Based on Shelton (2013), on the research mentioned in Chapter 14, and my own professional experience.

- Learning a new language
- Reading books or articles, ideally from diverse fields
- Working on puzzles
- Thinking about or solving problems distant from one's own area of expertise
- Pursuing a hobby or a new work skill
- Playing a musical instrument and/or listening to music
- Traveling and exploring new cultures and nature
- Writing (e.g., memoires, novels, or poems)
- Dancing in a way that requires synchronizing with your partner (probably the most important)
- Having fun (but not disregarding, undermining, or hurting others)
- Playing simulation games (especially exchanging roles with grandchildren)
- Exercising imagination (especially if one experiences physical limitations)
- Volunteering (e.g., helping children to understand the world, sharing one's own experiences with primary school children)
- Doing something outside one's routine (e.g., organizing an unexpected family event)

The most important recommendation, which touches all of these activities, is that these activities should be performed with empathy. We've mentioned the critical role of empathy, and it's important to add that empathetic relationships (e.g., "reading" and reacting to a dance partner's bodily messages while sending one's own "readable" messages) enhance the brain's functions.[8] Empathy is also positively related to creativity (Carlozzi *et al.*, 1995) and can be explored through games that encourage "getting into another's shoes," thereby augmenting creativity (Dani, 2012).

The Empowerer and the Family

So how do Empowering methods link child rearing and aging?

Empowering others using methods delineated here also engages the "helper's" creative mind, and in doing so, paves the way for harmonious aging. The complexity of life's processes transgresses all possible borders and stages. Laughing with children affects your own brain. The ever-changing cerebral cortex is powerfully shaped by life experiences. An enriched

---

[8] Dancing integrates different brain parts and activities at the same time; some claim that frequent dancing can reduce the risk of dementia more than 70 percent (Majd, 2012).

environment affects the brain, and hence behavior, regardless of age or the role one plays (Diamond, 2011). In that way, Empowerers enhance their own creativity willy-nilly and prepare themselves for harmonious aging.

Chapter Coda

- The role of an Empowerer in child rearing
- The paradox of an Empowerer: acting from outside (exogenously) to empower people (create an endogenous process)
- The Empowerer and aging in harmony
- The Empowerer and the family

PART III

Future

SECTION 6

How to Foresee the Future

Don't make predictions, especially when they concern the future.
Samuel Goldwyn

One of the oldest human desires is to be able to predict the future. In
the Hellenistic period the temple in Delphi was perceived to be the center of the world. Throughout ancient times generations of oracles were
kept busy as people traveled to Delphi to receive prophecies or consult the
famous high priestess, Pythia, before making their important decisions.
Interestingly, in modern times there is still a longing for the ancient proph-
esies reflected, for example, in the names of the forecasting method developed during the Cold War – the "Delphi method" – and a well-known IT
corporation – Oracle.

However, we have become increasingly embedded in complex systems,
and unpredictability is intrinsic to complexity (see Chapter 5). The multiple feedback loops that influence each other may cause, at some point, a
sudden jump. A market product may unexpectedly become trendy (e.g.,
3D printing), or some prosperous company may suddenly go bankrupt.
For decades KODAK was a market leader in the paper-photo industry.
At the end of the 1990s, it had 170,000 employees and sold 85 percent of
all photo paper worldwide. Within a few years the company was broke
(Goldman, 2016). At the time of KODAK's rapid growth, could anyone
have predicted that in a few years paper pictures would be replaced by
digital photography?

The ancient world was comparatively simple. Would Pythia manage
complexity? Would she be able to give us advice on whether to invest in
the growing industry of self-driving cars? Take, for example, the intricacy
of some 2016 predictions (Goldman, ibid):

In 2018 the first self-driving cars will appear for the public. Around 2020,
the complete industry will start to be disrupted. You won't want to own a
car anymore. You will call a car with your phone, and it will show up at
your location and drive you to your destination. You won't need to park it,

only pay for the distance driven. And you can be productive while driving. Our kids will never get a driver's license and will never own a car. It will change the cities, because we will need 90–95% fewer cars –. We can transform former parking lots into parks. Each year, 1.2 million people die in car accidents worldwide. With autonomous driving we now have one accident every 100,000 km, which will drop to one accident in 10 million km. That will save a million lives each year.

Most car companies may become bankrupt. Traditional car companies will try the evolutionary approach and just build a better car, while tech companies (Tesla, Apple, Google) will take the revolutionary approach and build a computer on wheels.

And what if Goldman is wrong? What if self-driving cars are too easy to be taken over by hackers or terrorists who might use them to cause massive catastrophes? Or what if, instead of cars, the real market boom happens in the field of flying vehicles? The *Forbes* article on flying cars sounds quite compelling (Guerrini, 2014).

Complexity challenges us to think differently. Samuel Goldwyn's bon mot at the beginning and the title of this chapter suggest that the real way to deal with the future is to play with it. But, before we look at the ways to *play* with the future, let's review more traditional methods for predicting it.

This section will focus both on the traditional approach to predicting the future (Chapter 16) as well as some unconventional methods (Chapter 17).

Exploring the Future

The Adjacent Possible

The Empowerer should be well embedded in the present but also "feel" the future as something close by – the *adjacent possible*. Professor Stuart Kauffman coined this term to define a set of things that is only one step away from actual existence (Kauffman, 2000). The space of unexplored possibilities includes all kinds of things that are easily imagined and expected. But it's more complex than that. It's also full of things that are entirely unexpected and hard to imagine. Each innovation changes the landscape of future possibilities, so that, at every instant, the adjacent possible is also changing (Emerging Technology, 2017).

The adjacent possible is fascinating to explore, especially given that the most effective way to predict the future in a complex environment is to simulate, imagine, play, or dance it, rather than to apply typical "A to B" logic.

Forecasting

The Delphi model, one of the first large-scale prediction methods, was initiated during the Cold War in the 1950s and 1960s, by the global think tank RAND Corporation. Operating under the assumption that personal interactions positively influence intellectual outcomes and that group judgments are typically better than individual judgments, RAND used a panel of experts for its prediction model.

First, each expert was asked to give his or her opinion on a critical issue, e.g., the possibility of an enemy attack. Then a facilitator shared these opinions with the group, without attribution. This process was repeated until consensus emerged (Dalkey, 1968; Brown, 1968). The method was used for a few decades, though it had some limitations: e.g., it relied on scientific methods, neglecting intuition, and the group's consensus opinion wasn't always better than an individual expert's prediction (Pill, 1971). Moreover, the experts used their knowledge of the past to project into the future – but new knowledge often develops at the fringes, not necessarily linearly evolving from the experts' current knowledge (Pill, 1971; Mason, 2016).

It's important to note that people tend to be terrible forecasters; for example, one study documented that experts' predictions are only slightly better than mere guesses (Tetlock & Gardner, 2016). Also, many scenario analysts emphasize that scenarios are hypothetical constructs and what they create doesn't necessarily represent reality (Kosow & Gaßner, 2008).

On the other hand, one of the initiators of Shell Oil Company's large-scale future scenarios analysis of the 1970s reflected that

> forecasts are not always wrong; more often than not, they can be reasonably accurate. And that's what makes them so dangerous. They're usually constructed on the assumption that tomorrow's world will be much like today's. They often work because the world doesn't always change. But sooner or later forecasts will fail when they are needed most: in anticipating major shifts in the business environment that make whole strategies obsolete. (Wack, 1985)

Keeping this (and the complexity theory of sudden jumps) in mind let's look at some other forecasting options.

Simulations

If you can't conjure up the vision of the evolving future then you can build models that might approximately reflect possible scenarios. This model building is called simulation, defined as the imitation of the operation of a real-world process or system over time (Banks *et al.*, 2014). Following are some examples.

Computer Simulations

Computer simulation can be run on a single computer or a network of computers, to reproduce the behavior of a system (Strogatz, 2007).

As discussed, complexity theory describes how interactions on a lower level may result in a new emergent phenomenon on a higher level. In business and in life one small and seemingly meaningless individual decision and action can cause significant consequences for large groups. This was compellingly illustrated by Thomas C. Schelling (2006).[1] One of

[1] First edition in 1978.

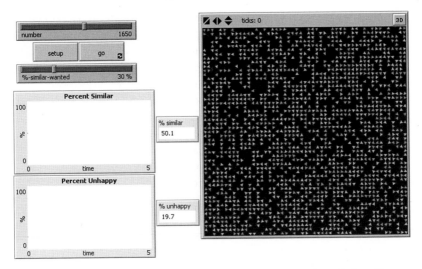

Figure 34. Initial setup (indicated by the "ticks-0" message, above the board).

his well-known examples deals with segregation. Schelling showed that slight (though far from malicious) preferences for neighbors of the same race eventually led to a completely segregated population. This discovery prompted the introduction of formal prediction methods in the social sciences and the design of the well-known Schelling simulation. The computerized simulation program adjusted pixels on a grid using preset rules. Each pixel (red or green) represented the race of a community member and was programmed to have, for example, a relatively small desire to have neighbors of similar race (let's say 30 percent on a scale of 0 percent – race makes no difference to 100 percent – absolutely no neighbors of another race). To each pixel was then assigned a rule that, in each step of computing, it would attract (with 30 percent strength) pixels of similar colors and repel pixels of different colors. (See the following simulations designed by Wilensky [1997, 1999].)

Figure 34 illustrates the initial state (the board on the right), where the green and red pixels are randomly scattered. The interface (on the left) provides two scroll bars. One is for choosing the number of dwellers in the community preset – in this case 1,650. The other is the "similar desire" scroll bar, preset for 30 percent.

The "go" button starts the program. Each computer tick is a move toward 30 percent similarity around each pixel. Figure 35 reflects the results after

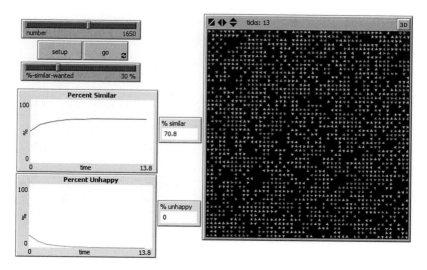

Figure 35. Islands of segregation after thirteen computer ticks.

thirteen computer ticks. Note that like colors are more closely grouped. At the same time the charts on the left display the percentage of similar colors joining together (70.8 percent) and the percentage of unhappy dwellers, i.e., those that want to be surrounded by a similar race, but are not (already 0 percent). Can you see the islands of segregation starting to form?

If we assume that one computer tick represents one year, then the prediction is that during thirteen years, community dwellers will keep moving, finally reaching the desired state of semi-isolated islands of red and similar islands of green.

Now let's see what happens if the rate of desire for a similar race is set at 70 percent (see Figure 36).

Schelling's simulation allows researchers to consider a variety of scenarios, adjusting for larger or smaller communities, or for a stronger or weaker desire to be surrounded by similar individuals. More advanced systems allow users to adjust the pace of computer ticks, to show the process evolving slowly or quickly.

Computer simulations can create a multitude of scenarios. They can model the transmission and perpetuation of a virus in a certain human population to show how many people are infected and how many may remain immune. They can forecast the dynamics of social networks, the flow of traffic on a highway, and – most familiar to us all – the weather,

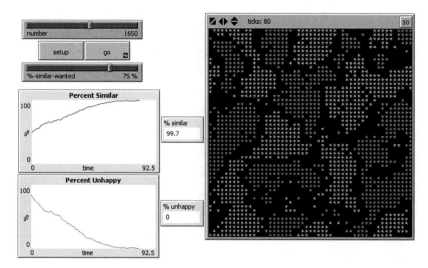

Figure 36. It took eighty ticks for the computer to reach an equilibrium with 70 percent of dwellers wanting neighbors of similar race.

knowing that prediction of weather entails a high level of complexity (and requires the fastest computers available). And especially critical are simulations of human behavior in a disaster (not possible to simulate in real life). Some see sophisticated predictive computer systems as essential. For example, Chen *et al.* (2003) claim that their nonlinear aggregation mechanisms vastly outperform both the imperfect market and the best of the experts. However, other authors doubt that this kind of computer analysis would yield a better result than feedback from a qualified group of people. In other words, good forecasting may not require powerful computers. Rather, it involves gathering evidence from a variety of sources, thinking probabilistically, working in teams, and being willing to admit error and change course (Tetlock & Gardner, 2016).

Some skepticism is warranted when we look at technological techniques to predict human behavior, but the recent development of mathematical models aimed at depicting the process of innovativeness is intriguing. For example, Loreto *et al.* (2016), drawing from Kauffman's term, developed the so-called adjacent possible model, encompassing all kinds of things that are easily imaginable and expected (called novelties), as well as things that are entirely unexpected and hard to imagine (called innovations). The former are new to the individual who finds them (e.g., newly discovered online songs), and the latter are entirely new to the world (e.g., making new comments to Wiki). The real challenge in modeling these processes is that each innovation changes the landscape of future possibilities so that, at every instant, the *adjacent possible* is changing.

Education through Simulations

Education through simulations is popular in many fields, including aircraft pilot training, which incorporates computer game, and military training, as we often see in movies. Education through simulations is also used in business, where simulations and games provide increasingly powerful and flexible educational tools (Fripp, 1993). Similar to a role-play simulation, often a scenario is played out in a simulated business environment, and the students are asked to make individual or team-based decisions. Often multiple-choice options are offered and then the scenario is played out to show the results of the decision.

These can be useful, but the world of business is changing fast. "If simulations are to remain relevant, they must keep abreast of these changes, and preferably anticipate them," says Fripp (1997).

Live Action Role-Playing (LARP) Games

In live action role-playing (LARP) games participants physically act out their characters' actions. The players pursue goals within a fictional setting representing the real world while interacting with each other in character. They create their characters' speech and movements like actors in improvisational theater (Kilgallon *et al.*, 2001).

LARPs may be played in public or private area networks, and the game may last for hours or days. There is usually no audience. Players may dress as their characters and carry appropriate props, and sometimes the setting is decorated to resemble a real-world environment (Tychsen *et al.*, 2005). Arrangers, called game masters (GMs), determine the rules and setting of a LARP. "In essence, the GM creates the magical circle around the game" (Tychsen *et al.*, 2005, p. 215).

LARP games have become quite popular since the 1980s. There are still multiple available LARP scenarios,[2] LARP summer camps[3] and an

[2] See https://wiki.rpg.net/index.php/LARP_Scenarios; retrieved February 24, 2017.
[3] www.wayfinderexperience.com/; retrieved February 24, 2017.

operating Larpwriter Summer School.[4] So-called larping is used for entertainment, as well as for social good: e.g., social activists are using LARPs to foster empathy among adults, who act out scenarios of real world injustices in order to spotlight emotions and complexities inherent in social or culture clashes (Graham, 2016).

For some people LARPing has become a primary social outlet. Some participants at the annual Pennsylvania-based Alliance game have attended for several years, and every year the Alliance sees fifty to one hundred new faces (Jacobs, 2014). LARPing can become so engaging that many games issue warnings, such as:

- Always keep IC (In Character, the character you play in the fictional world) and OOC (Out of Character, the real world character) knowledge/motivations separate.
- Don't conflate player's (your personal) and character's (from the fictional world) success!

An interesting account of LARPing's popularity and some good illustrations can be found on the Business Insider Web site (e.g., Jacobs, 2014).

Chapter Coda

- Forecasting methods of the 1950s and 1960s, especially the Delphi approach
- Computer simulations, e.g., Schelling's segregation simulation
- Live action role-playing games (LARPs)

---

[4] http://larpschool.blogspot.com/p/mixing-desk.html; retrieved February 24, 2017.

CHAPTER 17

Playing and Dancing the Future

From our perspective, using LARP pragmatics as a means to explore the future seems overstructured. The game manuals have more than seventy pages of detailed instructions for the particular characters as well as for the game master (GM), and the margin for improvisation is preset and limited. However, any kind of future trends analysis is invaluable. For example, the prestigious Organization for Economic Co-operation and Development (OECD) says that in scenario development, trend analysis can be a powerful tool for erasing prejudices and opening minds by exploring and combining far-reaching developments that might affect the social environment.[1]

Here we propose a handful of future-oriented, open, flexible, and adaptable games that may be played at home, with your kids, relatives, and friends, but also in business, in various settings.

An important caveat for business play: The following games are intended to complement existing techniques for exploring market trends, e.g., computer simulations. They should be treated as one of the forecasting methods, reinforcing other feasible techniques. Indirectly they could serve as a method for team bonding and building, providing a comfortable forum for togetherness and the release of instinctual (precognitive) hunches. Most people have some intuitional cognition but are often suppressed by fear of criticism and ridicule.

The future games presented here could serve either as a routine, perhaps as a once-a-month think tank exercise, or as an icebreaker preceding a discussion to consider information from various sources, including computer simulations and soft intelligence. In this case, it's best if they are played by a diverse team, with representation from various divisions, such as engineering, R&D, marketing, finances, and sales.

---

[1] www.oecd.org/site/schoolingfortomorrowknowledgebase/futuresthinking/trends/trendanalysisasamethod.htm; retrieved February 24, 2017.

These games can be also played ad hoc, when needed, to support a particular project. For example, the process of preparing high-level requirements for a new product may include future games that explore the group's instinctual potential.

Instinct-Mining Games

I believe, following Mason (2016), that major changes can originate with people at the fringes who surprise us with their ideas, developed far away from the mainstream. Often these ideas are introduced by so-called positive deviants, as described by Sternin: "In communities throughout the world, there are a few 'deviant' individuals whose uncommon behaviors or practices enable them to … find better solutions to pervasive problems than their neighbors with whom they share the same resource base" (Sternin, 2002, p. 58). By seeing solutions where others don't positive deviants spread and sustain needed change (Pascale *et al.*, 2010).

Hence, while not ignoring the mainstream lines, we should also look around the corners, seeking potential nontypical solutions. We need to step into the shoes of positive deviants. To do this we need to be creative. Typical LARP scenarios leave just a small margin for your own expression, presetting multiple rules and assignments to each character. To be creative we need to stimulate the brain's plasticity and new neuronal connections and have a lot of joy, fun, music, and dance (following recommendations from Chapter 14).

To explore the future we should not reject "crazy" ideas but look openly for something based on imagination, something enjoyable and possibly – danceable (see the following discussion). As a consequence you may become open to whimsical ideas. (Remember serendipity from Chapter 8?) Here, some might say, "Hold on; exploring the future is a serious undertaking, and you can't make fun of it." My answer is that the more serious the need for exploring the future is, the more fun you should have doing it, and, in fact, serious future explorations usually yield poor results.

Among the most important functions of this kind of game are reaching and exploring our instincts and thus discovering "gems," often well-hidden and unapproachable. We want to uncover and release the power of intuition, which embraces lifelong experience as well as unexpected and nonobvious insights. In that way we are entering an instinct-mining experience.

Move the Narratives to the Future

As we look at a handful of ideas to adapt and modify, it's important to remember that *distance* and *metaphors* help to enhance creative thinking. As we move into the future, we should try metaphorized scenarios that are spatially and temporally distant. And the further we "project" our narratives the better.

The field is open for your own exploration, and you may probe a variety of mutations. Following are three creative methods for predicting the future: future theater, guided imagery, and dancing the future. They should be seen more as a source of inspiration than as a script to follow. Consider whom you would choose as the GM or whether to involve a smaller group or the entire team in the process of preparing the outlines.

Also keep in mind that these scenarios kill two birds with one stone. First, they enable "instinct mining" and exploring imagination; second, they boost individual as well as group creativity. In this way a helpful feedback loop may develop between instinct mining and creativity, reinforcing both. Additionally, these games may contribute to team building.

Future Theater

Meet with the team to design a scenario related to how they imagine a situation might evolve in the next three to five years. In this scenario people may stay with their real-life positions and/or introduce some modifications. Perhaps in the future someone will retire and be replaced by a new hire. Another might marry and move to another city. In that vein, game participants should create fictional newcomers to the group. Try various mutations of the game, e.g., one with all participants maintaining their current positions, and the other with roles changing. Perhaps someone plays the role of the boss, and the boss plays the role of a subordinate. You can also create a scenario around upheavals affecting your company.

At some point you might modify the scenario and invite more staff members to fill some external roles, i.e., your competitors, strategic partners, etc. Include some "geek" characters – those who explore the fringes or peripheries for whimsical, but potentially valuable, ideas.

Future theater lets you play various variations of envisioned future situations and build new scenarios on the most useful fragments drawn and merged from what was played before.

As you may remember, horizontal communication augments serendipity and creativity, in this case, helping to explore the future. You may also assume that embedded in some of the played out scenarios will be real forecasts.

Guided Imagery

In Chapter 14 we presented a creativity-enhancing guided imagery technique for use with a family. This method can also be useful for business or social sectors, with the idea of "projecting" the team into the future.

Following is an example. However, you should use your own imagination to modify and adapt it.

To begin, the GM asks everyone to close his or her eyes, sit comfortably, and imagine the venture in three years. How would the office design look? How will people be dressed? What roles will the team members play?

Imagine that everybody is preparing for a strategic meeting. You can sense some tension. Reports on competitors' possible plans will be discussed. Imagine the meeting in the conference room. Who is sitting where? Who is facilitating the discussion?

The first person (who?) gives an account of rumors he or she has heard about a competitor's secret plans. It's new information that could be low-hanging fruit for your group. Try to imagine what that could be.

During the discussion someone (who?) mentions another weird rumor: A group of students is preparing something they're keeping in deep secrecy. The person giving this account tried to talk to one of the students while hanging out in a bar, but didn't get far. Imagine the team's discussion that followed the report.

The GM then tells all the participants to return slowly to the room and open their eyes then share with the group what they've imagined. The conjecture is that the individuals might have embedded in their imaginations some real "gems," which are easier to tease out without the pressure of current reality.

One important caveat: To detach people's imagination from the current reality, it's important to focus on what the future looks like – the décor, how people are dressed, methods of communication, etc. Even the most mundane detail could spark inspiration, so everything matters.

Dancing the Future

We've talked about how dance augments creativity and used the example of difficult relationships among a director, deputy director, and secretary transformed into choreography. Similarly, you may also dance to predict the future. A conclusion drawn from my professional experience is that everything can be translated into choreography. You just extract the essence of each reaction and "translate" it into a move. Next you do the same with the response, reflecting it by assigning it another characteristic (metaphorical) move. The set of those metaphorical moves makes the choreography. A "master choreographer" can help – not a real dance professional, rather someone from your team who likes and understands dancing. This person can harmonize all the moves into a dance.

You can use dance to conjure whatever is currently needed. This could be a search for innovation, understanding that somewhere out there novel ideas are ready to sprout. In that case, some team members may dance like mystics cooking up arcane "mixtures," while others can dance a search team looking for ideas just around the corner and out of sight. The dance could also be launched into the future as a means to explore ideas of future novelties and trends. The team could reflect through dance possible future markets. Really, the creative options are limitless.

If for some reason it's not possible actually to dance, a backup option is simply to imagine particular dancing variations. Also, as mentioned in Chapter 14, simply observing dance can enhance creativity. After imaging their dance, team members can report their experiences.

Why Dancing? Why Not Traditional Discussion?

These future games may sound odd. Business is serious, after all. Resources are stressed and there's no time for nonsense or play, some might say. Why not just order a report by a future-trends expert or discuss future options in a "normal" fashion?

These are valid options, and we don't mean to suggest doing away with traditional or computational methods. On the contrary, they should complement a future-games approach. However, because the future in a complex environment may deliver highly unpredictable discontinuities, jumps, new solutions, etc., we need creativity-enhancing methods of exploration and prediction. It's also important to keep in mind that the novelties we seek may be situated around fringes, not accessible through A-to-B analytic analysis. To explore these possible "untypical" scenarios, we need both convergent and divergent thinking.

Trying to predict the future may deliver some real "gems" and opportunities indisputably worth an investment of time and resources, especially in a <u>multimethod approach</u>. For example, each future game could be followed by a regular discussion and analysis that also take into consideration the results of computer forecasting simulations. One might also consider a more methodologically strict approach: Divide the group into two teams; the first plays the future games (theater, imagination, and dance); the second may use traditional experts' analysis and computer simulations. The results of both groups could then be compared and discussed at a joint meeting.

Intuition-mining techniques are not only useful for exploring the future; they also have important indirect consequences such as boosting the propensity for creativity and preparing team members to tackle other problems creatively and generate novel initiatives (long-term result). These games can also have a lasting effect on a team's propensity for cooperation, enhanced trust, and development of social capital.

Chapter Coda

- Playing and dancing the future:
- future theater
- future choreography
- future guided imagery
- Integrating various forecasting techniques into a multimethod approach; short- and long-term consequences

Précis
The Empowering Leadership Model

> Organization charts are frozen, anachronistic photos of a work place
> that ought to be as dynamic as the external environment around you.
> If people really followed organization charts, companies would col-
> lapse. General Colin Powell

Probably the best way to sum up the content of this book is to look at
the juxtaposition of two articles: The first one is from *Harvard Business
Review*, titled "Beyond Empowerment: Building a Company of Citizens"
(Manville & Ober, 2003). It examines the Hellenistic era, when Athens
dominated the region:

Some 2,500 years ago, the city-state of ancient Athens rose to unprecedented political and economic power by giving its citizens a direct voice
and an active role in civic governance. The city's uniquely participative
system of democracy helped unleash the creativity of the Athenian people
and channel it to produce the greatest good for society. The system succeeded in bringing individual initiative and common cause into harmony.
And that is precisely the synthesis today's companies need to achieve if
they're to realize the full power of their people and thrive in the knowledge
economy.

The authors refer to the agora, which, between the sixth and first centuries BC, was the heart of the government and the judiciary, as well as a
public place of debate, and not least of all, a marketplace. The beginnings
of democracy were evident in the macroscale politics of the time, and in
the region's microscale leadership. In the fourth century BC, Epicurus
founded his "Philosophy of the Garden." The Garden was a gathering and
deliberation place open to all. Epicurus even admitted women, not as an
exception but as a rule, which was probably a first in human history. "The
circle" was a prototype for today's round table discussions and the Garden
Philosophy presumably the inspiration for later associations. For centuries Epicurus was admired for his cultivation of friendship (Long, 1986),
but disdained for his philosophy of individual pleasure and happiness.

(From our perspective we know that joy enhances creativity, so kudos to Epicurus!)

The second article, from Strategy+Business School, looks at the same agora and Philosophy of the Garden phenomena as they manifest twenty-five hundred years later:

> Self-organizing teams and participative management endow[s] people throughout an enterprise with the skills, understanding, processes, and authority they need to make their own decisions on behalf of quality and business success, instead of having all the ideas and commands flow from the top. Experiments in self-managing teams were once controversial, but they created so many solid performance gains at companies such as Procter & Gamble, Crown-Zellerbach, General Foods and General Motors that they are now in the mainstream. I have seen firsthand how powerful and profitable it can be to give people the room to design their own workflow and manage their own processes. (Sink, 2007)

Agora, the Garden Philosophy, and Sink's "giving people the room" provided inspiration for this book and prompted us to delve more deeply into the structure of this intriguing model.

The Empowering Leadership Model

To introduce the concept of Empowering Leadership, we first laid the theoretical groundwork by:

- Giving an overview of leadership styles (Chapters 1 and 2) and innovative ways of influencing people, especially through an empowering kind of charisma (Chapters 3 and 4);
- Presenting complexity theory in depth (Chapter 5), illustrated by examples of big social movements (Chapter 6) and features that make networks efficient (Chapter 8); also introducing the preconditions for endogenous change, so as to enable chaos-to-order instead of chaos-to-chaos dynamics (Chapter 10);
- Delineating the mechanism of creativity, at both the neuroscience and psychosocial levels (Chapter 7), and looking at ways to boost creativity (Chapter 14).

This set the stage for the concept of Empowering Leadership (Chapter 9), and a diverse portfolio of illustrative case studies (Chapters 11 and 12). Next we concluded that being an Empowerer delivers results not only at work but also as a life attitude (Chapters 13 and 15).

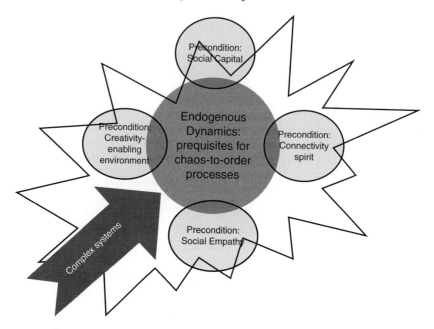

Figure 37. Preconditions for complex systems' chaos-to-order dynamics.

And finally, we delineated a variety of methods for predicting possible future scenarios in a complex environment, both computational as well as through life simulations (Chapters 16 and 17).

This makes for a complex tapestry, illustrated by Figures 37 to 39 that follow.

Inherent in a complex system is the challenge to ensure that random (chaotic) interactions of elements on the lower level will evolve into a new order on a higher level. It's especially critical because systems tend to become gradually more chaotic. Everything depends on preconditions' influencing the process. With that in mind, we presented four preconditions for complex dynamics to be channeled into the higher-level order: complexity as a way of thinking, connectivity spirit, social empathy, and a creativity-enabling environment; see Figure 37.

Next we elaborated on what constitutes an Empowering Leader, highlighting creativity and specific kinds of woven networks. See the model presented in Figure 38.

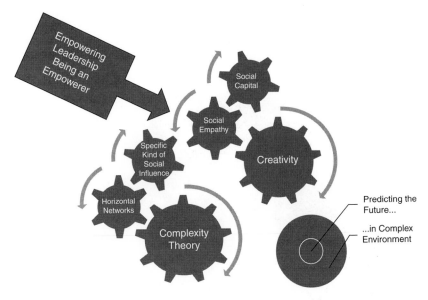

Figure 38. The Empowering Leadership model.

Adding to this intricacy one may also consider a palette of multiple feedback loops. For example, a creativity-enabling environment is a precondition for endogenous dynamics, and Empowering Leadership has (through mediating variables such as psychological empowerment and intrinsic motivation) a positive influence on creativity (Zhang & Bartol, 2010; Özaralli, 2015). Social capital may influence social empathy, and vice versa, and social empathy may foster building social capital (i.e., networks analysis, Venkatanathan *et al.*, 2013). In another example of a possible feedback loop, empathy may be interrelated with creativity as documented by the analysis of role reversal (Yaniv, 2012), which may be yet another indication for simulating future scenarios. Inevitably, a graph capturing even a fraction of these interrelations would look a bit jumbled: see Figure 39.

As we add more interconnections the result grows even messier. On the other hand, neat A-to-B boxes couldn't grasp these complex systems. (See General Powell's insight at the beginning of this Précis.)

Empowering Spirit

The downside of such a delineated model is that it looks very mechanical. Could Empowering Leaders be driven solely by efficiency? Would

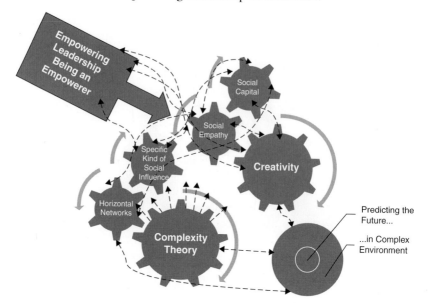

Figure 39. The snarl of interrelations.

it be possible to become empathetic and caring only as a "tool" for achieving better results? Could one foster an environment that helped people realize their potential, with the sole aim of making money? It may be important to look into the roots, i.e., the empowerment philosophy that is based on the premise that human beings have the capacity to make choices and are responsible for the consequences of their choices (Feste, 1995; Feste & Anderson, 1995). Recall that it was Thomas Jefferson who, writing the Declaration of Independence in 1776, laid the cornerstone of American political philosophy, i.e., the empowerment of people and the belief that every man should be empowered (Hess, 1984).

The leaders featured in this book all strongly believe in the potential of others. They are convinced that if people are treated with dignity and empowered to flourish, they will deliver tremendous results. Take, for example, the successful business leaders mentioned in Chapter 11, who all trust in people's empowerment as a value per se.

Bill Gore (W. L. Gore & Associates, Inc.) dreamed of a company devoted to innovation, where imagination and initiatives would flourish and people would be free to search and invent. At Gore employees are all called associates and are provided with a free space for contact, cooperation, and innovation in areas outside the firm's profile. Their horizontal interactions are encouraged, as assembled groups often produce novel ideas.

At Chris Rufer's Morning Star, all employees, regardless the education or position, are called colleagues, with no bosses and no top-down control. Rufer created a space where people said they couldn't wait for the weekend to be over, so they could get back to playing the "game of work as self-managers." Rufer believes that people, when self-driven, can achieve much more than if managed top-down.

Ricardo Semler (Semco Partners) believes that the purpose of work is to enable workers to feel good about life. He also believes that employees' freedom and satisfaction are the priority and, hence, introduces a working environment with no job titles, no written policies, no HR department, not even headquarters. Actually, he handed over total control of the company to the workforce. There is no doubt that the iconic hammocks where employees may relax whenever they want are provided not because of the drive to make money, but out of a deep respect for people and a belief in the core value of coresponsibility. Hence, the hammocks are never overused.

This goes even further: The well-known routine is performance reviews and ratings. This consumes a great deal of time and places the leader–employee relationship on a formal platform. However, the growing empowerment trend is reflected in the increasing tendency to reject quantified performance ratings. In 2015, more than fifty large firms, including GE, Juniper, and Adobe, eliminated traditional employee evaluation systems, and 70 percent of the companies on the IT market considered a similar shift (Rock & Jones, 2015a). This shift reduced the administrative burden and, most importantly, led to a dramatic increase in the frequency of manager–employee conversations (Rock & Jones, 2015b). A next step might be to abandon manager–employee structures for an all-associate (Gore) or all-colleague (Morning Star) organization and introduce a peer-to-peer reporting system.

Our look at extraordinary leaders also shows that social entrepreneurs are driven by their mission and social values. For example, Steve Bigari (Chapter 9) was a fast-advancing manager at McDonald's but postponed his profitable career in order to launch his America's Families Association to spread the idea of empowering low-income workers. Similarly, Jos de Blok from Holland resigned from a good job with a good salary to launch a movement of self-managing nurses. Ahmad Edilbi, a Syrian emigrant based in Dubai and a well-paid specialist in branding and visual communications, devoted himself utterly to launching a platform that empowered

Syrian emigrants. (Both are profiled in Chapter 12.) Ramesh Kumar from India (Chapter 4) postponed his successful career at the State Bank of India to introduce valuable, affordable, high-quality houses in the most disadvantaged rural areas by building self-governing housing communities and an appropriate bank-loan system. If we look at all seventeen stories of social entrepreneurs mentioned in this book, we'll find the same drive based on human values and the belief that people, when empowered, can "change the world."[1]

The Bottom of the Pyramid – New Apprehension

The book *The Fortune at the Bottom of the Pyramid:; Eradicating Poverty through Profits* is well known. Its author, C. K. Prahalad, posits that there can be a win–win relationship between business and the poor, especially if the business acknowledges the opportunities to sell large volume at low cost to the many "at the bottom of the pyramid" (BOP). In his vision the low-income social stratum presents astounding opportunity for seeking fortunes, on the one hand, and spreading prosperity to the aspiring poor, on the other (Prahalad, 2010).

The philosophy of Empowering Leadership opens another BOP avenue: access to the undiscovered gems and potential embedded among coworkers at all levels. Empowering people thorough an enabling environment to cocreate and take coresponsibility makes them more identified with the internalized mission. The best metaphor for the release of the BOP's potential is a magic spell that releases an outburst of good energy.

Closing Remarks

This book is only a first step on the way to understanding the phenomenon of Empowering Leadership. There is still much to explore, including the many ways complexity theory may translate into real-life actions, further studies on how to boost creativity, and lessons on how to shape the structure of networks – specifically the role of horizontal connections and social capital, as well as how to create an empathetic and supportive environment for others to thrive and take coleadership. Additionally, it would be worthwhile to look at ways to operate in an increasingly complex environment, where predicting the future becomes a huge challenge.

---

[1] Following David Bornstein's book titled *How to Change the World* (Bornstein, 2004).

Another avenue of exploration could be methods to teach Empowering Leadership in schools and universities. Rather than a "preachy" approach, it seems that a more participatory method that includes simulations and firsthand experience would be most effective. For example, instead of teaching the traditional method of "planning the change" we might want to try "dancing (or simulating) the change." Methods for teaching EL most likely warrant another book.

Finally, we find still unresolved the search for one's personal footing in the complex environment. What is our bedrock when changes accelerate, events are unpredictable, and efficient management can no longer rely on schemes, charts, and tidy arrows? Fundamentally, EL requires elasticity. So how are we to stay flexible and operate in a fluid and changing world, while maintaining a solid personal foundation?

As an author and explorer, I am thinking about a new project that will capture Empowering Leaders' accounts of how they find their personal base, whether it be through religion, philosophy, a personal creed, or something else. At this point I can only share my own experience: I found my fulcrum in Scripture and inspiration from Jesus' leadership. Moreover, I was struck by the way Christianity spread at such an incredible speed throughout the Mediterranean, especially considering that communication at the time moved at the speed of a donkey ride.

Rodney Stark, a well-known sociologist of religion, shed some light on that fast-spreading phenomenon in his popular book *The Rise of Christianity: How the Obscure, Marginal Jesus Movement Became the Dominant Religious Force in the Western World in a Few Centuries* (Stark, 1997). Interestingly, essential for that spread to occur were social capital and social networks, both prerequisites for EL.

I also draw from Pope Francis' teaching on the importance of joy: "Joy is the gift of Lord. It fills us internally with a spirit."[2] And joy is the basic pillar for augmenting creativity and, hence, for Empowering Leadership.

Closing this book I would like to advance a simple conjecture that it is fun and joy that will be pivotal for the leadership of the future.

---

[2] From his exhortation *Apostolicum Gaudium*. "The Joy of the Gospel."

References

Adams, R. (2008). *Empowerment, Participation and Social Work*. New York: Palgrave Macmillan.

Adler, P. S., & Kwon, S.-W. (2002). Social capital: Prospects for a new concept. *The Academy of Management Review*, 27(1): 17–40.

Aharon, I., Etcoff, N., Ariely, D., Chabris C. F., O'Connor E. & Breiter H. C. (2001). Beautiful faces have variable reward value: fMRI and behavioral evidence. *Neuron*, 32(3): 537–551.

Aldrich, H. E. & Zimmer, C. (1986). Entrepreneurship through social networks. In D. Sexton & R. Smilor (Eds.), *The Art and Science of Entrepreneurship* (pp. 3–23). Cambridge, MA: Ballinger.

Allen, S. L., Smith, J. E. & Da Silva, N. (2013). Leadership style in relation to organizational change and organizational creativity: Perceptions from non-profit organizational members. *Nonprofit Management and Leadership*, 24(1): 23–42.

Amabile, T. M. (1996). *Creativity in Context: Update to the Social Psychology of Creativity*. Boulder, CO: Westview Press.

Andel, Pek Van (1994). Anatomy of the unsought finding: Serendipity: Origin, history, domains, traditions, appearances, patterns and programmability. *British Journal for the Philosophy of Science*, 45(2): 631–648.

Andrews, K. T. (2004). *Freedom Is a Constant Struggle. Freedom Is a Constant Struggle*. Chicago: University Of Chicago Press.

Armbruster, H. (2014). Enabling others to act a leaders quality. *Pulse*. Retrieved February 2, 2017 from: www.linkedin.com/pulse/2014072911 4522-119974072-enabling-others-to-act-a-leaders-quality

Arnold, J. A., Arad, S., Rhoades, J. A. & Drasgow, F. (2000). The empowering leadership questionnaire: The construction and validation of a new scale for measuring leader behaviors. *Journal of Organizational Behavior*, 21(3): 249–269.

Aronson, E. (1999). The power of self-persuasion. *American Psychologist Press*, 54(11): 875–884.

Arthur, W. B. (1999). Complexity and the economy. *Science*, 284(5411): 107–109.

Asch, S. E. (1956). Studies of independence and conformity. I. A minority of one against a unanimous majority. *Psychological Monographs: General and Applied*, 70(9): 1–70.

Ash, T. G. (2002). *The Polish Solidarity*. New Haven, CT: Yale University Press.

Axelrod, R. & Cohen, M. D. (2000). *Harnessing Complexity: Organizational Implications of a Social Frontier*. New York: Basic Books.

Baber, A., Waymon, L., Alphonso, A., & Wylde, J. (2015). *Strategic Connections: The New Face of Networking in a Collaborative World*. New York: AMACOM.

Ballard, I. C., Murty, V. P., Carter, R. M., MacInnes, J. J., Huettel, S. A. & Adcock, R. A. (2011). Dorsolateral prefrontal cortex drives mesolimbic dopaminergic regions to initiate motivated behavior. *The Journal of Neuroscience*, 31(28): 10340–10346.

Bandura, A. (1976). *Social Learning Theory*. Englewood Cliffs, NJ: Prentice Hall.

Banks, J., Carson, J. S., Nelson, B. L. & Nicol, D. M. (2014). *Discrete-Event System Simulation*. Harlow, UK: Pearson.

Barabási, A. L. (2003). *Linked*. Cambridge, MA: A Plume Book.

Barbuto Jr., J. E. (1997). Taking the charisma out of transformational leadership. *Journal of Social Behavior & Personality*, 12(3): 689–697.

Barnett, M. A., Tetreault, P. A. & Masbad, I. (1987). Empathy with a rape victim: The role of similarity of experience. *Violence Victims*, 2(4): 255–262.

Barsade, S. G. (2002). The ripple effect: Emotional contagion and its influence on group behavior. *Administrative Science Quarterly*, 47(4): 644–675.

Bar-Tal, D. (2007). Sociopsychological foundations of intractable conflicts. *American Behavioral Scientist*, 50(11): 1430–1453.

Basadur, M. S. (2004). Leading others to think innovatively together: Creative leadership. *The Leadership Quarterly*, 15(1): 103–121.

Bass, B. M. (1985). *Leadership and Performance Beyond Expectations*. New York: Free Press.

Bass, B. M. & Riggio, R. E. (2006). *Transformational Leadership*. Mahwah, NJ: Lawrence Erlbaum.

Bateson, P. & Martin, P. (2013). *Play, Playfulness, Creativity and Innovation*. New York: Cambridge University Press.

Baumrind, D. (1964). Some thoughts on ethics of research: After reading Milgram's "Behavioral Study of Obedience. *American Psychologist*, 19(6): 421–423.

Bedau, M. A. & Humphreys, P. (2008a), Introduction. In Bedau, M. A., Humphreys, P. (Eds.), *Emergence: Contemporary Readings in Philosophy and Science* (pp. 1–6). Cambridge, MA: A Bradford Book.

(2008b), Philosophical perspective of emergence. In M. A. Bedau & P. Humphreys (Eds.), *Emergence: Contemporary Readings in Philosophy and Science* (pp. 1–6). Cambridge, MA: A Bradford Book.

Belasco, J. A. & Stayer, R. C. (1993). *Flight of the Buffalo: Soaring to Excellence, Learning to Let Employees Lead*. New York: Warner Books.

Bellows, R. (1959). *Creative Leadership*. Oxford, UK: Prentice-Hall.

Bem, D. J. (1967). Self-perception: An alternative interpretation of cognitive dissonance phenomena. *Psychological Review*, 74(3): 183–200.

Bennett, N., Wise, C., Woods, Ph. A. & Harvey, J. A. (2003). *Distributed Leadership*. National College of School Leadership, Nottingham.

Bergland, C. (2013). Why Is Dancing So Good for Your Brain? *Psychology Today*. Retrieved January 27, 2017 from: www.psychologytoday.com/blog/the-athletes-way/201310/why-is-dancing-so-good-your-brain.

Berkowitz, M. W. & Bier, M. C. (2007). What works in character education. *Journal of Research in Character Education*, 5(1): 29–48.

Betz, A. (2016). Jos de Blok, the founder of Buurtzorg, speaks of his journey. *Enlivening Edge*. Retrieved January 31, 2017 from: www.enliveningedge.org/features/jos-de-blok-founder-buurtzorg-speaks-journey/.

Beversdorf, D. Q. (2013). Pharmacological effects on creativity. In O. Vartanian, & A. S. Bristol (Eds.), *Neuroscience of Creativity* (pp. 151–173). Cambridge, MA: The MIT Press.

Blair, H. (2005). Civil society and pro-poor initiatives in rural Bangladesh: Finding a workable strategy. *World Development*, 33(6): 921–936.

Blanchard, K. H., Zigarmi, P. & Zigarmi, D. (1985). *Leadership and the One Minute Manager: Increasing Effectiveness through Situational Leadership*. New York: Morrow (updated 2013).

Blodgett, J. M. (2016). How to find a flying squirrel: Citizen scientists are enlisted to help scientists. *The Washington Post*. Retrieved January 31, 2017 from: www.washingtonpost.com/national/health-science/how-to-find-a-flying-squirrel-citizen-scientists-are-enlisted-to-help-scientists/2016/03/21/6c32ffd2-cb63-11e5-ae11-57b6aeab993f_story.html

Boden, M. A. (2004). *The Creative Mind: Myths and Mechanisms*. London: Routledge.

——— (2013). Creativity as a neuroscientific mystery. In Oshin Vartanian & Adam S. Bristol (Eds.), *Neuroscience of Creativity* (pp. 3–18). Cambridge, MA: The MIT Press.

Boecker, H., Sprenger, T., Spilker, M. E., Henriksen, Koppenhoefer, M., Wagner, K., J., Valet, M., Berthele, A. & Tolle, T. R. (2008). The runner's high: Opioidergic mechanisms in the human brain. *Oxford Journals*, 18(11): 2523–2531.

Bolden, R. (2011). Distributed leadership in organizations: A review of theory and research. *International Journal of Management Reviews*, 13(4): pp. 423–451.

Bolton, R. (2005, February). Habermas's theory of communicative action and the theory of social capital. Paper delivered at the meeting of Western Regional Science Association, San Diego, California. Retrieved January 27, 2017 from: http://web.williams.edu/Economics/papers/Habermas.pdf

Bono, J. E. & Judge, T. A. (2003). Self-concordance at work: Toward understanding the motivational effects of transformational leaders. *Academy of Management Journal*, 46(5): 554–571.

Booth, J. (2015). Why genuine empathy is good for business. *Fast Company*. Retrieved January 27, 2017 from: www.fastcompany.com/3052337/why-genuine-empathy-is-good-for-business

Borgatti, S. P., Jones, C. & Everett, M. G. (1998). Network measures of social capital. *Connections*, 21(2): 27–36.

Bornstein, D. (1998). Changing the world on a shoestring. *The Atlantic Monthly*, 281: 34–39.

Bornstein, D., (2004). *How to Change the World: Social Entrepreneurs and the Power of New Ideas*. New York: Oxford University Press.

Bouma, J., Bulte. E. & van Soest, D. (2008). Trust and cooperation: Social capital and community resource management. *Journal of Environmental Economics and Management*, 56(2): 155–166.

Bovee, C. L., & Thill, J. V. (2011). *Business Communication Today*. Boston: Pearson.

Bourdieu, P. (1986). Hasley, A. H., Lauder, H., Brown, P. & Wells, A. S. (Eds.), The forms of capital. In *Education, Culture, Economy, Society*, pp. 46–58. New York: Oxford University Press.

(2003). The forms of capital. In Halsey, A. H., Lauder, H., Brown, P., & Wells, A. S. (Eds.), *Education: Culture, Economy, Society* (pp. 46–58). Oxford: Oxford University Press.

Boyers, J. (2013). Why empathy is the force that moves business forward. *Forbes*. Retrieved January 27, 2017 from: www.forbes.com/sites/ashoka/2013/05/30/why-empathy-is-the-force-that-moves-business-forward/#710216fa8fb8

Boyle, M. E., & Ottensmeyer, E. (2005). Solving business problems through the creative power of the arts: Catalyzing change at Unilever. *Journal of Business Strategy*, 26(5): 14–21.

Braiker, H. (2004). *Who's Pulling Your Strings? How to Break the Cycle of Manipulation and Regain Control of Your Life*. New York: McGraw-Hill.

Brehm, J. & Rahn, W. (1997). Individual-Level Evidence for the Causes and Consequences of Social Capital. *American Journal of Political Science*, 41(3): 999–1023.

Breiter, H. C., Aharon, I., Kahneman, D., Dale, A. & Shizgal, P. (2001). Functional imaging of neural responses to expectancy and experience of monetary gains and losses. *Neuron*, 30(2): 619–639.

Brinckerhoff, P. C. (2000). *Social Entrepreneurship: The Art of Mission-Based Venture Development*. New York: John Wiley & Sons.

Brown, B. (2003). *The Private Revolution: Women in the Polish Underground Movement*. London: Hera Trust.

Brown, B. B. (1968). Delphi Process: A Methodology Used for the Elicitation of Opinions of Experts. RAND, Document No: P-3925. Retrieved February 2, 2017 from: www.rand.org/content/dam/rand/pubs/papers/2006/P3925.pdf

Brown, J. M. (2008). *Gandhi and Civil Disobedience: The Mahatma in Indian Politics 1928–1934*. New York: Cambridge University Press.

Brown, M. E., Treviño, L. K. & Harrison, D. A. (2005). Ethical leadership: A social learning perspective for construct development and testing. *Organizational Behavior and Human Decision Processes*, 97(2): 117–134.

Brown, S., Martinez, M. J. & Parsons, L. M. (2006). The neural basis of human dance. *Cerebral Cortex*, 16(8): 1157–1167.

Bruner, R. F. (2002). *Socrates' Muse: Reflections on Effective Case Discussion Leadership*. New York: McGraw.

Bryant, L. L., Corbett, K. K. & Kutner, J. S. (2001). In their own words: A model of healthy aging. *Social Science & Medicine*, 53(7): 927–941.

Buechler, S. M. (1995). New social movement theories. *The Sociological Quarterly*, 36(3): 441–464.

(1999). *Social Movements in Advanced Capitalism: The Political Economy and Cultural Construction of Social Activism*. New York: Oxford University Press.

(2011). *Understanding Social Movements: Theories from the Classical Era to the Present*. Boulder, CO: Paradigm.

Burns, J. M. (2003). *Transforming Leadership*. New York: Grove Press.

Burt, R. S. (1992). *Structural Holes: the Social Structure of Competition*. Cambridge, MA: Harvard University Press.

(1997). The contingent value of social capital. *Administrative Science Quarterly*, 42(2): 339–365.

(2000). The network structure of social capital. *Research in Organizational Behavior*, 22: 345–423.

(2001). Structural holes versus network closure as social capital. In N. Lin, K. S. Cook, & R. S. Burt, (Eds.), *Social Capital: Theory and Research* (pp. 31–56). New York: Aldine de Gruyter.

(2005). Structural holes and good ideas. *American Journal of Sociology*, 110(2): 349–399.

(2011). *Brokerage and Closure: An Introduction to Social Capital*. New York: Oxford University Press.

Carlozzi, A. F., Bull, K. S., Eells, G. T. & Hurlburt, J. D. (1995). *The Journal of Psychology*, 129(4): 365–373.

Carey, P. (2000). Community health promotion and empowerment. In J. Kerr (Ed.), *Community Health Promotion: Challenges for Practice* (pp. 27–50). Oxford: Bailliere Tindall.

Carlozzi, A. F., Bull, K. S., Eells, G. T. & Hurlburt, J. D. (1995). Empathy as related to creativity, dogmatism, and expressiveness. *The Journal of Psychology: Interdisciplinary and Applied*, 129(4): 365–373.

Carlyle, T. (1988). *On Heroes, Hero-Worship, and the Heroic in History*. New York: Frederick A. Stokes & Brother.

Carson, J. B., Tesluk, P. E. & Marrone, J. A. (2007). Shared leadership in teams: An investigation of antecedent conditions and performance. *Academy of Management Journal*, 50(5): 1217–1234.

Carstensen, L. L., Mikels, J. A., & Mather, M. (2006). Aging and the intersection of cognition, motivation, and emotion. In J. E. Birren & K. W. Schaire, *Handbook of the Psychology of Aging* (6th ed., pp. 343–362). Amsterdam, The Netherlands: Elsevier.

Casserly, M. (2012). Top five personality traits employers hire most. Forbes. Retrieved February 8, 2016 from: www.forbes.com/sites/meghancasserly/2012/10/04/top-five-personality-traits-employers-hire-most/#399e875eeec3

Castells, M. (2010). *The Power of Identity: The Information Age: Economy, Society, and Culture*. Oxford, UK: Wiley-Blackwell.

Cespedes, F. V. (2014). Stop using battle metaphors in your company strategy. *Harvard Business Review*. Retrieved January 27, 2017 from: https://hbr.org/2014/12/stop-using-battle-metaphors-in-your-company-strategy

Chan, S. (2001). Complex Adaptive Systems. MIT, ESD.83 Research Seminar in Engineering Systems, October 31, 2001/November 6, 2001. Retrieved January 27, 2017 from: http://web.mit.edu/esd.83/www/notebook/Complex%20Adaptive%20Systems.pdf

Chaney, W. H. (2007). *Dynamic Mind*. Las Vegas: Houghton-Brace.

Chemers M. M. (1997). *An Integrative Theory of Leadership*. Mahwah, NJ: Lawrence Erlbaum Associates.

Chemers, M. M. (2000). Leadership research and theory: A functional integration. *Group Dynamics: Theory, Research, and Practice*, 4(1): 27–43.

Chen, K-Y., Fine, L. R. & Huberman, B. A. (2003). Predicting the future. Information Systems Frontiers, 5(1): 47–61.

Chermahini, S. A. & Hommel, B. (2010). The (b)link between creativity and dopamine: Spontaneous eye blink rates predict and dissociate divergent and convergent thinking. *Cognition*, 115(3): 458–465.

Chia, R. (1996). Teaching paradigm shifting in management education. *Journal of Management Studies*, 33(4): 409–428.

Chiu, C., Dweck, C. S., Tong, J. Y. & Fu, J. H. (1997). Implicit theories and conceptions of morality. *Journal of Personality and Social Psychology*, 73(5): 923–940.

Chong, L., & Gibbons, P. (1997). Corporate entrepreneurship: The roles of ideology and social capital. *Group and Organization Management*, 22(1): 10–30.

Cialdini, R. B. & Goldstein, N. J. (2004). Social influence: Compliance and conformity. *Annual Review of Psychology*, 55: 591–621.

Ciulla, J. B. (2004). Ethics and leadership effectiveness. In Antonakis, J., Cianciolo, A. T. & Sternberg,R. J. (Eds.), *The Nature of Leadership* (pp. 302–327). Thousand Oaks, CA: Sage.

Claridge, T. (2004). Benefits and *Importance of Social Capit*al. *Social Capital Research*. Retrieved January 27, 2017 from: www.socialcapitalresearch.com/literature/theory/benefits.html

Clark, K. (2013). *Leadership, the Art of Empowering: Attitudes and Skills for Transformative Leadership*. Appleton, WI: CreateSpace Independent Publishing Platform.

Cohen, G. D. (2006). *The Creativity and Aging Study: The Impact of Professionally Conducted Cultural Programs on Older Adults; Final Report*. Washington, DC: National Endowment For The Arts (NEA).

Coleman, J. S. (1988). Social capital in the creation of human capital. *The American Journal of Sociology*, 94: 95–12.

(1990). *The Foundations of Social Theory*. Cambridge, MA: Belknap Press of Harvard University Press.

(2000). *Foundations of Social Theory*. Cambridge, MA: Belknap Press.

Conger, J. A. (1989). *The Charismatic Leader: Behind the Mystique of Exceptional Leadership*. San Francisco: Jossey-Bass.

Conger, J. A. & Kanungo, R. N. (1988). The empowerment process: Integrating theory and practice. *Academy of Management Perspectives*, 13(3): 471–482.

(1998). *Charismatic Leadership in Organizations*. Thousand Oaks, CA: Sage.

(1989). Leadership: The art of empowering others. *Academy of Management Perspectives*, 3(1): 17–24.

Cook, K. S., Hardin, R. & Levi, M. (2005). *Cooperation without Trust?* New York: Russell Sage Foundation.

Couger, J. D. (1995), *Creative Problem Solving and Opportunity Finding*. Danvers, MA: Boyd & Fraser.

Criswell, C. & Martin, A. (2007). 10 Trends. A Study of Senior Executives' Views on the Future. Center for Creative Leadership, White Paper. Retrieved January 27, 2917 from: http://insights.ccl.org/wp-content/uploads/2007/03/TenTrends.pdf

Csermely, P. (2009). *Weak Links: The Universal Key to the Stability of Networks and Complex Systems*. Berlin: Springer.

Csikszentmihályi, M. (1991). *Flow: The Psychology of Optimal Experience*. New York: Harper Perennial.

Csikszentmihályi, M. (1997). *Creativity: Flow and the Psychology of Discovery and Intention*. New York: Harper Perennial.

Cyert, R. M. (1990). Defining leadership and explicating the process. *Nonprofit Management and Leadership*, 1(1): 29–38.

Czyżewski, K. (2008). *The Return Line [Linia powrotu]*. Sejny: Pogranicze.

Daft, R. L. (2015). *Organization Theory and Design*. Boston: Cengage Learning.

Dal Forno A. & Merlone, U. (2013). Nonlinear dynamics in work groups with Bion's basic assumptions. *Nonlinear Dynamics, Psychology, and Life Sciences*, 17(2): 295–315.

Dalkey, N. C. (1968). Predicting the Future. The RAND Corporation, working paper. Santa Monica, CA. Retrieved February 2, 2017 from: http://130.154.3.8/content/dam/rand/pubs/papers/2008/P3948.pdf.

Dani, Y. (2012). Dynamics of creativity and empathy in role reversal: Contributions from neuroscience. *Review of General Psychology*, 16(1): 70–77.

Darbellay, F., Moody, Z., Sedooka, A. & Steffen, G. (2014). Interdisciplinary research boosted by serendipity. *Creativity Research Journal*, 26(1): 1–10.

da Silva, M. F. (2006). Cooperation, social capital and economic performance. *Revista de Economia Política*, 26(3). Retrieved January 27, 2017 from: www.scielo.br/scielo.php?script=sci_arttext&pid=S0101-31572006000300002

(2006). Cooperation, social capital and economic performance. *Revista de Economia Política*, 26(3). Retrieved February 2, 2017 from: www.scielo.br/scielo.php?script=sci_arttext&pid=S0101-31572006000300002

Davis, G. A. (1993). Personalities of creative people. *R&D Innovator*, 2(4). Retrieved January 27, 2017 from www.winstonbrill.com/brill001/html/article_index/articles/1-50/article34_body.html

Davis, M. H. (1996). *Empathy: A Social Psychological Approach*. Boulder, CO: Westview Press.

de Blok, J. & Kimball, M. (2013). Buurtzorg Nederland: Nurses leading the way! *AARP Journal, American Association of Retired Persons.* Retrieved January 31, 2017 from: http://journal.aarpinternational.org/a/b/2013/06/Buurtzorg-Nederland-Nurses-Leading-the-Way

de Bono, E. (1995). Serious creativity. *The Journal for Quality and Participation,* 18(5): 12–18.

——— (1996). *Serious Creativity: Using the Power of Lateral Thinking to Create New Ideas.* New York: HarperCollins.

Deci, L. E. (1975). *Intrinsic Motivation.* New York, NY: Springer.

Dee W. Hock (2000). *Birth of the Chaordic Age.* San Francisco: Berrett-Koehler.

Degenne. A. & Forsé, M. (1999). *Introducing Social Networks.* London: Sage.

Deiglmeier, K. (2013). Social entrepreneurship and social innovation. In Shapiro, R. A. (Ed.), *The Real Problem Solvers; Social Entrepreneurs in America,* (pp. 132–140). Stanford, CA: Stanford University Press.

De Rosnay, J. (1997). Homeostasis. *Principia Cybernetica Web.* Retrieved January 27, 2017 from http://pespmc1.vub.ac.be/HOMEOSTA.html

De Tocqueville, A. (2003). *Democracy in America and Two Essays on America.* New York: Penguin Books.

Deutsch, M. & Gerard, H. B. (1955). A study of normative and informational social influences upon individual judgment. *Journal of Abnormal and Social Psychology,* 51(3): 629–636.

de Veer, A. J. E. et al. (2009). Ervaringen van Buurtzorgeclienten in landelijk perspectief. *NIVEL.* Retrieved January 31, 2017 from: www.nivel.nl/sites/default/files/bestanden/Rapport-Buurtzorg-addendum.pdf

De Waal, F. (2009). *The Age of Empathy: Nature's Lessons for a Kinder Society.* New York: Three Rivers Press.

Deutschman, A. (2004). The fabric of creativity. *Fast Company.* Retrieved January 31, 2017 from: www.fastcompany.com/51733/fabric-creativity

De Vignemont, F. & Singer, T. (2006). The empathic brain: How, when and why? *Trends in Cognitive Sciences,* 10(10): 435–441.

Diamond, M. C. (2011). Response of the brain to enrichment. *Anais da Academia Brasileira de Ciências,* 73(2): 211–220.

Doidge, N. (2007). *Brain That Changes Itself: Stories of Personal Triumph.* New York: Penguin Books.

Dooley, K. J. (2009). Organizational psychology. In S. J. Guastello, M. Koopmans & D. Pincus (Eds.), *Chaos and Complexity in Psychology* (pp. 434–451). Cambridge: Cambridge University Press.

Douglas, B. (1979). Rank, power, authority: A reassessment of traditional leadership in South Pacific societies. *The Journal of Pacific History,* 14(1): 2–27.

Draft, R. L. (2015). *Organization Theory and Design.* Boston: Cengage Learning.

Drayton, W. (2000). *Selecting Leading Social Entrepreneurs.* Arlington, VA: Ashoka.

Drayton W. (2002). The citizen sector: Becoming as entrepreneurial and competitive as business. *California Management Review,* 44(3): 119–131.

Drayton, W. (2004). Needed: A new social financial services industry. *Alliance.* Retrieved January 27, 2017 from www.alliancemagazine.org/feature/needed-a-new-social-financial-services-industry/

(2005). Where the real power lies. *Alliance*, 10(1): 29–30.

(2013). Collaborative entrepreneurship. In Shapiro, R. A. (Ed.), *The Real Problem Solvers; Social Entrepreneurs in America*, pp. 165–176. Stanford, CA: Stanford University Press.

Drucker, P. F. (1995). *Managing in a Time of Great Change*. New York: Truman Talley Books/Dutton.

(1999). *Management Challenges for the 21st Century*. New York: HarperCollins.

Dubakov, M. (2009, March 23). Simple rules, complex systems and software development. *Edge of Chaos*. Retrieved January 27, 2017 from: www .targetprocess.com/blog/2009/03/simple-rules-complex-systems-and.html

Duhigg, C. (2016). What Google Learned From Its Quest to Build the Perfect Team. *New York Times Magazine*. Retrieved January 27, 2017 from: www .nytimes.com/2016/02/28/magazine/what-google-learned-from-its-quest-to-build-the-perfect-team.html

Durkheim, E. (1984). *The division of labor in the society*. New York: The Free Press.

Dweck, C. S. (2000). *Self-Theories: Their role in motivation, personality, and development*. Philadelphia, PA: Psychology Press.

Dweck, C. S. (2006). *Mindset. The new psychology of success*. New York: Random House.

Edles, L. D. & Appelrouth, S. (2014). *Sociological Theory in the Classical Era*. Thousand Oaks, CA: SAGE Publications.

Edwards, J., Cheers, B., & Graham, L. (2003). Social change and social capital in Australia: A solution for contemporary problems? *Health Sociology Review*, 12(1): 68–85.

Eisenberg, N. (2002). Empathy-related emotional responses, altruism, and their socialization. In R. J. Davidson & A. Harrington (Eds.), *Visions of Compassion: Western Scientists and Tibetan Buddhists Examine Human Nature* (pp. 131–164). New York: Oxford University Press.

Eisenberg, N. & Strayer, J. (1990). Critical issues in the study of empathy. In N. Eisenberg & J. Strayer (Eds.), *Empathy and its development* (pp. 3–13). Cambridge, Cambridge University Press.

Eisenberger, R. & Shanock, L. (2003). Rewards, intrinsic motivation, and creativity: A case study of conceptual and methodological isolation. *Creativity Research Journal*, 15(2 & 3): 121–130.

Elkington, J., & Hartigan, P. (2008). *The power of unreasonable people*. Boston: Harvard Business Press.

Ellison, N. B., Steinfield, C., & Lampe, C. (2007). The benefits of Facebook "friends:" Social capital and college students' use of online social network sites. *Journal of Computer-Mediated Communication*, 12(4): 1143–1168,

Emerging Technology (2017). Mathematical Model Reveals the Patterns of How Innovations Arise. MIT Technology Review. Retrieved February 2, 2017 from: www.technologyreview.com/s/603366/mathematical-model-reveals-the-patterns-of-how-innovations-arise/

Eoyang, G. H. & Holladay, R. J. (2013). *Adaptive Action: Leveraging Uncertainty in Your Organizations*. Stanford: Stanford Business Books.

Érdi, P. (2008). *Complexity explained*. Berlin: Springer.

Erickson, E. H., Erickson, J. M., & Kivnick, H. Q. (1986). *Vital involvement in old age: The experience of old age in our time.* New York: W. W. Norton & Company.

Evans, M. G. (1970). The effects of supervisory behavior on the path-goal relationship. *Organizational Behavior and Human Performance,* 5(3): 277–298.

Faucette, J. (2012). The Power of Business Imagination. *Entrepreneur.* Retrieved January 27, 2017 from: www.entrepreneur.com/article/223429

Faulkner, D. (2011). Angels, tooth fairies and ghosts: Thinking creatively in an early years classroom. In Faulkner, D. & Coates. E. (Eds.), *Exploring Children's Creative Narratives* (pp. 39–62). New York: Routledge.

Feste, C. (1995). Empowerment: From philosophy to practice. *Patient Education and Counseling,* 26(1–3): 139–44.

Feste, C. & Anderson, R. M. (1995). Empowerment: From philosophy to practice. *Patient Education and Counseling,* 26(1–3): 139–144.

Festinger, L. (1957). *A theory of cognitive dissonance.* Stanford, CA: Stanford University Press.

Festinger, L., Riecken, H. W., & Schachter, S. (2009). *When prophecy fails.* London: Pinter & Martin.

Fiedler, F. E. (1967). *A theory of leadership effectiveness.* New York: McGraw-Hill.

Field, J. (2008). *Social capital.* London: Routledge.

Findlay, C. S. & Lumsden, C. J. (1988).The creative mind: Toward an evolutionary theory of discovery and innovation. *Journal of Social and Biological Structures,* 11(1(): 3–55.

Fine, B. (2001). *Social capital versus social theory: Political economy and social science at the turn of the millennium.* London: Routledge.

Fisher, Lawrence. M. (2005). Ricardo Semler Won't Take Control. Business Thought Leaders. Retrieved January 31, 2017 from: www.strategy-business .com/article/05408?gko=3291c

Fisher, Len (2009). *The perfect swarm. The science of complexity in everyday life.* New York: Basic Books.

Flaherty, A. W. (2005). Frontotemporal and dopaminergic control of idea generation and creative drive. *The Journal of Comparative Neurology,* 493(1): 147–153.

Fleishman, E. A. (1953). The description of supervisory behavior. *Journal of Applied Psychology,* 37(1): 1–6.

Foley, M. W & Edwards, B. (1998). Beyond Tocqueville: Civil society and social capital in comparative perspective. *American Behavioral Scientist,* 42(1): 5–20.

Foster, A. & Ford, N. (2003). Serendipity and information seeking: An empirical study. *Journal of Documentation,* 59(3): 321–340.

Förster, J., Friedman, R. S., & Liberman, N. (2004). Temporal construal effects on abstract and concrete thinking: Consequences for insight and creative cognition. *Journal of Personality and Social Psychology,* 87(2): 177–189.

Förster, J., Epstude, K. & Özelse, A. (2009). Why love has wings and sex has not: How reminders of love and sex influence creative and analytic thinking. *Personality and Social Psychology Bulletin,* 35(11): 1479–1491.

Förster, J., Friedman, R. S., & Liberman, N. (2004). Temporal construal effects on abstract and concrete thinking: Consequences for insight and creative cognition. *Journal of Personality and Social Psychology*, 87(2): 177–189.

Freedman, J. L. & Fraser, S. C. (1966). Compliance without pressure: The foot-in-the-door technique. *Journal of Personality and Social Psychology*, 4(2): 195–202.

Fripp, J. (1993). *Learning through simulation: A Guide to the Design and Use of Simulations in Business and Education*. London, UK: McGraw-Hill.

(1997). A future for business simulations? *Journal of European Industrial Training*, 21(4): 138–142.

Friszke, A. (2006). Regionalny Komitet Wykonawczy Mazowsze: Powstanie, struktura, działalność (1981–1989) [Regional Mazovian executive committee: Origin, structure and activity]. In A. Friszke (Ed.), *Solidarność Podziemna 1981–1989 [Underground Solodarity 1981–1989]*, (pp. 405–487). Warszawa: Instytut Studiów Politycznych PAN.

Frost, S. (2014). Learning to brainstorm: Fun activities for kids. *Livestrong. com*. Retrieved February 2, 2017 from: www.livestrong.com/article/273215-how-to-learn-to-brainstorm-fun-activities-for-kids/

Fukuyama, F. (1996). *Trust: The social virtues and the creation of prosperity*. New York: A Free Press Paperbacks.

Fukuyama, F. (2001). Social capital, civil society and development. *Third World Quarterly*, 22(1): 7–20.

Gabbay, S. M., & Zuckerman, E. W. (1998). Social capital and opportunity in corporate R&D: The contingent effect of contact density on mobility expectations. *Social Science Research*, 27(2): 189–217.

Gallese, V. (2003). The roots of empathy: The shared manifold hypothesis and the neural basis of intersubjectivity. *Psychopathology*, 36(4): 171–180.

(2005). Embodied simulation: From neurons to phenomenal experience. *Phenomenology and the Cognitive Sciences*, 4(1): 23–48.

(2006). Intentional attunement: A neurophysiological perspective on social cognition and its disruption in autism. *Brain Research*, 1079(1): 15–24.

(2009). Mirror neurons, embodied simulation, and the neural basis of social identification. *Psychoanalytic Dialogues*, 19(5): 519–536.

(2011). Mirror neurons and art. In Bacci F & Melcher D (Eds.), *Art and the Senses* (pp. 445–463). New York: Oxford University Press.

(2014). Bodily selves in relation: Embodied simulation as second-person perspective on intersubjectivity. *Philosophical Transactions of the Royal Society B*, 369(1644): 1–10.

Gandhi, M. K. (2001). *Non-Violent Resistance (Satyagraha)*. New York: Dover.

Gass. R. H. & Seiter, J. S. (2013). *Persuasion, Social Influence, and Compliance Gaining*. Harlow, UK: Routledge.

Gardikiotis, A. (2011). Minority influence. *Social and Personality Psychology Compass*, 5(9): 679–693.

Gardner, W. L., Cogliser, C. C., Davis, K. M. & Dickens, M. P. (2011). Authentic leadership: A review of the literature and research agenda. *Leadership Quarterly*, 22(6): 1120–1145.

Gelb, M. J. (2000). *How to Think Like Leonardo da Vinci: Seven Steps to Genius Every Day.* New York: Bantam Bell.

Gendron, G. (1966). Flashes of genius: Interview with Peter Drucker. *Inc. Magazine,* 18(7): 30–39.

Gentile, M. C. (2002). *Social Impact Management and Social Enterprise: Two Sides of the Same Coin or Totally Different Currency.* New York: Aspen Institute for Social Innovation in Business. Retrieved February 5, 2010 from www .aspeninstitute.org/sites/default/files/content/docs/business%20and%20 society%20program/SOCIMPACTSOCENT.PDF

Gibney, E. (2016). "Open-hardware" pioneers push for low-cost lab kit; Conference aims to raise awareness of shared resources for building lab equipment. *NATURE.* Retrieved January 31, 2017 from: www.nature.com/ news/open-hardware-pioneers-push-for-low-cost-lab-kit-1.19518

Gladwell, M. (2002). *The Tipping Point: How Little Things Can Make a Big Difference.* Boston: Back Bay Books.

———. (2011). *Outliers: The Story of Success.* New York: Little, Brown.

Gleick, J. (2008). *Chaos: Making a New Science.* New York: Penguin Books.

Goldman, R. (2016). Future predictions. *The Farming Forum.* Retrieved February 2, 2017 from: https://thefarmingforum.co.uk/index.php?threads/ dr-robert-goldman-future-predictions.122536/

Goldsmith, M. (2010). Empowering your employees to empower themselves. *Harvard Business Review.* Retrieved January 27, 2017 from: https://hbr.org/ 2010/04/empowering-your-employees-to-e/

Goldstein, J. (1999). Emergence as a construct: History and issues. *Emergence: Complexity and Organization,* 1(1): 49–72.

Gordon, M. (2005). *Roots of Empathy: Changing the World Child by Child.* Toronto: Thomas Allen.

Gordon, W. J. J. (1961). *Synectics: The Development of Creative Capacity.* New York: Harper & Brothers

Gosling, J., Bolden, R. & Petrov, G. (2009). Distributed leadership in higher education: What does it accomplish? *Leadership,* 5(3): 299–310.

Goss, H. V. (2011). How to jumpstart your child's mind with brainstorming. Retrieved February 2, 2017 from: www.education.com/magazine/article/ brainstorming-solutions-jumpstart-child-mind/

Goyder, C. (2014). *Gravitas: Communicate with Confidence, Influence and Authority.* London: Vermilion.

Graham, R. (2016). LARPing for social good: The power of live action role play. Kill Screen. Retrieved February 2, 2017 from: https://killscreen.com/articles/ larping-for-social-good-the-power-of-live-action-role-play/

Granovetter, M. S. (1973). The strength of weak ties. *The American Journal of Sociology,* 78(6): 1360–1380.

———. (1983). The strength of weak ties: A network theory revisited. *Sociological Theory,* 1(1): 201–233.

———. (1985). Economic action and social structure: The problem of embeddedness. *The American Journal of Sociology,* 91(3): 481–510.

(1995). *Getting a Job: A Study of Contacts and Careers.* Chicago: University of Chicago Press.

Grant, A. M. & Berry, J. W. (2011). The necessity of others is the mother of invention: Intrinsic and prosocial motivations, perspective taking, and creativity. *Academy of Management Journal*, 54(1): 73–96.

Gray, B., Sarnak, D. O. & Burgers, J. (2015). Home care by self-governing nursing teams: The Netherlands' Buurtzorg Model, The Commonwealth Fund. *The Commonwealth Fund*. Retrieved January 31, 2017 from: www.common wealthfund.org/publications/case-studies/2015/may/home-care-nursing-teams-netherlands

Gray, P. (2013). *Free to Learn: Why Unleashing the Instinct to Play Will Make Our Children Happier, More Self-Reliant, and Better Students for Life.* New York: Basic Books.

Gronn, P. (2002). Distributed leadership as a unit of analysis. *The Leadership Quarterly*, 13(4): 423–451. [Earlier version of this article was presented as a paper to the Organisation Theory Special Interest Group at the annual meeting of the American Educational Research Association, Montreal, Canada, April 1999.

(2009). Leadership configurations. *Leadership*, 5(3):381–394.

Guerrini, F. (2014). Are flying cars the future of transportation? *Forbes*. Retrieved February 2, 2017 from: www.forbes.com/sites/federicoguerrini/2014/10/29/the-skys-the-limit-not-for-the-aeromobils-flying-car/#4ceca31618a2

Guilford, J. P. (1950). Creativity. *American Psychologist*, 5(9): 444–454.

Guthrie, D. (2012). Creative leadership: Humility and being wrong. *Forbes*. Retrieved February 2, 2017 from: www.forbes.com/sites/dougguthrie/2012/06/01/creative-leadership-humility-and-being-wrong/#461c277f5084

Habermas, J. (1985). *The Theory of Communicative Action*, Vol. 2. Boston: Beacon Press.

Hackman, J. R. (2002). *Leading Teams: Setting the Stage for Great Performances.* Boston: Harvard Business Review Press.

Håkansson. J. (2003). Exploring the Phenomenon of Empathy. Doctoral dissertation. Stockholm: Stockholm University, Department of Psychology.

Hall, E., Hall, C., Stradling, P. & Young, D. (2014). *Guided Imagery: Creative Interventions in Counselling & Psychotherapy.* London: Sage.

Halpin, A. W. & Winer, B. J. (1957). A factorial study of the leader behavior descriptions. In R. M. Stogdill & A. E. Coons (Eds.), *Leader Behavior: Its Description and Measurement*. Columbus: Bureau of Buisness Research, Ohio State University.

Hamel, G. (2007). *The Future of Management.* (pp. 83–99). Boston: Harvard Business Review Press.

(2010a). W. L. Gore: Lessons From a management revolutionary. Resource document. *Wall Street Journal*. Retrieved January 27, 2017 from: http://blogs.wsj.com/management/2010/04/02/wl-gore-lessons-from-a-management-revolutionary-part-2/

Hamel, G.(2010b). Innovation democracy: W. L. Gore's original management model. MIX: It's Time to re-invent management. Resource document. *Management, Innovation, Exchange.* Retrieved January 27, 2017 from www.managementexchange.com/story/innovation-democracy-wl-gores-original-management-model

Hamel, G. (2011). First, let's fire all the managers. Resource document. *Harvard Business Review.* Retrieved January 31, 2017 from: https://hbr.org/2011/12/first-lets-fire-all-the-managers

Hammonds, K. H. (2005). A lever long enough to move the world. *Fast Company*, 90: 60–63.

Hannam, R. G (1993). *Kaizen for Europe: Customizing Japanese Strategies for Success.* San Francisco: IFS.

Harris, A. & Spillane, J. (2008). Distributed leadership through the looking glass. *Management in Education*, 22(1): 31–34.

Hart, J. G. (2006). Exploring tribal leadership: Understanding and working with tribal people. *Journal of Extension*, 44(4). Retrieved January 27, 2017 from: www.joe.org/joe/2006august/a3.php

Hartnell, C. (2015). Interview with Bill Drayton. *Alliance.* Retrieved January 27, 2017 from www.alliancemagazine.org/interview/interview-with-bill-drayton/

Hasson, U., Ghazanfar, A. A., Galantucci, B., Garrod, S. & Keysers C., (2012). Brain-to-brain coupling: A mechanism for creating and sharing a social world. *Trends in Cognitive Science*, 16(2): 114–121.

Hawkes, C. H. (1992). Endorphins: The basis of pleasure? *Journal of Neurology, Neurosurgery and Psychiatry*, 55(4): 247–250.

Hegar, K. W. (2012). *Modern Human Relations at Work.* Mason, OH: Mountain View College.

Herman, P. (2010). *The HIP Investor: Make Bigger Profit by Building a Better World.* Hoboken, NJ: John Wiley & Sons.

Hersey, P. H., Blanchard, K. H. & Johnson, D. E. (2012). *Management of Organizational Behavior: Leadership Human Resources.* Upper Saddle River, NJ: Prentice Hall.

Hess, R. (1984). Thoughts on empowerment. *Prevention in Human Services*, 3(2–3): 227–230.

Hess, T. M. (2006). Attitudes toward agig and their effects on behavior. In J. E. Birren & K. W. Schaire, *Handbook of the Psychology of Aging* (6th ed., pp. 379–406). Amsterdam, The Netherlands: Elsevier.

Hobman, E. V., Jackson, C. J., Jimmieson N. L. & Martin, R. (2011). The effects of transformational leadership behaviours on follower outcomes: An identity-based analysis. *European Journal of Work and Organizational Psychology*, 20(4): 553–580.

Hock, D. W. (2000). *Birth of the Chaordic Age.* San Francisco: Berrett-Koehler.

Hockenbury, D. & Hockenbury, S. E. (2011). *Discovering Psychology.* New York: Worth.

Hoffman, M. L. (1987). The contribution of empathy to justice and moral judgment. In N. Eisenberg & J. Strayer (Eds.), *Empathy and Its Development* (pp. 47–80). Cambridge: Cambridge University Press.

Holland, J. H. (1999). *Emergence: From Chaos to Order*. Cambridge, MA: Perseus Books.

Holling, C. S., Peterson, G. D. & Allen, C. R. (2008). Panarchies and discontinuities. In C. R. Allen & C. S. Holling (Eds.), *Discontinuities in Ecosystems and Other Complex Systems* (pp. 3–19). New York: Columbia University Press.

Hope, M. (2000). *On Socrates*. Independence, KY: Cengage Learning.

House, R. J. (1971). A path goal theory of leader effectiveness. *Administrative Science Quarterly*, 16(3): 321–338.

Howard-Jones, P., Taylor, J. & Sutton, L. (2002). The effect of play on the creativity of young children during subsequent activity. *Early Child Development and Care*, 172(4): 2002.

Iacoboni, M. (2009). *Mirroring People: The Science of Empathy and How We Connect with Others*. New York: Picador.

Ibáñez, A. (2007). Complexity and cognition: A meta-theoretical analysis of the mind and brain as a topological dynamical system. *Nonlinear Dynamics, Psychology, and Life Sciences*, 11(1): 51–90.

Ickes, W. (1997). *Empathic Accuracy*. New York: Guilford Press.

Imai, M. (1986). *Kaizen: The Key to Japan's Competitive Success*. New York: McGraw-Hill.

Inkson, K. (2002). Thinking creatively about careers: The use of meaphor. In M. Peiperl, M. Arthur, R. Goffee, & N. Anand (Eds.), *Career Creativity* (pp. 15–34). New York: Oxford University Press.

Jacobs, H. (2014). Here are some of the American adults who started live-action role playing and never stopped. Business Insider. Retrieved February 2, 2017 from: www.businessinsider.com/why-people-love-larping-2014-10?IR=T

Jäncke, L. (2009). The plastic human brain. *Restorative Neurology and Neuroscience*, 27(5): 521–538.

Jervis, R. (1998). *System Effects: Complexity in Political and Social Life*. Princeton, NJ: Princeton University Press.

Jia, L., Hirt, E. R. & Karpen, S. C. (2009). Lessons from a faraway land: The effect of spatial distance on creative cognition. *Journal of Experimental Social Psychology*, 45(5): 1127–1131.

Johansson, B. B. (2004). Brain plasticity in health and disease. *The Keio Journal of Medicine*, 53(4): 231–246.

Johnson, N. (2009). *Simply Complexity: A Clear Guide to Complexity Theory*. Oxford, UK: OneWorld.

Johnson, S. (2002). *Emergence: The Connected Lives of Ants, Brains, Cities, and Software*. New York: Touchstone.

Jones, E. E. (1964). *Ingratiation: A Social Psychological Analysis*. New York: Appleton-Century-Croft.

Judge, T. A. & Piccolo, R. F. (2004). Transformational and transactional leadership: A meta-analytic test of their relative validity. *Journal of Applied Psychology*, 89(5): 755–768.

Kaplan, B. & Kaiser, R. (2006). *The Versatile Leader: Make the Most of Your Strengths Without Overdoing It*. San Francisco: Pfeiffer.

Kastens, K., Manduca, C. A., Cervato, C., Frodeman, R., Goodwin, C., Liben, L. S., Mogk, D. W., Spangler, T. C., Stillings, N. A. & Titus, S. (2009). How geoscientists think and learn. *Eos, Transactions, AGU*, 90(31): 265–266.

Kauffman, S. A. (2000). *Investigations*. New York: Oxford University Press.

Kauffmann, S. (1995). *At Home in the Universe: The Search for Laws of the Self-Organization and Complexity*. Oxford: Oxford University Press.

Kaufman, S. B. (2010). Why creative folks blink a lot. *Psychology Today*. Retrieved January 27, 2017 from: www.psychologytoday.com/blog/beautiful-minds/201004/why-creative-folks-blink-lot

Kelly, J. G. (1971). Qualities for the community psychologist. *American Psychologist*, 26(10): 897–903.

(2013). *A Guide to Conducting Prevention Research in the Community: First Steps*. New York: Routledge.

Kelman, H. (1958). Compliance, identification, and internalization: Three processes of attitude change. *Journal of Conflict Resolution*, 1: 51–60.

Kenney, P. (2001). Framing, political opportunities, and civic mobilization in the eastern European revolutions: A case study of Poland's freedom and peace movement. *Mobilization*, 6(2): 193–210.

(2008). *A Carnival of Revolution: Central Europe 1989*. Princeton, NJ: Princeton University Press.

Kenworthy, L. 1997. Civic engagement, social capital, and economic cooperation. *American Behavioral Scientist*, 40(5): 645–656.

Keysers, C. (2011). *The Empathic Brain*. Seattle: CreateSpace.

Keysers, C. & Gazzola, V. (2010). Social neuroscience: Mirror neurons recorded in humans. *Current Biology*, 20(8): 353–354.

Kilgallon, John, Sandy Antunes, & Mike Young (2001). Rules to Live by: A Live Action Roleplaying Conflict Resolution System. Interactive link. Retrieved February 2, 2017 from: www.interactivitiesink.com/mechanics/download/RTLB2.pdf

Kim, W. C. & Mauborgne, R. (2005). *Blue Ocean Strategy: How to Create Uncontested Market Space and Make Competition Irrelevant*. Cambridge, MA: Harvard Business Review Press.

King, A. J., Johnson, D. D. P. & Van Vugt, M. (2009). The origins and evolution of leadership. *Current Biology*, 19(9): R911–R916.

King, M, L., Jr. (2001). *The Autobiography of Martin Luther King, Jr*. Boston MA: Grand Central.

Kirby, J. T. (1997). Aristotle on Metaphor. *The American Journal of Philology*, 118(4): 517–554.

Kirkpatrick, D. (2011). *Beyond Empowerment: The Age of the Self-Managed Organization*. Morning Star Self-Management Institute.

(2015). 12 keys to the workplace of the future. *Huffington Post, HuffPost Business*. Retrieved January 31, 2017 from: www.huffingtonpost.com/great-work-cultures/twelve-keys-to-the-workpl_b_7986378.html

Kirkpatick, S. A. & Locke, E. A. (1991). Leadership: Do traits matter? *Academy of Management Perspectives*, 5(2): 48–60.

Knack, S. & Keefer, P. (1997). Does social capital have an economic payoff? A cross-country investigation. *The Quarterly Journal of Economics*, 112(4): 1251–1288.

Knoll, N. & Schwarzer, R. (2004). "Prawdziwych przyjaciół..." Wsparcie społeczne, stres, choroba i śmierć. In H. Sęk & R. Cieślak (Eds.), *Wsparcie społeczne, stres i zdrowie* (pp. 29–48). Warszawa: PWN.

Koestler, A. (1964). *The Act of Creation*. London: Hutchison.

(2009). The three domains of creativity. In M. Krausz & D. Dutton (Eds.), *The Idea of Creativity* (pp. 251–266). Leiden, Netherlands: Brill.

Kolar, Tomaž (2012). Using metaphors as a tool for creative strategic sense-making. *Economic and Business Review*, 14(4): 275–297.

Koo, Mee-Hyoe (2013). Interview with Bill Drayton, pioneer of social entrepreneurship. *Forbes*. Retrieved January 27, 2017 from www.forbes.com/sites/meehyoekoo/2013/09/30/interview-with-bill-drayton-pioneer-of-social-entrepreneurship/#2715e4857a0b5e948c784692

Kosow, H. & Gaßner, R. (2008). Methods of Future and Scenario Analysis. German Development Institute. Retrieved February 2, 2017 from: http://edoc.vifapol.de/opus/volltexte/2013/4381/pdf/Studies_39.2008.pdf

Kosslyn S. M., Ganis G. & Thompson W. L. (2001). Neural foundations of imagery. *Nature Reviews Neuroscience*, 2(9): 635–642.

Kouzes, J. M. & Posner, B. Z. (1987). *The Leadership Challenge: How to Get Extraordinary Things Done in Organizations*. San Francisco: Jossey-Bass.

(1992). Ethical leaders: An essay about being in love. *Journal of Business Ethics*, 11(5/6): 479–484.

(1993). *Leadership practices inventory (Lpi): A self-assessment and analysis*. San Francisco: Jossey-Bass/Pfeiffer.

(2008). *The leadership challenge*. San Francisco: Jossey Bass.

(2011). *The Truth about Leadership: The No-fads, Heart-of-the-Matter Facts You Need to Know*. San Francisco: Jossey-Bass

Krackhardt, D., & Hanson, J. R. (1993). Informal networks: The company behind the chart. *Harvard Business Review*, 71(4): 104–111.

Kramer, M. R. (2005). Measuring innovation. Evaluation in the field of social entrepreneurship. *The Skoll Foundation*. Retrieved January 27, 2017 from https://business.ualberta.ca/-/media/business/centres/cccsr/ccse/documents/generalinformation/reports/reportkramer.pdf

Krill, T. L., Carter, R. I. & Williams, D. L. (1997). An exploration of the leadership practice enabling others to act: A case study. *Journal of Agricultural Education*, 38(4): 42–49.

Kruse, K. (2013). What is leadership? Resource document. *Forbes*, retrieved January 27, 2017 from: www.forbes.com/sites/kevinkruse/2013/04/09/what-is-leadership/

Kubik, J. (1994). *The Power of Symbols Against the Symbols of Power*. University Park, PA: Pen State Press.

Kulisevsky, J., Pagonabarraga, J. & Martinez-Corral, M. (2009). Changes in artistic style and behaviour in Parkinson's disease: Dopamine and creativity. *Journal of Neurology*, 256(5): 816–819.

Lakoff, G. & Johnson, M. (2003). *Metaphors We Live by*. Chicago: University of Chicago Press.

Laloux, F. (2014). *Reinventing Organizations*. Brussels: Nelson Parker.

La Porta, R., Lopez-de-Silanes, F., Shleifer, A. & Vishny, R. W. (1996). Trust in large organizations. *National Bureau of Economic Research*, Working Paper 5864. Retrieved February 2, 2017 from: www.nber.org/papers/w5864.pdf

Laraia, A. C., Moody, P. E. & Hall, R. W. (1999). *The Kaizen Blitz: Accelerating Breakthroughs in Productivity and Performance*. New York: John Wiley & Sons.

Laumer, U., Bauer, M., Fichter, M., & Milz, H. (1997). Therapeutische Effekte der Feldenkrais-Methode "Bewusstheit durch Bewegung" bei Patienten mit Essstoerungen. *Psychotherapie Psychosomatik Medizinische Psychologie*, 47: 170–180. Translation: 2004, Therapeutic effects of the Feldenkrais method (awareness through movement) in eating disorders. *Feldenkrais Research Journal*, 1: 1–17.

Leadbeater, C. (1997). *The Rise of the Social Entrepreneur*. London: Demos.

Lederach, J. P. (2003). *The Little Book of Conflict Transformation*. Intercourse, PA: Good Books.

Leimbach, M. (2009). Versatile communication: Avoiding the hidden costs of communication misalignment. *Global Research and Development for Wilson Learning Worldwide*. Retrieved January 27, 2017 from: www .mooballmailer.com/admin/temp/newsletters/1439/attachments/ Versatile%20Communications%20Avoiding%20the%20Hidden%20 cost%20of%20Communication%20Misalignment.pdf

Lewin, K., Lippitt, R. & White, R. K. (1939). Patterns of aggressive behavior in experimentally created "social climates." *Journal of Social Psychology*, 10(2): 271–299.

Lewin, K. (2004). *Resolving Social Conflicts. Field Theory in Social Science*. Washington DC: American Psychological Association.

Levin, F. M. (2000). Learning, development, and psychopathology: Applying chaos theory to psychoanalysis. *Annual of Psychoanalysis*, 28: 85–104.

Levin, S. R. (1982). Aristotle's theory of metaphor. *Philosophy & Rhetoric*, 15(1): 24–46.

Levy, S. R., Stroessner, S. J. & Dweck, C. S. (1998). Stereotype formation and endorsement: The role of implicit theories. *Journal of Personality and Social Psychology*, 74(6): 1421–1436.

Liang, J. & Luo, B. (2012). Toward a discourse shift in social gerontology: From successful aging to harmonious aging. *Journal of Aging Studies*, 26(3): 327–334.

Liberman, N. & Shapira, O. (2009). Does falling in love make us more creative? *Scientific American*. Retrieved January 27, 2017 from: www.scientificamerican .com/article/does-falling-in-love-make/

Likert, R. (1961). *New Patterns of Management*. New York: McGraw-Hill.

(1967). *The Human Organization: Its Management and Value*. New York: McGraw-Hill.

Lin, N. (2001). *Social Capital: A Theory of Social Structure and Action*. Cambridge: Cambridge University Press.

Lin, N, Cook, K. & Burt, R. S. (2001). Preface. In Lin, N, C ook, K. & Burt, R. S. (Eds.), *Social Capital: Theory and Research* (pp. vii–xii). New York: Aldine de Gruyter.

Lindstrom, M. (2016). *Small Data: The Tiny Clues That Uncover Huge Trends.* New York: St. Martin's Press.

Lindenmayer, M. (2013). Ask great questions: Leadership skills of Socrates. *Forbes.* Retrieved January 27, 2017 from: www.forbes.com/sites/ michaellindenmayer/2013/06/18/ask-great-question-leadership-skills-of-socrates/#7b9c0f597a9f

Lindsay, Greg (2014). Engineering serendipity. *Aspen Ideas Festival.* Retrieved January 27, 2017 from: https://medium.com/aspen-ideas/engineering-serendipity-941e601a9b65#.eicshe5kn

(2015). How to engineer serendipity. *TIME.* Retrieved January 27, 2017 from: http://time.com/3951029/engineer-serendipity/

Llopis, G. (2014). Leadership is about enabling the full potential in others. *Forbes.* Retrieved February 2, 2017 from: www.forbes.com/sites/glennllopis/2014/07/ 29/leadership-is-about-enabling-the-full-potential-in-others/#2d33e92a6a87

Long, A. A. (1986). *Hellenistic philosophy: Stoics, Epicureans, Sceptics.* Berkeley, CA: University of California Press.

Loreto, V., Servedio, V. D. P., Strogatz, S. H. & Tria, F. (2016). Dynamics on expanding spaces: Modeling the emergence of novelties. In M. D. Esposti, E. G. Altmann, & F. Pachet (Eds.), *Creativity and Universality in Language* (pp. 59–83). New York: Springer.

Lunenburg, F. C. (2010). Formal communication channels: Upward, downward, horizontal, and external. *Focus on Colleges, Universities, and Schools,* 4(1): 1–7.

Macionis, J. J. (2010). *Sociology.* Upper Saddle River, NJ: Prentice Hall.

MacLean Jr., W. E., Lewis, M. H., Bryson-Brockmann, W. A., Ellis, D. N., Arendt, R. E. & Baumeister, A. A. (1985). Blink rate and stereotyped behavior: Evidence for dopamine involvement? *Biological Psychiatry,* 20(12): 1321–1326.

Mair, J., & Martí, I. (2006). Social entrepreneurship research: A source of explanation, prediction, and delight. *Journal of World Business,* 41: 36–44.

Majd, S. (2012). *How to Live with a Young Brain?* Australia: Amazon Australia Services.

Manville, B. & Ober, J. (2003). Beyond empowerment: Building a company of citizens. *Harvard Business Review:* 48–53. Retrieved February 1, 2017 from: https:// hbr.org/2003/01/beyond-empowerment-building-a-company-of-citizens

Manz, C. C. & Sims, H. P. (1991). Super leadership: Beyond the myth of heroic leadership. *Organizational Dynamics,* 19(4): 18–35.

Manz, C. C., Shipper, F. & Stewart, G. L. (2009). Everyone a team leader: Shared influence at W. L. Gore & Associates. *Organizational Dynamics,* 38(3): 239–244.

Mapes, J. J. (2003). *Quantum Leap Thinking.* Naperville, IL: Sourcebooks.

Maresco, P. A. & York, C. C. (2005). Ricardo Semler: Creating organizational change through employee empowered leadership. resource document. *Academic Leadership Online Journal.* Retrieved January 31, 2017 from:

www.newunionism.net/library/case%20studies/SEMCO%20-%20
Employee-Powered%20Leadership%20-%20Brazil%20-%202005.pdf

Martin, M. (2007). Intervening at the inflection point. *UBS Philanthropy Services Viewpoints*, Retrieved January 27, 2017, from www.tusev.org.tr/userfiles/image/Viewpoints%20v6%20%282%29.pdf

Martin, R. L., & Osberg, S. (2007). Social entrepreneurship: The case for definition. *Stanford Social Innovation Review*, Spring 2007: 29–39.

Martin, R. & Hewstone, M. (2007). Social-influence processes of control and change: Conformity, obedience to authority, and innovation. In M. Hogg & J. M. Cooper (Eds.), *The SAGE Handbook of Social Psychology* (pp. 312–332). London: Sage.

Maskell, P. (2000). Social capital, innovation, and competitiveness. In S. Baron, J. Field, & T. Schuller (Eds.), *Social Capital: Critical Perspective* (pp. 111–123). New York: Oxford University Press.

Mason, M. K. (2016). Future Scenarios: The Art of Storytelling. Retrieved February 2, 2017 from: www.moyak.com/papers/scenarios-future-planning.html

Maurer, R. (2014). *One Small Step Can Change Your Life: The Kaizen Way*. New York: Workman.

Maxwell, E. (2013). Influence vs. manipulation. *Social-Engineering.org*, 4(45). Retrieved January 27, 2017 from www.social-engineer.org/newsletter/Social-Engineer.Org%20Newsletter%20Vol.%2004%20Iss.%2045.htm

Maxwell, J. C. (2002). *Teamwork Makes The Dreamwork*. Nashville, TN: Thomas Nelson. (Maxwell, 2002).

Mayo, M., Meindl, J. R. & Pastor, J. C. 2003. Shared leadership in work teams: A social network approach. In C. L. Pearce & J. A. Conger (Eds.), *Shared Leadership: Reframing the Hows and Whys of Leadership* (pp. 193–214). Thousand Oaks, CA: Sage.

Maxwell, John C. (2002). *Teamwork Makes the Dreamwork*. Nashville, TN: Thomas Nelson.

Mead, G. H. (1967). *Mind, Self, and Society: From the Standpoint of a Social Behaviorist*. Chicago: University of Chicago Press.

McAdam, D. (1999). *Political Process and the Development of Black Insurgency, 1930–1970*. Chicago: The University of Chicago Press.

McChrystal, S. (2015). *Team of Teams: New Rules of Engagement for a Complex World*. New York: Portfolio.

McFadzean, E. (1998). Enhancing creative thinking within organisations. *Management Decision*, 36(5): 309–315.

McLeod, S. (2007). Moscovici and minority influence. *Simply Psychology*. Retrieved January 27, 2017 from www.simplypsychology.org/minority-influence.html

(2008). Asch experiment. *Simply Psychology*. Retrieved January 27, 2017 from: www.simplypsychology.org/asch-conformity.html

McNamara, C. (2010). *Field Guide to Leadership and Supervision in Business*. Minneapolis: Authenticity Consulting.

Meinhardt, H. (2003). *The Algorithmic Beauty of Sea Shells*. Berlin: Springer.

Miall, H. (2004). Conflict transformation: A multi-dimensional task. In A. Austin, M. Fischer, & N. Ropers, *Transforming Ethnopolitical Conflict* (pp. 67–89). Wiesbaden, Germany: The Berghof Handbook Verlag.

Milgram, S. (1963). Behavioral study of obedience. *Journal of Abnormal and Social Psychology*, 67(4): 371–8.

(2009). *Obedience to Authority: An Experimental View*. New York: Harper Perennial.

Miller, J., Wroblewski, M. & Villafuerte, J. (2013). *Creating a Kaizen Culture*. McGraw-Hill Education.

Miller, J. M. & Page, S. E. (2007). *Complex Adaptive Systems*. Princeton, NJ: Princeton University Press.

Milway, K. S. (2014). How social entrepreneurs can have the most impact. *Harvard Business Review*. Retrieved January 27, 2017 from https://hbr.org/2014/05/how-social-entrepreneurs-can-have-the-most-impact/

Mischel, W. (1969). Continuity and change in personality. *American Psychologist*, 24(11): 1012–1018.

(1973). Toward a cognitive social learning reconceptualization of personality. *Psychological Review*, 80(4): 252–283.

Mitchel, M. (2009). *Complexity: A Guided Tour*. New York: Oxford University Press.

Monsen, K. & de Blok, J. (2013). Buurtzorg Nederland. *American Journal of Nursing*, 113(8): 55–59.

Moody, J. & White, D. R. (2003). Structural cohesion and embeddedness: A hierarchical concept of social groups. *American Sociological Review*, 68(1): 103–127.

Morgan, G. (1980). Paradigms, metaphors, and puzzle solving in organization theory. *Administrative Science Quarterly*, 25(4): 605–622.

Morris, A. (2006). Freedom is a constant struggle: The Mississippi civil rights movement and its legacy by Kenneth T. Andrews. *Contemporary Sociology*, 35(4): 413–415.

Mukamel, R., Ekstrom, A. D., Kaplan, J., Iacoboni, M. & Fried, I. (2010). Single-neuron responses in humans during execution and observation of actions. *Current Biology*, 20(8): 750–756.

Naparstek, B. (1995). *Staying Well with Guided Imagery*. New York: Warner Books.

Neace, M. B. (1999), Entrepreneurs in emerging economies: Creating trust, social capital, and civil society. *The ANNALS of the American Academy of Political and Social Science*, 565(1): 148–161.

Neil, A. S. (1977). *Summerhill: A Radical Approach to Childrearing*. New York: Pocket Books.

Nieto, M. J. & Santamaría, L. (2007). The importance of diverse collaborative networks for the novelty of product innovation. *Technovation*, 27(6–7): 367–377.

North, M. J. & Macal, C. M. (2007). *Managing Business Complexity: Discovering Strategic Solutions with Agent-Based Modeling and Simulation*. New York: Oxford University Press.

Northouse, P. G. (2010). *Leadership: Theory and Practice*. Thousand Oaks, CA: Sage.

Nowak, A. (2004). Dynamical minimalism: Why less is more in psychology? *Personality and Social Psychology Review*, 8(2): 183–193.

Nowak, A. & Vallacher, R. R. (1998a). *Dynamical Social Psychology*. New York: Guildford Press.

(1998b). Toward computational social psychology: Cellular automata and neural network models of interpersonal dynamics. In S. J. Read & L. C. Miller (Eds.), *Connectionist Models of Social Reasoning and Social Behavior* (pp. 277–311). Mahwah, NJ: Lawrence Erlbaum.

Nowak, A., Vallacher, R. R. & Miller, M. E. (2003). Social influence and group dynamics. In T. Millon & M. J. Lerner, *Handbook of Psychology*, Vol. 5: *Personality and Social Psychology* (pp. 383–417). New York: John Wiley & Sons.

Nowak, A. & Vallacher, R. R. (2005). Information and influence in the construction of shared reality. *IEEE: Intelligent Systems*, 1: 90–93.

Osa, M. (2003). *Solidarity and Connections: Networks of Polish Opposition.* Minneapolis: University of Minnesota Press.

Özaralli, N. (2015). Linking empowering leader to creativity: The moderating role of psychological (Felt) empowerment. *Proceedings of the 3rd International Conference on Leadership, Technology and Innovation Management*, 181: 366–376.

Özbebek, A. & Toplu, E. K. (2011). Empowered employees' knowledge sharing behavior. *International Journal of Business and Management Studies*, 3(2): 1309–8047.

Page, N. & Czuba, C. E. (1999). Empowerment: What is it? *Journal of Extension*, 37(5). Retrieved January 27, 2017 from: www.joe.org/joe/1999october/comm1.php

Papa, M. J., Daniels, T. D. & Spiker, B. K. (2007). *Organizational Communication Perspectives and Trends*. Thousand Oaks, CA: Sage.

Pascale, R., Sternin, J. & Sternin, M. (2010). *The Power of Positive Deviance: How Unlikely Innovators Solve the World's Toughest Problems*. New York: Harvard Business Press.

Pascual-Leone, A., Amedi, A., Fregni, F. & Merabet, L. B. (2005). The plastic human brain cortex. *Annual Review of Neuroscience*, 28: 377–401.

Pascual-Leone, A., Freitas, C., Oberman, L., Horvath, J. C., Halko, M., Eldaief, M. et al. (2011). Characterizing brain cortical plasticity and network dynamics across the age-span in health and disease with TMS-EEG and TMS-fMRI. *Brain Topography*, 24: 302–315.

Pavlovich, K. & Krahnke, K. (2012). Empathy, connectedness and organization. *Journal of Business Ethics*, 105(1): 131–137.

Pearce, C. L. & Conger, J. A. (2003). *Shared Leadership: Reframing the Hows and Whys of Leadership*. New York: Sage.

(2002). All those years ago. In C. L. Pearce & J. A. Conger (Eds.), *Shared Leadership: Reframing the Hows and Whys of Leadership* (pp. 1–18). New York: Sage.

Pearson D. G. (2007). Mental imagery and creative thought. *Proceedings of the British Academy*, 147: 187–212.

Pellis, S. & Pellis, V. (2009). *The Playful Brain: Venturing to the Limits of Neuroscience*. London: Oneworld.

Petty, R. E., Wheeler, S. C. & Tormala, Z. L. (2003). Persuasion and attitude change. In T. Millon & M. J. Lerner (Eds.), *Handbook of Psychology* (pp. 353–382). Hoboken, NJ: John Wiley & Sons.

Piaget, J. (2008). *The Moral Judgment of the Child*. New York: Free Press Paperbacks.

Pill, J. (1971). The Delphi method: Substance, context, a critique and an annotated bibliography. *Socio-Economic Planning Sciences*, 5(1): 57–71.

Piper, J. (2008). 6 Messages: Psalms: Thinking and Feeling with God. Retrieved January 27, 2017 from: www.desiringgod.org/messages/by-series/psalms-thinking-and-feeling-with-god

Piven, F. F. (2008). Can power from below change the world? *American Sociological Review*, 73(1): 1–14.

Podolny, J. M., & Baron, J. N. (1997). Resources and relationships: Social networks and mobility in the workplace. *American Sociological Review*, 62(5): 673–693.

Pomerenke, J. (2014). Empathy in business is vital to an entrepreneur's success. *Entrepreneur*. Retrieved January 27, 2017 from: www.entrepreneur.com/article/238935

Port, R. F. & van Gelder, T. (1995). It's about time: An overview of the dynamical approach to cognition. In Port, R., van Gelder, T. J. (Eds.), *Mind as Motion: Explorations in the Dynamics of Cognition* (pp 1–43). Cambridge, MA: MIT Press.

Porter, J. (2007). Weak ties and diversity in social networks. *Bokardo Social Web Design*. Retrieved February 2, 2017 from: http://bokardo.com/archives/weak-ties-and-diversity-in-social-networks

Portes, A. (1998). Social capital: Its origins and applications in modern sociology. *Annual Review of Sociology*, 24: 1–24.

Portugal, S. J., Hubel, T. Y., Fritz, J., Heese, S., Trobe, D., Voelkl, B., Hailes, S., Wilson, A. M. & Usherwood, J. R. (2014). Upwash exploitation and downwash avoidance by flap phasing in ibis formation flight. *Nature*, 505: 399–402.

Prahalad, C. K. (2010). *The Fortune at the Bottom of the Pyramid: Eradicating Poverty through Profits*. Upper Saddle River, NJ: Pearson FT Press.

Praszkier, R. (2012). Social entrepreneurs open closed worlds: The transformative influence of weak ties. In A. Nowak, D. Bree & K. Nowak-Winkowska (Eds.), *Complex Human Dynamics. From Mind to Societies* (pp. 111–129). New York: Springer.

——— (2014). Empathy, mirror neurons and SYNC. *Mind and Society*, 15(1): 1–25.

——— (2015). Empowering leadership: Embracing endogenous dynamics. *Journal of Positive Management*, 6(2–4): 34–58.

Praszkier, R., Nowak, A. & Coleman, P. (2010). Social entrepreneurs and constructive change: The wisdom of circumventing conflict. *Peace and Conflict*, 16: 153–174.

Praszkier, R., Nowak, A. & Zablocka-Bursa, A. (2009). Social capital built by social entrepreneurs and the specific personality traits that facilitate the process. *Social Psychology [Psychologia Społeczna]*, 4(1–2): 42–54.

Praszkier, R. & Nowak, A. (2012). *Social Entrepreneurship: Theory and Practice.* Cambridge: Cambridge University Press.

Praszkier, R., Nowak, A. & Zablocka-Bursa, A. (2009). Social capital built by social entrepreneurs and the specific personality traits that facilitate the process. *Social Psychology [Psychologia Społeczna]*, 4(1–2): 42–54.

Praszkier, R. & Nowak, A. (2012b). Social entrepreneurship: Paving the way for peace. In A. Bartoli, Z. Mampilly & S. A. Nan (Eds.), *Peacemaking: A Comprehensive Theory and Practice Reference* (pp. 159–167). Santa Barbara, CA: Praeger.

Puccio, G. J., Mance, M. & Murdock, M. C. (2010). *Creative Leadership: Skills That Drive Change.* Thousand Oaks, CA: Sage.

Putnam, R. D. (1993). The prosperous community: Social capital and public life. *The American Prospect*, 13: 35–42.

(1996). Who killed civic America? *Prospect*, 6: 66–72.

(2000). *Bowling Alone: The Collapse and Revival of American Community.* New York: Simon & Shuster.

Putnam, R. D. & Gross, K. A. (2002). Introduction. In R. D. Putnam (Ed.), *Democracies in Flux* (pp. 3–19). New York: Oxford University Press.

Raelin, J. A. (2003). *Creating Leaderful Organizations: How to Bring Out Leadership in Everyone.* San Francisco: Berrett-Koehler.

(2005). We the leaders: In order to form a leaderful organization. *Journal of Leadership and Organizational Studies*, 12(2): 18–30.

(2011). From leadership-as-practice to leaderful practice. *Leadership*, 7(2): 195–211.

Ramachandran, V. S. (2000). Mirror neurons and imitation learning as the driving force behind "the great leap forward" in human evolution. *Edge, 69.* Retrieved January 27, 2017 from: www.edge.org/3rd_culture/ramachandran/ramachandran_p1.html

Ramachandran, V. S. & Oberman, L. M. (2006). Broken mirrors: A theory of autism. *Scientific American*, 295(5): 62–69.

Rappaport, J. (1987). Terms of empowerment/exemplars of prevention: Toward a theory for community psychology. *American Journal of Community Psychology*, 15: 121–148.

(2013). Studies in empowerment: Introduction to the issue. In J. Rappaport, C. Swift & R. Hess (Eds.), *Studies in Empowerment: Steps toward Understanding and Action* (pp. 1–8). New York: Routledge.

Raymond, E. S. (2001). *The Cathedral and the Bazaar: Musings on Linux and Open Source by an Accidental Revolutionary.* Sebastopol, CA: O'Reilly Media.

Reingold, J. (2007). A job that lets you pick your own boss, Resource document. *FORTUNE Magazine.* Retrieved January 27, 2017 from http://archive.fortune.com/2007/10/08/magazines/fortune/goretex.fortune/index.htm

Reynolds, C. W. (1987). Flocks, herds, and schools: A distributed behavioral model. *Computer Graphics*, 21(4): 25–34.

Rickards, T. & Moger, S. (2000). Creative leadership processes in project team development: An alternative to tuckman's stage model. *British Journal of Management,* 11(4): 273–283.

Rivas, M. F. & Suttery, M. (2009). Leadership in public goods experiments – on the role of reward, punishment and endogenous leadership. Resource document. JEL classification, C72, C92, H41. Retrieved January 27, 2017 from: http://campus.usal.es/~ehe/Papers/Leadership_FernandaRivas.pdf

Rizzolatti, G. & Fabbri-Destro, M. (2008). The mirror system and its role in social cognition. *Current Opinion in Neurobiology,* 18(2): 179–184.

Roberts, Royston M. (1989). *Serendipity: Accidental Discoveries in Science.* Somerset, NJ: John Wiley & Sons.

Robinson, W. P. (2010). *Leading People from the Middle: The Universal Mission of Heart and Mind.* New York: iUniverse.

Rock, D. & Jones, B. (2015a). Why more and more companies are ditching performance ratings. *Harvard Business Review.* Retrieved February 1, 2017 from: https://hbr.org/2015/09/why-more-and-more-companies-are-ditching-performance-ratings

(2015b). What really happens when companies nix performance ratings. *Harvard Business Review.* Retrieved February 1, 2017 from: https://hbr.org/2015/11/what-really-happens-when-companies-nix-performance-ratings

Rodrigue, R. (2013). Leadership Behavior Description Questionnaire (LBDQ & LBDQ-XII). In M. C. Bocarnea, R. A. Reynolds & J. D. Baker (Eds.), *Online Instruments, Data Collection, and Electronic Measurements: Organizational Advancements* (pp. 97–117). Hershey, PA: IGI Global.

Roehborn, B. (2012). *Social Competences of Children Participating in Playgroups [Kompetencje społeczne dzieci biorących udział w zajęciach Grup Zabawowych].* Warszawa: Foundation for Children [Fundacja Rozwoju Dzieci].

Rogers, E. M. (2003). *Diffusion of Innovation.* New York: Free Press.

Rosenzweig, M. R. & Bennett, E. L. (1966). Psychobiology of plasticity: Effects of training and experience on brain and behavior. *Behavioral Brain Research,* 78(1): 57–65.

Rost, J. (1993). *Leadership for the Twenty-First Century.* Westport, CT: Praeger.

Roth, T. & Leimbach, M. (2015). Versatility: The engine of success. *Training.* Retrieved January 27, 2017 from: https://trainingmag.com/versatility-engine-success

Roy, S. (2010). The psychology of empathy. *Futurehealth.* Retrieved January 27, 2017 from: www.futurehealth.org/articles/The-Psychology-of-Empathy-by-Saberi-Roy-100620-281.html

Ruef, M. (2002). Strong ties, weak ties and islands: Structural and cultural predictors of organizational innovation. *Industrial and Corporate Change,* 11(3): 427–449.

Runco, M. A. (2007). *Creativity: Theories and Themes: Research, Development and Practice.* Burlington: Elsevier Academic Press.

Russ, S. W. (2003). Play and creativity: Developmental issues. *Scandinavian Journal of Educational Research,* 47(3): 291–303.

Russ, S. W. (2016). *Affect and Creativity: The Role of Affect and Play in the Creative Process*. New York: Lawrence Erlbaum Associates.

Rusu, I. (2013). Dopamine, endorphins and epinephrine. *European Journal of Science and Theology*, 9(6): 1–3.

Sadowska, B. (2009). *New Opening: The Social Market Economy*. Poznan: The Barge Foundation.

Sale, A., Berardi, N. & Maffei, L. (2014). Environment and brain plasticity: Towards an endogenous pharmacotherapy. *Physiological Reviews*, 94(1): 189–234.

Sarason, B. R. (1981): The dimensions of social competence: Contributions from a variety of research areas. In J. D. Wine & M. D. Smye (Eds.), *Social Competence* (pp. 100–124). New York: The Guilford Press.

Sarnoff, D. & Remer, P. (1982). The effects of guided imagery on the generation of career alternatives. *Journal of Vocational Behavior*, 21(3): 299–308.

Sawyer, R. K. (2007). *Social Emergence: Societies as Complex Systems*. Cambridge: Cambridge University Press.

Schelling, T. C. (2006). *Micromotives and Macrobehavior*. New York: W. W. Norton.

Scheve, T. (2014). What are endorphins? How stuff works. *Science*. Retrieved January 27, 2017 from: http://science.howstuffworks.com/life/endorphins1.htm

Schilit, W. K. & Locke, E. A. (1982). A study of upward influence in organizations. *Administrative Science Quarterly*, 27(2): 304–316.

Schneidr, B. D. (2007). *Energy Leadership: Transforming Your Workplace and Your Life from the Core*. Hoboken, NJ: John Wiley & Sons.

Schumpeter (2016). Team spirit. *The Economist*. Retrieved January 27, 2017 from: www.economist.com/news/business-and-finance/21694962-managing-them-hard-businesses-are-embracing-idea-working-teams

Scott, A. 1990. *Ideology and the New Social Movements*. London: Unwin Hyman.

Seibert, S. E., Wang, G. & Courtright, S. H. (2011). Antecedents and consequences of psychological and team empowerment in organizations: A meta-analytic review. *Journal of Applied Psychology*, 96(5): 981–1003.

Semler, R. (1994). Why my former employees still work for me. *Harvard Business Review*. Retrieved January 31, 2017 from: https://hbr.org/1994/01/why-my-former-employees-still-work-for-me

(1995). *Maverick: The Success Story behind the World's Most Unusual Workplace*. New York: Warner Books.

(2004). *The Seven-Day Weekend: Changing the Way Work Works*. New York: Portfolio.

Senge, P. (1990). *The Fifth Discipline*. New York: Currency Doubleday.

Senge, P., Kleiner, A., Roberts, C., Ross, R., Roth, G. & Smith, B. (1999). *The Dance of Change*. New York: Currency Doubleday.

Sęk., H. (2001). *Wprowadzenie do psychologii klinicznej*. Warszawa: Wydawnictwo Naukowe Scholar.

Shapira, O. & Liberman, N. (2009). An easy way to increase creativity. *Scientific American*. Retrieved January 27, 2017 from: www.scientificamerican.com/article/an-easy-way-to-increase-c/

Shelton, C. D. (2013). *Brain Plasticity: Rethinking How the Brain Works.* London, Canada: Choice PH.

Sheridan C. L. & Radmacher S. A. (1998). *Psychologia zdrowia. Wyzwanie dla biomedycznego modelu zdrowia* pp. 217–223). Warszawa: Instytut Psychologii Zdrowia PTP.

Shridharani, K. J. (1973). *War without Violence.* Munchen: Dissertations-G.

Sink, R. (2007). My unfashionable legacy. *Strategy + Business.* Retrieved July 10, 2017 from: www.strategy-business.com/article/07302

Skarda, C. A. & Freeman, W. J. (1990). Chaos and the new science of the brain. *Concepts in Neuroscience,* 1(2): 275–285.

Society for Neuroscience (2008) *Mirror neurons.* Washington, DC: Society for Neuroscience, November 2008. Retrieved January 27, 2017 from: https://docs.google.com/document/d/1B3GvHFOzSFiOo69dt9ngqNsoAp47IWw PbvNrVejwHv8/edit?hl=en_US&pref=2&pli=1

Solomon, R. C. (2014). Ethical leadership, emotions and trust: Beyond "charisma." In J. B. Ciulla (Ed.), *Ethics, the Heart of Leadership* (pp. 83–102). Santa Barbara, CA: Praeger.

(2014). Ethical leadership, emotions and trust: Beyond "charisma." In J. B. Ciulla (Ed.), *Ethics, the Heart of Leadership* (pp. 83–102). Santa Barbara, CA: Praeger.

Soule, A. B. (2008). The creative family: How to encourage imagination and nurture family. *Connections.* Boston: Trumpeter Books.

Sprouse-Blum, A. S, Smith, G., Sugai, D. & Parsa, F. D. (2010). Understanding endorphins and their importance in pain management. *Hawaii Medical Journal,* 69(3): 70–71.

Srivastava, A., Bartol, K. M. & Locke, E. A. (2006). Empowering leadership in management teams: Effects on knowledge sharing, efficacy, and performance. *Academy of Management Journal,* 49(6): 1239–1251.

Stanley, D. J. (2005). The impact of empowered employees on corporate value. *Graziadio Business Review,* 8(1).

Stark, R. (1997). *The Rise of Christianity: How the Obscure, Marginal Jesus Movement Became the Dominant Religious Force in the Western World in a Few Centuries.* San Francisco: HarperCollins.

Stark, S. (1977). Toward a psychology of charisma. *Psychological Reports,* 40(3): 683–696.

Stein, M. I. (1953). Creativity and culture. *Journal of Psychology,* 36(2): 311–322.

(1974). *Stimulating Creativity,* Vol. 1. New York: Academic Press.

Stephens, G. J., Silbert, L. J. & Hasson, U. (2010). Speaker-listener neural coupling underlies successful communication. *Proceedings of the National Academy of Sciences of the USA,* 107(32): 14425–14430.

Sternberg, R. J., & Lubart, T. I. (2004). The concept of creativity: Prospects and paradigms. In Robert J. Sternberg (Ed.), *Handbook of Creativity* (pp. 3–15). Cambridge: Cambridge University Press.

Sternin, J. (2002). Positive deviance: A new paradigm for addressing today's problems today. *The Journal of Corporate Citizenship,* 5: 57–62.

Steyaert, C. & Hjorth, D. (2006). Introduction: What is social entrepreneurship? In C. Steyaert & D. Hjorth (Eds.), *Entrepreneurship as Social Change* (pp. 1–18). Cheltenham, UK: Edward Elgar.

Stodgill, R. M., Goode, O. S. & Day, D. R. (1962). New leader behavior description subscales. *Journal of Psychology*, 54(2): 259–269.

Stoppler, M. C. (2014). Endorphins: Natural pain and stress fighters. *MedicineNet.com*. Retrieved January 27, 2017 from: www.medicinenet.com/script/main/art.asp?articlekey=55001

Stotland, E. (1969). Exploratory investigations of empathy. *Advances in Experimental Social Psychology*, 4: 271–314.

Strogatz, S. (2003). *Sync: How Order Emerges from Chaos in the Universe, Nature, and Daily Life*. New York: Hyperion.

(2007). The end of insight. In J. Brockman (Ed.), *What Is Your Dangerous Idea? Today's Leading Thinkers on the Unthinkable* (pp. 130–131). New York: Harper Perennial.

Sull, D. & Eisenhardt, K. M. (2015). *Simple Rules: How to Thrive in a Complex World*. New York: Houghton Mifflin Harcourt.

Sveiby, K. E. (2010). Perplexity and indigenous leadership. In S. Lowe (Ed.), *Managing in Changing Times: A Guide for the Perplexed Manager* (pp. 281–315). Thousand Oaks, CA: Sage.

Talbot, P. A. (2003). Corporate generals: The military metaphor of strategy. *Irish Journal of Management*, 24(2): 1–10.

Taleb, N. N. (2010). *The Black Swan: The Impact of the Highly Improbable*. New York: Random House.

Tardy C. H. (1985). Social support measurement; *American Journal of Community Psychology*, 13(2): 187–202.

Tetlock, P. E. & Gardner, D. (2016). *Superforecasting: The Art and Science of Prediction*. New York: Broadway Books.

Thietart, R. & Forgues, A. B. (1995). Chaos theory and organization. *Organization Science*, 6(1): 19–31.

Thomas, K. W. & Velthouse, B. A. (1990). Cognitive elements of empowerment: An "interpretive" model of intrinsic task motivation. *Academy of Management Perspectives*, 15(4): 666–681.

(2009). *Intrinsic Motivation at Work: What Really Drives Employee Engagement*. San Francisco: Berrett-Koehler.

Thompson, L. (2013). *Creative Conspiracy: The New Rules of Breakthrough Collaboration*. Boston: Harvard Business Review Press.

Tourish, D. (2005). Critical upward communication: Ten commandments for improving strategy and decision making. *Long Range Planning*, 38(5): 485–503.

Tourish, D. & Robson, P. (2003). Critical upward feedback in organisations: Processes, problems and implications for communication management. *Journal of Communication Management*, 8(2): 150–167.

Tripathi, P. & Burleson, W. (2012). Predicting creativity in the wild: Experience sample and sociometric modeling of teams. *Proceedings of the ACM Conference on Computer Supported Cooperative Work, CSCW*: 1203–1212.

Tsai, W. & Ghoshal, S. (1988). Social capital and value creation: The role of intrafirm networks. *The Academy of Management Journal*, 41(4): 464 – 476. DOI: http://dx.doi.org/10.2307/257085

Tucker, A. A. (2007). Leadership by the Socratic method. *Air and Space Power Journal*, Summer 2007: 80–87.

Tucker, R. C. (1968). The theory of charismatic leadership. *Daedalus*, 97(3): 731–756.

Tychsen, A., Michael, H., Thea, B. & Manolya, K. (2005). *The Game Master: The Second Australasian Conference on Interactive Entertainment* (pp. 215–222). Sydney, Australia: Creativity and Cognition Studios Press. Retrieved February 2, 2017 from: http://dl.acm.org/citation.cfm?id=1109214&dl= ACM&coll=DL&CFID=682999451&CFTOKEN=26166580

Tyler, T. R. (2003). Why do people rely on others? Social identity and social aspects of trust. In K. S. Cook (Ed.), *Trust in Society* (pp. 285–306). New York: Russell Sage Foundation.

Twardowski, J. (2014). 6 Steps to setting boundaries in relationships. *The Huffington Post*. Retrieved February 2, 2017 from: www.huffingtonpost.com/jennifer-twardowski/6-steps-to-setting-boundaries-in-relationships_b_6142248.html

Uhl-Bien, M., Marion, R. & McKelvey, B. (2007). Complexity leadership theory: Shifting leadership from the industrial age to the knowledge era. *The Leadership Quarterly* 18(4): 298–318.

Uzzi, B. (1996). The sources and consequences of embeddedness for the economic performance of organizations: The network effect. *American Sociological Review*, 61(4): 674–698.

    (1997). Social structure and competition in interfirm networks: The paradox of embeddedness. *Administrative Science Quarterly*, 42(1): 35–67. DOI:10.2307/2393808.

Vallacher, R. R. & Nowak, A. (2007). Dynamical social psychology: Finding order in the flow of human experience. In A. W. Kruglanski & E. T. Higgins (Eds.), *Social Psychology: Handbook of Basic Principles* (pp. 734–758). New York: Guilford.

Vallacher, R. R., Read, S. J. & Nowak, A. (2002). The dynamical perspective in personality and social psychology. *Personality and Social Psychology Review*, 6(4): 264–273.

Vallacher, R. R., Coleman, P. T., Nowak, A. & Bui-Wrzosinska, L. (2010). Rethinking intractable conflict: The perspective of dynamical systems. *American Psychologist*, 65(4): 262–278.

Vallerand, R. J. (2008). On the psychology of passion: In search of what makes people's lives most worth living. *Canadian Psychology*, 49(1): 1–13.

Van Praag, H., Kempermann, G., & Gage, F. H. (2000). Neural consequences of environmental enrichment. *Nature Reviews Neuroscience*, 1(3): 191–198.

Van Vugt, M. (2006). Evolutionary origins of leadership and followership. *Personality and Social Psychology Review*, 10(4): 354–371.

Van Vugt, M. & Ahuja, A. (2011). *Naturally Selected: The Evolutionary Science of Leadership*. New York: HarperCollins.

Venkatanathan, J., Karapanos, E., Kostakos, V. & Gonçalves, J. (2013). A network science approach to modelling and predicting empathy. *ASONAM '13 Proceedings of the 2013 IEEE/ACM International Conference on Advances in Social Networks Analysis and Mining*. Niagara Falls, Canada.

Von Oech, R. (1983). *A Whack on the Side of the Head: How You Can Be More Creative*. London: Creative Think.

Vroom, V. H. (1964). *Work and Motivation*. New York: Wiley. (New edition: 1994, San Francisco: Jossey-Bass).

Vroom, V.H. & Yetton, P.W. (1973). *Leadership and Decision-making*. Pittsburgh, PA: University of Pittsburgh Press.

Wack, P. (1985). Scenarios: Uncharted waters ahead. *Harvard Business Review*. Retrieved February 2, 2017 from: https://hbr.org/1985/09/scenarios-uncharted-waters-ahead

Waddock, S. A. & Post, J. E. (1991). Social entrepreneurs and catalytic change. *Public Administration Review*, 51(5): 393–401.

Wageman, R., Nunes, D. A., Burruss, J. A. & Hackman, J. R. (2008). *Senior Leadership Teams: What It Takes to Make Them Great*. Boston: Harvard Business Review Press.

Waldrop, M. M. (1992). *Complexity: The Emerging Science at the Edge of Order and Chaos*. New York: Simon & Schuster.

Walker, G., Kogut, B. & Shan, W. (1997). Social capital, structural holes and the formation of an industry network. *Organization Science*, 8(2): 109–125.

Wartzman, R. (2012). If self-management is such a great idea, why aren't more companies doing it? Resource document. *Forbes*. Retrieved January 31, 2017 from: www.forbes.com/sites/drucker/2012/09/25/self-management-a-great-idea/#236400a942a2

Wasko, M. M. & Faraj, S. (2005). Why should I share? Examining social capital and knowledge contribution in electronic networks of practice. *Management Information Systems Quarterly*, 29(1): 35–57.

Watts, D. J. & Strogatz, S. H. (1998). Collective dynamics of "small-world" networks. *Nature*, 393: 440–442.

Watts, T. (2008). *Business Leaders' Values and Beliefs Regarding Decision Making Ethics*. Morrisville, NC: LuLu.com.

Weber, M. (1978). *Economy and Society*. Berkley: University of California Press.

Welch, R. L. (1980). Vertical and horizontal communication in economic processes. *The Review of Economic Studies*, 47(4): 733–746.

Whitebread, D. & Bingham, S. (2013). Too much, too young: Should schooling start at age 7? *New Scientist*. Retrieved February 2, 2017 from: www.newscientist.com/article/mg22029435.000-too-much-too-young-should-schooling-start-at-age-7.html#.UoxwXeKQOdw

Wilensky, U. (1997). *NetLogo Segregation model*. Center for Connected Learning and Computer-Based Modeling. Evanston, IL: Northwestern University. Retrieved February 2, 2017 from: http://ccl.northwestern.edu/netlogo/models/Segregation

(1999). *NetLogo*. Center for Connected Learning and Computer-Based Modeling. Evanston, IL: Northwestern University. Retrieved February 2, 2017 from: http://ccl.northwestern.edu/netlogo/

Williams, J. (2002). *Eyes on the Prize: America's Civil Rights Years, 1954–1965*. New York: Penguin Books.

Wolfram S. (2002). *A New Kind of Science*. Champlain, IL: Wolfram Media.

Wood, W. (2000). Attitude change: Persuasion and social influence. *Annual Review of Psychology*, 51: 539–570.

Woolcock, M. (1998). Social capital and economic development: Toward a theoretical synthesis and policy framework. *Theory and Society*, 27(2): 151–208.

(2004). Social capital and economic development: Toward a theoretical synthesis and policy framework. *Theory and Society*, 27(2): 151–208.

Woolcock, M. & Narayan, D. (2000). Social capital: Implications for development; theory, research, and policy. *The World Bank Research Observer*, 15(2): 225–249.

Xin, L. & Qin, K. (2011). Embeddedness, social network theory and social capital theory: Antecedents and consequence. *Management and Service Science (MASS)*: 1–5. DOI: 10.1109/ICMSS.2011.5997958.

Yang, K. (2007). Individual social capital and its measurement in social surveys. *Survey Research Methods*, 1(1): 19–27.

Yaniv, D. (2012). Dynamics of creativity and empathy in role reversal: Contributions from neuroscience. *Review of General Psychology*, 16(1): 70–77.

Youngblood, M. D. (1997). Leadership at the edge of CHAOS: From control to creativity. *Strategy & Leadership*, 25(5): 8–14.

Zablocka, A., Praszkier, R, Petrushak, E. & Kacprzyk-Murawska, M. (2016). Measuring the propensity for building social capital depending on ties-strength. *Journal of Positive Management*, 7(4): 19–39.

Zhang, X. & Bartol, K. (2010). Linking empowering leadership and employee creativity: The influence of psychological empowerment, intrinsic motivation and creative process engagement. *Academy of Management*, 53(1): 107–128.

Zhu, W., Wang, G., Zheng, X., Liu, T. & Miao, Q. (2013). Examining the role of personal identification with the leader in leadership effectiveness: A partial nomological network. *Group Organization Management*, 38(1): 36–67.

Zimmerman, M. A. (1995). Psychological empowerment: Issues and illustrations. *American Journal of Community Psychology*, 23(5): 581–599.

(2000). Empowerment theory: Psychological, organizational and community levels of analysis. In J. Rappaport & E. Seidman (Eds.), *Handbook of Community Psychology* (pp. 43–63). New York: Springer.

Index